RELUCTANT BREAK

WITH BRITAIN

From Stamp Act to Bunker Hill

GREGORY T. EDGAR

Published 1997 by

HERITAGE BOOKS, INC.
1540E Pointer Ridge Place
Bowie, Maryland 20716
1-800-398-7709

ISBN 0-7884-0585-3

A Complete Catalog Listing Hundreds of Titles
On History, Genealogy, and Americana
Available Free Upon Request

"Thou profane wicked monster of falsehood and perfidy: Your late infamous proclamation is full of notorious lies, as a toad or rattlesnake of deadly poison. Without speedy repentence, you will have an aggravated damnation in Hell. You are not only a robber, a murderer, and usurper, but a wicked rebel: a rebel against the authority of truth, law, equity, the English constitution of government, these colony states, and humanity itself."

> *- Reverend Roger Cleveland, pastor of the Ipswich, Mass., Congregational Church, writing to British General Thomas Gage, June, 1775*

ALSO BY GREGORY T. EDGAR

Available from Heritage Books:

> *"Liberty or Death!" The Northern Campaigns in the American Revolutionary War.* Nominated for the 1995 Cincinnati Award.

> *Campaign of 1776: The Road to Trenton.* Nominated for the 1996 Fraunces Tavern Museum Book Award.

Available directly from Gregory T. Edgar, at 131 Pinnacle Road, Ellington, CT 06029:

> *"Are the Yankees Cowards Now?" A Story of Bunker Hill.*

> *Gone to Meet the British, A Novel of the American Revolution.*

INTRODUCTION

The American Revolutionary War was a war for independence. But it didn't start out that way. When the fighting started on April 19, 1775, at Lexington, Massachusetts, the American Whigs, or "patriots," wished to stay within the British Empire. They had only taken up arms to force Parliament to recognize the inviolability of American liberties.

The patriots were not willing to let Parliament enforce new restrictive laws that were contrary to the liberties set down in their colonial charters and the English Constitution of 1688. After all, the American colonists were English citizens, too. Even in England, where there was much pro-American sentiment, many a Whig argued that King George III's ministers were the true rebels, since they were rebelling against the English Constitution; and that the American patriots were fighting to protect the rights of all Englishmen.

Gradually, starting with the Proclamation of 1763 which prohibited Americans from pushing the frontier westward across the Appalachians, and continuing with several new tax laws, Parliament was nibbling away at the colonists' right to self-government. Patriots founded local revolutionary organizations, such as the Sons of Liberty and Committees of Correspondence, to oppose Parliament. "No taxation without representation!" became a common theme in political pamphlets.

It is tempting for us to use this catchy phrase to oversimplify the patriot view. But if Parliament had reversed course and allowed the colonies representation, the new members of Parliament from America would have formed too small a minority to have much effect. This would only have postponed the inevitable war. Rather, if I had to select a single quotation to explain the mindset of the patriots, I would choose the words of 91-year-old Levi Preston, from Danvers, Massachusetts. In 1843, when pressed by a young man to say why he'd taken up arms against the British he replied, "We always had governed ourselves and we always meant to. They didn't mean we should."

In the spring of 1775, with the outbreak of the war, and the Continental Congress asking the colonial legislatures to raise troops for a truly continental army, a patriotic and martial fervor swept the colonies. A colonist from Philadelphia wrote to a correspondent in London: "The *rage militaire*, as the French call a passion for arms, has taken possession of the whole continent." This spirit contrasted sharply with the disillusionment that would come a year later, in 1776, when each new report from the war would tell of another American defeat.

Confidence was high in 1775. Many patriots expected the conflict to last only as long as it took for news to reach London, alerting Parliament that America was deadly serious about its willingness to fight a war to preserve American liberties. Congress appointed one of its own, George Washington, to command its army. Before leaving Philadelphia to ride north to the war, Washington would write home to his wife, Martha, assuring her, "I shall return safe to you in the fall." But it was not to be. The British were also in earnest, and the war would drag on for years.

King George III, contrary to popular American misconception, was not neutral on the American question. In fact, he was just starting to speak out on it, revealing publicly for the first time that his true feelings lay with his ministers and other hard-liners in Parliament. Indeed, he would not even deign to have the rebel Congress's petition read aloud to him - the so-called "Olive Branch Petition" asking him to intercede on America's behalf in its dispute with Parliament. Rather, the King declared, "The die is now cast. The colonies must either submit or triumph." He proceeded to aggressively pursue a military solution, hiring mercenaries from Germany to help his army force America's submission to Parliament.

By the summer of 1776, with a full-scale war thrust upon them, and their offers of reconciliation rebuffed, American patriots would reluctantly break their allegiance to their sovereign, King George III, and declare independence.

CONTENTS

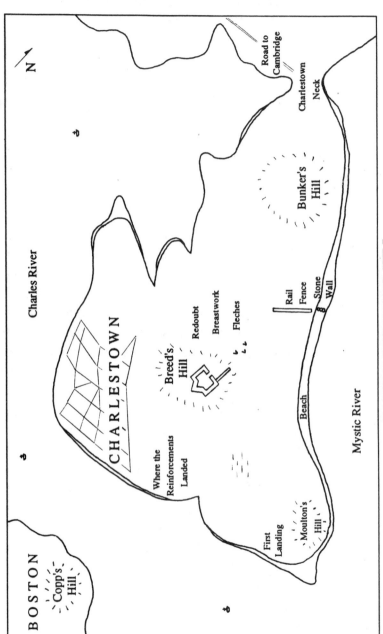

BATTLE OF BUNKER HILL

CHAPTER ONE
SETTING THE STAGE FOR
THE BREAK WITH BRITAIN

*"They are a race of convicts, and ought to be thankful for anything
we allow them short of hanging."*

> *- Dr. Samuel Johnson, English man
> of letters*

Before examining the events of the revolutionary period, an understanding is needed of what Americans were like in the 1760s, and what their role was within the British Empire.

The population of the thirteen colonies, from Georgia northward to Maine (then a part of Massachusetts Bay), in 1763 was approximately 1,750,000. Of these, perhaps 350,000, one-fifth, were Negroes, most of them slaves in the southern colonies. In comparison, Britain at that time had about 7,500,000 people. America's population had been doubling every twenty-five years since the previous century, and would continue to do so, making the total about 3,000,000 by the end of the Revolutionary War in the early 1780s.

The most populous colonies were Virginia, Massachusetts, Maryland and Pennsylvania. Almost the entire population was rural, no more than one out of every twenty people living in towns of more than 2,000. The largest towns in 1763 were seaports, with Philadelphia at 25,000 leading the way, followed by Boston and New York at 17,000 apiece, and Charleston, South Carolina, next with only 8,000.

The vast majority of Americans were farmers who owned enough land to be economically independent, although for most of them it was at or near a subsistence level. The abundance of cheap land meant that almost any free man could own land in America, described by one European as "the best poor man's country in the world." American society was a mobile one, in which a man could rise on his own merits. In 1763, nearly half of all white Americans were indentured servants bound by contract to work, typically seven years, to repay their employer for their passage to America. However, once they earned their freedom, many became very successful, among them Matthew Thornton, one of the signers of the Declaration of Independence. There was no titled nobility and little landed gentry to act as a restrictive force, as in England. In the words of J. Hector St. Jean Crevecoeur, a Frenchman who moved to America in 1754, land ownership meant Americans were

> all animated with the spirit of an industry which is unfettered and unrestrained, because each person works for himself. Wives and children gladly help their father to clear those fields whence exuberant crops arise to feed and clothe them all, without any part being claimed either by a despotic prince, a rich abbot or a mighty lord.

Under the inheritance laws of primogeniture, the oldest son inherited the land. Since the typical family had eight children, this meant there was always a substantial number of young men seeking lands of their own. They did not have far to search, the frontier being a short journey inland. Population growth and migration also meant there was a constant need for tradesmen. Benjamin Franklin observed in 1751, "No man continues long a laborer for others, but gets a plantation of his own; no man continues long a journeyman to a trade, but goes among those new settlers and sets up for himself." Debtors running away from creditors, adventurers of all kinds, and persons not willing to tolerate "civilized ways" all added to the swell of those migrating to the frontier.

What were these farmers like, who braved the dangers and rigors of the frontier, and were disdained by the townspeople? In 1766, Charles

Woodmason left the relatively comfortable life of Charleston, South Carolina, to work as a missionary among the "backwoods" people of the frontier. He was impressed with their desire to hear the word of God, noting that, "Many of these people walk ten or twelve miles with their children in the burning sun to hear it." However, he was not favorably impressed with their social habits. They came to church wearing "no shoes or stockings" and there was "no making them sit still during service, but they will be in and out, forward and backward the whole time, women especially, as bees to and fro in their hives."

The farmers' motivation to industry was also characteristic of a good proportion of the inhabitants of the coastal towns, such as the seamen who sailed the Atlantic in search of whales, cod, or profit through trade. Of the whalers, Crevecoeur observed:

> The motives that lead them to the sea are very different from those of most other seafaring men ... a settled plan of life, a well-founded hope of earning a livelihood. They go to whaling with as much pleasure, with as strong an expectation of success, as a landsman undertakes to clear a piece of swamp.

The towns were populated mainly by merchants and others directly or indirectly involved in the mercantile trade. Raw materials had to be exported to the mother country, or between colonies, and manufactured goods had to be imported from Britain. The towns also had the usual variety of artisans, such as blacksmiths, coopers, printers, etc. In the seaports, one could find a large number of widows, owing to the many wars and the dangerous occupations of fishing, whaling, and trading on the high seas. In Boston, nearly one out of every three adult women was a widow.

Most Americans in 1763 were literate, even the farmers. Of the thirteen colonies, fully eleven of them could each boast at least twenty newspapers. This was also a great period for correspondence. The wealth of original material available to people researching the revolutionary period is due mainly to the common practice of writing long, descriptive letters, and keeping journals. Newspapers of the time did not have staffs of reporters as they do today. Instead, the "publick printer" relied on local citizens to provide firsthand accounts of events. These were usually letters the citizens had received from distant relatives or friends who were eyewitnesses. If the letter related news of universal interest, it might be reprinted in more than one newspaper; for example, in Boston, Philadelphia and Charleston.

As the political crisis with Parliament developed, subscriptions skyrocketed, and newspapers became public forums. Editorials submitted by concerned citizens, usually with Latin pen names, were rebutted in subsequent issues by writers holding the opposite views. Patriot propagandists, such as James Otis, Jr., Silas Downer, John Dickinson and others, stirred up resistance against each new law enacted by Britain's Parliament.

These grievances and ideas about liberty did not reach an apathetic audience. Americans for one hundred and fifty years had been gradually testing their ability to wrest power, bit by bit, from the King's official representatives - the colonial governors. In all the colonies, except Connecticut and Rhode Island, the governor was appointed by the King. Each colony had a bicameral legislature, composed of an Assembly and a Council. Members of the Council (the upper house) were appointed by the governor or the King (except in Massachusetts, where they were elected by the Assembly). In all the colonies, Assemblymen were elected by the people they represented. By 1763, about three of every four white adult males could vote.

It was in each colony's Assembly that resistance to Parliamentary taxation would be hotly debated. Here lay the real threat to the bond between England and her colonies, as Sir Guy Carleton pointed out in 1768: "A popular Assembly, in a country where all men appear nearly upon a level, must give a strong bias to republican principles." The governor had important powers - to appoint his favorites for the Council and other government positions, to exercise the veto, to dissolve a legislative session, etc. - but he could not initiate legislation,

4

nor could he force the Assembly to vote for his views.

Americans were conscious of what they considered their "rights as Englishmen." They were proud of Britain's tradition of political liberties and civil rights guaranteed by the English Constitution. However, these theoretical rights were much more likely to be put into actual practice by English subjects not in England itself, but in the American colonies. In England, where only one out of every twenty free men could vote, the upper classes gave lip service to the principles of English justice and freedom, and were callously indifferent to the conditions of the urban and rural poor.

Americans probably enjoyed the most freedoms of any people in the "civilized" world at the time. There were no tithes to be paid to support an established church. Naval press gangs were rarely a threat to inhabitants of the seaports. Americans were more advanced in self-government along democratic lines than the people of England or any other country. Since New York's Zenger court case in 1735, the colonists had enjoyed almost complete freedoms of speech, assembly, and the press. The trades and professions were open to anyone with the talent, there being no restrictive guilds or associations. Even debtors could be free from imprisonment by simply moving to the frontier, where creditors rarely dared follow.

Creveoeur summed up the character of the typical American militia man as that of

> a new man. He is independent; he is impatient of discipline. He is equalitarian, and has little patience with those who claim to be his superiors. He is literate, takes an active part in the business of politics, and carries into camp the habits of self-government.

One might say, someone who very likely would stand up for what he felt were his rights, should anyone attempt to take any of those rights away. The well-read American public was being influenced by eighteenth century English and French philosophers, who wrote that man should be ruled by the law of nature. The law of nature held that man owes no allegiance to superiors, but should act as he would be inclined to in a perfect state of nature without rulers and privileged classes. This "natural rights of man" philosophy was right at home in New England, which, because of its pattern of develpment, had no aristocracy such as found in some of the other colonies, where large landholders tended to dominate. Visitors traveling through New England never failed to be astounded by the "social leveling" exhibited there. One British visitor, Janet Shaw, wrote that a "most disgusting equality" prevailed.

Americans talked a lot about their "rights as Englishmen." Englishmen in Parliament, however, did not consider Americans the equals of residents of England. During the conflict over taxation, British propagandists found that one of the most effective ways to counter advocates of conciliation in Parliament was to remind them of the low birth and general inferiority of the colonists, and what an insufferable humiliation it would be to treat them as equals. The greatest British man of letters of that time, Samuel Johnson - who knew everything - knew about Americans. "They are a race of convicts, and ought to be thankful for anything we allow them short of hanging."

* * * * *

Now that we have seen what America and its inhabitants were like just prior to the Revolution, we can examine America's role within the British Empire. Essentially, the British view held that the American colonies existed for the financial profit of England. Just as the Parliament had passed laws preventing Ireland from selling its products to anyone but England, so too the Navigation Acts and other laws forced America's economy to be dependent on England's. A British columnist illustrated this view, when he wrote that the colonies were "to be regarded in no other light but as subservient to the commerce of their mother country." Another agreed, pointing out that, "The very word 'colony' implies dependency." General Thomas Gage felt it absolutely essential that America be kept dependent on Britain. Gage predicted that, if such restrictive "commerce with the mother country shall cease, an independency of her government will soon follow."

If the colonies' purpose was to provide for the economic well-being of Britain, their separate economies must be complementary with Britain's. Therefore, Parliament enacted laws encouraging the colonists to manufacture goods which Britain could not, and prohibiting them from producing those goods made in Britain. The interests of the colonies must always be subordinate to Britain's.

Because of this policy, there was little economic diversification in the colonies, and almost no manufacturing. Kitchenware, clocks, books, axes, shoes, clothing, farming and carpentry tools, etc., were all imported from England. The colonies could provide the raw materials, but were not allowed to use them to manufacture finished products.

The colonies provided the British West Indies with fish and wood products, while serving as a market for their molasses. New England rum, made from the molasses, was sold throughout the colonies, and used in both the slave trade and trade with Indians on the American frontier. New England also provided Britain with more than one-third of its newly-built ships. Tobacco, indigo and rice from the southern colonies, and wheat from Pennslyvania, gave English merchants the commodities that were much in demand throughout Europe. American iron provided an important raw material for England's foundries. But, more important than its exports, America provided a steady, large market for goods manufactured in Britain. The colonies suffered from an unfavorable balance of payments. Every year, more and more hard currency left America for Britain, and less came back.

As the London Magazine put it in 1766, "The American is apparelled from head to foot in our manufactures. He scarcely drinks, sits, moves, labours or recreates himself, without contributing to the emolument of the mother country."

As early as 1748, a Swedish visitor, Peter Kalm, noted a coolness in the feelings of Americans toward Great Britain. He felt the cause was "commercial oppression" by the mother country, and that this coolness was increased by the fact that many of the Americans did not take their roots from England. The many Dutch, Germans, French, and especially the Irish and Scots, had little reason to feel a loyalty to England. And how much loyalty was to be expected even from those of English descent, considering that, in most cases, their ancestors left England in resentment, escaping unfavorable religious or economic conditions?

Kalm believed that America's "exceeding freedom and prosperity nurse an untamable spirit." And that the only reason why the love of these colonies for England "does not utterly decline" was the presence of the French on the frontier, and the protection of the American coast provided by the British navy. "The English government has therefore reason to regard the French in North America as the chief power which urges their colonies to submission," Kalm wrote. Later, in 1763, this French threat disappeared, when the treaty ending the final French and Indian War gave Canada to England, opening the way for the full expression of America's "untamable spirit."

CHAPTER TWO
THE CONFLICT BEGINS
1763-1766

"What do we mean by the Revolution? The War? That was no part of the Revolution. It was only an effect and consequence of it. The Revolution was in the minds of the people, and this was effected, from 1760 to 1775, in the course of fifteen years before a drop of blood was drawn at Lexington."

> *- John Adams, writing to Thomas Jefferson in 1815*

The peace treaty of 1763 doubled the size of the American colonies south of Canada by adding the lands between the Appalachian Mountains and the Mississippi River. One of the most urgent matters before Parliament in 1763 was the need for a policy on the settlement of this vast new territory, inhabited almost solely by Indians.

The Hudson's Bay Company, a powerful lobby of London merchants that traded in furs, wanted to keep settlers out of these western lands, since settlement would quickly lead to the end of that area as a prime source of furs. But the end of the war meant a greatly reduced Indian threat. So the colonists, with their high birth and immigration rates, were ready to seek out virgin lands in greater numbers than ever before. They pushed the frontier steadily westward.

In response, an Ottawa warchief named Pontiac organized 36 tribes and, in an unprecedented show of unity and coordination, they attacked forts and settlements all along the frontier in 1763, killing 2,000 settlers. This came at a time when the British government was heavily in debt and desperately needed to reduce the size of its army.

It could not afford to maintain large forces on the American frontier.

Equally important was the prospect that Britain's monopoly as a provider of manufactured goods to the colonies would be jeopardized if the American population gradually shifted further away from the seaports. The Board of Trade's John Pownall declared that the establishment of inland colonies might

> induce a necessity for such remote settlements to ingage in the production and manufacture of those articles of necessary consumption which they ought, upon every principle of true policy, to take from the mother country, and would also give rise to a separation of interests and connections.

So the British government took two separate actions, which, together, were intended to halt the American westward migration. First, Parliament reorganized the fur trade, restricting it to trappers and traders who already held a license (that is, those selling to the Hudson's Bay Company). Second, King George III issued a proclamation in October, 1763, forbidding Americans from moving "beyond the heads of any rivers which fall into the Atlantic Ocean from the west and northwest." Lands west of the crest of the Appalacians would remain under royal control, reserved for the Indians.

> We do hereby strictly forbid, on pain of our displeasure, all our loving subjects from making any purchase or settlements whatever, [or] taking possession of the lands above reserved. And we do further strictly enjoin and require all persons forthwith to remove themselves from such settlements.

For years, military officers operating along the frontier had been sending recommendations to London, suggesting that the army be employed in a policing role, to protect red men from whites. This is exactly what was decided in the autumn of 1763. Fifteen regiments (8,000 to 10,000 men) would be allocated to North America. Sending them away from England would also make them less likely to arouse the traditional hostility and suspicion among the civilian population in England against a standing peacetime army. One reason for the existence in 1763 of such a large standing army, unprecedented in peacetime, was the fear that France might try to forcibly take back some of her lost North American territories. Sending them to the American frontier would not only work to inhibit French aggression, but also keep a lid on the colonists' western migration.

Until 1764, the colonists made no direct contribution to the upkeep of a peacetime army. To persuade Parliament to allocate the necessary funds for so many troops to be stationed so far away, the King's ministers promised that although the first year's expense would have to be paid by British taxpapers, one-third of the cost for subsequent years would be paid by new revenues to be raised in the American colonies. This was especially necessary because the recent war against France had increased the national debt to 123 million pounds. Merely paying the interest on this huge war debt would require new sources of revenue.

To refer to Parliament's efforts to raise new revenues from the colonies as "The New Imperial Policy" is somewhat misleading, because the various measures enacted for those purposes did not emanate from a well-thought out plan. Rather, each new law was an individual reaction to a new crisis.

First came the Revenue Act of 1764, pushed through Parliament by Lord George Grenville, the new Chancellor of the Exchequer and First Lord of the Treasury. Its purpose was to firmly enforce, for the first time, the old Navigation Acts which imposed duties on trade. Also, it would suppress the growing illegal trade between the colonies and foreign countries, especially Holland and the French West Indies. Millions of gallons of molasses and thousands of chests of tea were smuggled into America each year without duty being paid to British customs collectors. To the British, American smugglers had been especially odious during the recent war, when they had sold their American products to the British Empire's enemies (the French and Spanish) in the Carribbean. An inquiry into the administration of the customs service determined that it was inefficient and corrupt, and that it cost far more to operate than it collected. The new Revenue Act was designed to change that.

The Revenue Act (called the "Sugar Act" by Americans) greatly enlarged the list of American products which could legally be shipped only to Britain or its colonies. It also required duties be paid on sugar, Madeira wine, indigo, pimento, and coffee shipped to American ports from abroad. Customs collectors who previously served in absentia were now ordered to their posts in America, and they were forbidden from having their duties performed by their deputies. Many of these deputies were suspected of having taken bribes from smugglers.

To motivate customs collectors to vigorously execute their duties, the Revenue Act stipulated that they would receive one half of the proceeds from all ships and cargo they condemned after seizure. Colonial governors and army and navy commanders in America were ordered to assist the customs collectors in arresting smugglers and seizing their ships. A new vice-admiralty court was established at Halifax, Nova Scotia, where cases could be tried without juries, and in front of judges who were not vulnerable to threatening mobs. And, to further ensure that customs collectors would perform their duties, they were declared immune from being sued for damages in colonial courts.

Also passed in 1764 were: 1) a Currency Act, outlawing the colonies' practice of issuing paper money; and 2) a resolution stating that, if not enough revenue is raised by the Revenue Act, further revenue laws should be passed, using stamps as the medium. The proposal for such a stamp bill was introduced as a mere resolution, rather than actual legislation, because Grenville wished to have time to consult with the colonies on the idea. He stated in Parliamentary debate that it was his desire "to follow, to a certain degree, the inclination of the people in North America, if they will agree to the end."

In America, the Revenue Act was perceived as an ominous precedent, a law to be resisted, lest compliance invite passage of other, more restrictive laws. In New England, resistance was encouraged by the clergy, sparked by news that London's Anglican bishop was lobbying for the establishment of an Anglican bishopric in North America. Congregationalists felt that, if the Revenue Act succeeded, it would encourage an attack on the extraordinary religious freedoms that Americans enjoyed. New Englanders had always held that the partition between the Roman Catholic and Anglican Churches was dangerously thin. Now, with Roman Catholics no longer actively persecuted in England, many Americans suspected that England was about to return to Rome, and that the appointment of an Anglican bishop would lead to the subjugation of America by popery.

Merchants were especially hard hit by the Revenue and Currency Acts. Due to the limited number of products which could be made in America, the colonists had always faced a chronic shortage of the hard currency needed to purchase British manufactured goods. Now paper money printed in the colonies would no longer be acceptable. Some merchants decided to protest these new laws by ceasing to import British goods. Philadelphia's Samuel Rhodes wrote to his supplier in London, "I need not say much of future dealings, for I fear that all our trade with you must come to an end if your legislature will carry into execution those resolves."

In Boston, each section of town - the north end, the south end, and the middle - had a group of merchants and "mechanics" (tradesmen, like the silversmith Paul Revere) who met one night each week to discuss politics and its practical application. A penniless, middle aged lawyer named Samuel Adams belonged to all three groups: the North Caucus, Middle Caucus and South Caucus. (The term "caucus" originated from the fact that many of these mechanics were caulkers by trade.) Adams was the town's tax collector, and fared very poorly at it because of his habit of being overly sympathetic to citizens who could not afford to pay their taxes. This made Sam very popular, at least among some of the citizens.

Adams persuaded these caucuses to take action against these new

Parliamentary measures. One of these men was a young merchant named John Hancock, the richest man in the colony. Adams also went outside these small groups and coaxed the leaders of Boston's two large rival gangs into putting their love of rioting to a more positive purpose: terrorizing customs collectors and other notorious supporters of Parliament's new measures. To help win over these ruffians, he sometimes had Hancock provide the liquid refreshments for their gatherings. Ten years later, during the first Continental Congress, a "Tory" (loyalist) writer would describe Sam Adams and his relationship with the younger John Hancock:

> Mr. Adams's character may be defined in a few words. He is a hypocrite in religion, a republican in politics, of sufficient cunning to form a consummate knave, possessed of as much learning as is necessary to disguise the truth with sophistry, and so complete a moralist that it is one of his favorite maxims that "the end will justify the means."
>
> With his oily tongue he duped a man whose brains were shallow and pockets deep, and ushered him to the public as a patriot, too. He filled his head with importance and emptied his pockets, and as a reward kicked him up the ladder, where he now presides over the "Twelve United Provinces" and where they both are at the present plunging you, my countrymen, into the depths of distress.

While Adams inspired but did not actually partake in riots, he did personally lead other actions which would be more important to the movement - manipulation of the press and of Boston's Town Meetings, where any citizen was free to speak his mind. He made sure these meetings were packed with enough of his supporters to either ensure a majority or intimidate the Tories into acquiescence. Adams would also make frequent use of his skillful pen and, eventually, his position as Clerk in the Assembly, to mastermind a superb propaganda campaign that would influence opinions and events in Massachusetts and, to some extent, throughout the colonies.

In the spring of 1764, under Adams's leadership, a Boston Town Meeting resolved that Boston's representatives in the Assembly should take a firm stance against the Revenue Act:

> Those unexpected proceedings may be preparatory to more extensive taxation; for if our trade may be taxed, why not our lands and everything we possess? If taxes are laid upon us in any shape, without our having a legal representation where they are laid, are we not reduced from the character of free subjects to the miserable state of tributary slaves? This annihilates our charter right to govern and tax ourselves. We claim British rights, not by charter only; we are born to them. Use your endeavors that the weight of the other North American colonies may be added to that of this province, that by united application all may happily obtain redress.

Encouraged by its Boston delegation, the Massachusetts Assembly established a Committee of Correspondence, which on June 25, 1764, sent a circular letter to all the other colonial legislatures, describing the danger to their "most essential rights" and requesting "united assistance." The result was considerable debate in those legislatures, and the drafting of petitions of grievances, which were sent to Parliament. In Britain, the petition of grievance was a traditional method of nonviolently expressing political opposition. Typical of the reasoning put forth in these petitions from the colonies was the following excerpt, taken from the one that New York's Assembly sent on October 18, 1764:

> Exemption from burthen of ungranted, involuntary taxes must be the grand principle of every free state,

without which right there can be no liberty, no happiness, no security; it is inseparable from the very idea of property, for who can call that his own which may be taken away at the pleasure of another.

Nonviolent resistance was not limited to the legislatures, though. The New York Gazette reported on November 22, 1764:

> The young gentlemen of Yale College have unanimously agreed not to make use of any foreign spiritous liquors. The gentlemen [are] commended for setting so laudable an example. All gentlemen of good taste who visit the college will think themselves better entertained with a good glass of cider, than they could be with the best punch or Madeira.

For Rhode Island, in particular, the Revenue and Currency Acts posed severe impacts on the local economy. Because that small colony imported over a million gallons of molasses each year, the duty of three pence per gallon would amount to more than 14,000 pounds a year in taxes. This was, according to a Rhode Island pamphleteer, more hard money "than was ever in the colony at one time." As it turned out, the judges and prosecuting attorneys in that colony were sympathetic to smugglers. They frustrated the attempts of the customs collectors to prosecute the violators by arranging for the trials to take place when the collectors were out of town, so the cases could be dismissed for lack of evidence.

The most important development during this period was the education of the public concerning the conflict. It was claimed at the time that America was "a country where people more generally read, discuss, and judge for themselves than perhaps any other in the world." Political pamphlets for and against taxation were very popular, and newspapers published essays, as well as excerpts of letters from people in England writing to colonists about the crisis. These informed those who could read. Those who could not read learned of the taxation crisis at their local taverns, which soon gained a reputation as "nurseries of revolution."

American pamphleteers cited constitutional arguments along the theme of "no taxation without representation," a phrase made popular by Boston's James Otis, Jr. Newspapers in England also debated the issue. Supporters of the government's position cited the concept of "virtual representation." According to this theory, any member of Parliament's House of Commons, regardless of the location of his home constituency, represented the interests of all Englishmen, wherever they may reside within the empire.

However, a Marylander named Daniel Dulaney saw through it, arguing in his 1765 pamphlet, *Considerations on the Propriety of Imposing Taxes in the British Colonies*, that, "The notion of a virtual representation of the colonies is a mere cobweb, spread to catch the unwary and entangle the weak." And, Dulaney argued, an American's sovereignty was divided between the British Parliament and his colonial legislature. The next year, Virginia's Richard Bland took Dulaney's idea further by arguing, in his *An Enquiry into the Rights of the British Colonies*, that in coming to America the colonists' ancestors had exercised their natural right to quit one country in favor of another and, by forming a new government in the wilderness, had actually "become a sovereign state, independent of the state from which they separated." Bland was definitely a man whose ideas were ahead of his time; such ideas would not become commonly accepted until ten years later, when Thomas Paine would add his *Common Sense* to the debate on the practicality of declaring independence.

On both sides of the Atlantic, each populace was divided politically into Tories and Whigs. Tories favored the efforts of the King and the Tory-dominated Parliament to rule America with a firmer hand. In America, Tories often referred to themselves as "friends of government." Whigs in Parliament feared that if the King and his ministers succeeded in America, it would lead to similar and perhaps worse restrictions at home. The English Revolution of 1688 had taken some of the governing power from the Crown and given it to the Parliament. Through the effective use of patronage and other forms of bribery, King George III was beginning to shift the balance back to the Crown. The Whigs were fighting this trend, and therefore were great friends to American liberties.

* * * * *

The American colonies learned that a bill to raise revenue via tax stamps was under consideration long before the bill was proposed and debated in Parliament. The introduction of this new bill was especially frustrating to Benjamin Franklin, Jared Ingersall, and other colonial agents who had met with George Grenville beforehand. They'd been told by him:

> I am not set upon this tax. If Americans dislike it, and prefer any other method of raising the money themselves, I shall be content. Write, therefore, to your several colonies, and if they choose any other mode I shall be satisfied, provided the money be raised.

Several alternative methods of raising revenue in the colonies were offered by the colonial legislatures, but these fell on deaf ears. And the House of Commons refused to have their petitions against the stamp bill read aloud; the members had been irritated enough already by the colonies' questioning of Parliament's authority to levy the sugar tax on them. The Revenue Act had failed to raise the expected level of new revenues, so Parliament duly passed the new Stamp Act on March 22, 1765. During the debate in the House of Commons, only a few members spoke out against it, and the measure carried by a vote of 245 to 49.

If one examines the situation in Britain at the time, it is not surprising that the vote was so overwhelmingly in favor of the Stamp Act. Because of the inequitable system of taxation, most of the tax burden for the empire fell on the shoulders of the landowners in Britain, who complained that they were paying the bills for the recent French war, which benefitted only the merchants and the American colonies. John Wilkes, a pro-American member of the House of Commons, observed that the country squires clung obstinately to the conviction that a colonial revenue was essential to their welfare. Americans were wrong in their belief that the King's ministers were the only ones to blame for the new measures being passed in Parliament. Indeed, the Revenue Act of 1764 had passed by a nearly unanimous vote.

Americans were doubly incensed when they received news of the Stamp Act's passage, because they also learned that their petitions against it had not been read aloud in Parliament. This refusal was contrary to the traditional political right of Englishmen to have grievances aired. A New Yorker wrote that, "This single stroke has lost Great Britain the affection of all her colonies." Now, not only were the colonists not represented in Parliament, but their petitions were being ignored!

Under the provisions of the Stamp Act, beginning on November 1, 1765, virtually every use of paper or parchment would require payment of a tax. This tax would be in the form of a stamp whose embossment must be purchased with hard money. Examples of taxable transactions included: appointments to public office, liquor and attorney's licenses, land titles and other legal documents, and the sale of newspapers, pamphlets, calendars, playing cards, dice, etc. As with the Revenue Act, it also stipulated that all violators would be tried in admiralty courts without juries.

Sam's young lawyer cousin, John Adams, considered this provision "the most grievous innovation of all, where one judge presides alone!" That, according to Adams, was "directly repugnant to the Great Charter itself." Also passed that same month of March, 1765, was a Quartering Act, requiring the local colonists to feed and house the British army when stationed in or passing through their vicinity.

The Stamp Act, with its duties on legal documents, newspapers and pamphlets, would be costly to lawyers and "publick printers" - the most vocal sections of society. For this reason alone, it was a blunder of the first magnitude. Lawyers opposed to it used the press to gain the attention and support of the general populace. New York's loyal Lt. Governor Cadwallader Colden, in 1765, would blame the lawyers for inciting the Stamp Act riots that spread through the colonies like an epidemic:

> Every man's character who dares to discover his sentiments in opposition to theirs is loaded with infamy by every falsehood which malice can invent, and thereby exposed to the brutal rage of the mob. Nothing is too wicked for them to attempt which serves their purposes. The press is to them what the pulpit was in times of popery.

Parliament succeeded in alienating virtually every influential group in America: clergymen, merchants, lawyers, printers, and (since most were merchants or lawyers) assemblymen. In some areas, another group was added to this list - land speculators. Many of the wealthy landholders in Virginia's tidewater districts, for example, had planned on reaping huge profits from speculation in the trans-Appalachian lands won from the French - plans foiled by the Proclamation of 1763.

As soon as news of this new Stamp Act reached America, in May, 1765, Whigs began discussing what method of resistance to employ. Subscriptions to newspapers began increasing dramatically, as well as sales of political pamphlets, and would continue to do so for the next ten years while the conflict escalated. One colonist remarked that, "more attention is paid by many to the news paper than to sermons."

One pamphlet which had a particularly large circulation and made an impact both in England and America was written by James Otis, Jr., a leader in the Massachusetts Assembly. He had risen to prominence four years earlier, in 1761, in a court case challenging the legality of Writs of Assistance, which allowed customs collectors to search suspected smugglers' houses without warrants. It was during that trial that Otis had coined the phrase, "a man's house is his castle." Though he lost the case, his four hour summation speech created such a sensation that John Adams considered it the birth of independency.

In Otis's pamphlet, *Rights of the British Colonies Asserted and Proved*, he put forth virtually every major argument and doctrine that would be used over the next decade by other great patriot writers such as Livingston, Freneau, Hopkinson, Paine and Jefferson. Otis rebutted the reasoning that supported Parliament's new American policies, and he proposed that Parliament must consider admitting representatives from the American colonies. Thus, he coined another phrase: "no taxation without representation." The idea was not a new one. It had been debated in Parliament, and would be again, frequently, during the next few years.

American representation in Parliament would never come close to approval, though, mainly for two reasons: 1) the fear that Americans in Parliament would attach themselves to the King's ministers by being susceptible to their bribes, and thus strengthen the Crown at the expense of Parliament; and 2) the conviction that Americans were a rough, untutored lot, not fit for the company of gentlemen and, indeed, "not very unlike their half-brothers, the Indians."

When news of the Stamp Act's passage reached the Virginia legislature in late May, that session was in its last few days and soon due to recess for the hot season. Only 39 of the 116 Burgesses remained, the others having already left for home. Perhaps those still there were not representative of the entire body in their opinions of what should be done about the Stamp Act. A young lawyer named Patrick Henry had just arrived from one of the western districts to start his political career. Upon hearing the news about the Stamp Act, Henry had stayed up all night writing nine resolutions. The next day, Henry introduced seven of them. After furious debate, the first five passed, all by narrow margins. Each successive resolution was more inflammatory than the last, and passed by a narrower margin. After the sixth and seventh failed to carry a majority, he wisely decided not to introduce the eighth and ninth resolutions. His own account of what happened that day was found decades later among Henry's papers, he having written it on the back of a copy of the resolutions. This, he wrote, was

> the first opposition to the Stamp Act and the scheme of taxing America by the British Parliament. All the colonies, either through fear, or want of opportunity to form an opposition, or from influence of some kind or other, had remained silent. I had been for the first time elected a Burgess a few days before, was young, inexperienced, unacquainted with the forms of the House, and the members that composed it.
>
> Finding the men of weight averse to opposition, and the commencement of the tax at hand and that no person was likely to step forth, I determined to venture; and alone, unadvised, and unassisted, on a blank leaf of an old law-book wrote.
>
> Upon offering them to the House, violent debates ensued. Many threats were uttered, and much abuse cast on me by the party for submission. After a long and warm contest the resolutions were passed by a small majority, perhaps of one or two only.

The governor threatened to have Patrick Henry arrested, but as he reported to his superior in London, those Burgesses who had voted for the resolutions rallied round Henry, calling him a "noble patriot" and declaring that "if the least injury was offered to him they would stand by him to the last drop of their blood."

Passage of the resolutions was the beginning of a shift in political power within Virginia's legislature. This shift was accomplished primarily because Patrick Henry and Richard Henry Lee turned muckrakers and exposed the scandalous shortages in the official records of the treasury. The speaker of the House of Burgesses, during his earlier years as treasurer, had fallen into the habit of using Treasury funds to make "loans" to himself and his tidewater aristocrat friends. These loans had never been paid back. The scandal reduced the political influence of some of the Tory Burgesses from the tidewater districts and advanced the reputation and influence of the young Whigs now being elected from the western piedmont districts.

All five of Patrick Henry's resolutions were printed in newspapers throughout the colonies, even though the governor had stricken the fifth one from the record. Some printers changed the wording of the fifth one, making it even more inflammatory, in order to have it match their own views or to be more sensational and, thus, sell more copies. For example, Henry had asserted that Virginia had "the only and sole exclusive right and power" to lay taxes on Virginians. However, in Rhode Island, the Newport Mercury had it as: "Resolved that any person who shall, by speaking or writing, assert or maintain that any person or persons, other than the General Assembly of this Colony, have the power to impose or lay taxation on the people here, shall be deemed an enemy to his Majesty's colony."

In the Massachusetts Assembly, James Otis, Jr. prepared a circular letter requesting the other colonial legislatures each send three delegates to a "Stamp Act Congress," which he proposed be held in New York in October. Some of the wealthiest and most distinguished Americans were elected or appointed delegates to the Congress. This should have convinced the British government that opposition to Parliamentary taxation was not confined, as they thought, to the lower class "rabble and banditti" of the coastal seaports.

It was a long hot summer for the stamp masters, those few men selected by Parliament to collect the stamp duties. Grenville hoped by appointing Americans, rather than Britons, as stamp masters he would save them from the wrath of the rioters. He was wrong. They became the most hated people in America. The Whigs in America looked upon them as traitors, or in the Boston Gazette's analogy, slaves promoted to overseers:

> A foreigner we could more cheerfully endure, because he might be supposed not to feel our distresses.

But for one of our fellow slaves, who equally shares in
our pains, to rise up and beg the favor of inflicting them,
is not that intolerable?

Benjamin Franklin, soon after returning from London, observed the American reaction to the Stamp Act and wisely gave his commission as a stamp master to his cousin. At one point, while he was still in London, his wife in Philadelphia had collected a sizable supply of arms and ammunition, and prepared with her friends to withstand a siege. Franklin was not able to remove the stain on his reputation until almost a year later when, back in London, he urged repeal of the act.

In every American seaport, active Whigs banded together in local chapters of a new secret society known as the "Sons of Liberty." They took the name from a comment made in a speech to Parliament by the English Whig, Isaac Barre. Arguing against the Stamp Act, Barre had referred to those Americans who vigorously resisted the Revenue Act as "sons of liberty." Also called "Liberty Boys," the Sons had their own secret signs of recognition and, on public occasions when it was safe, each member wore around his neck a

medal, on one side of which was the figure of a stal-
wart arm, grasping in its hand a pole surmounted with a
Cap of Liberty, and surrounded by the words 'Sons of
Liberty.' On the reverse was the emblem of the Liberty
Tree.

Their goal, in the words of the New York chapter, was to "go to the last extremity, and venture our lives and fortunes, to prevent the Stamp Act from ever taking place," by protecting people who did business without stamps, and by showing "the highest resentment" toward those who sold or bought the stamps.

The custom of using a certain tree as the location for rituals of resistance spread throughout the colonies after it was started in Boston on August 14, 1765. On that day, an effigy of Boston's stamp master,

Andrew Oliver, was hung from a tree. Hanging next to it was a boot, with an effigy of the devil sticking out, meant to represent Lord Bute, the King's advisor and one of the chief proponents of the act.

At nightfall, the mob brought Oliver's effigy to a dock where Oliver had recently erected a small building that the mob assumed would be his stamp office. The mob destroyed the building, then proceeded to Oliver's home, but Oliver and his family had fled by then. So they broke windows, smashed furniture and used it to make a bonfire. Then they beheaded Oliver's effigy and threw it on the bonfire. Governor Francis Bernard gave orders to the colonel of the local militia to beat an alarm, but was told that all the drummers were members of the mob. He therefore decided to take up immediate residence in Castle William, a fort on Castle Island in Boston's harbor.

Lieutenant Governor Thomas Hutchinson, however, decided to go to the mob and talk them into dispersing. He was pelted with rocks, and fled to his house. Twelve days later, Hutchinson's house, as well as those of an admiralty court judge and a comptroller of customs, were all invaded by the mob, who left "nothing remaining but the bare walls and floors." Hutchinson wrote to a friend a few days later:

> Such ruin was never seen in America. Besides my plate and family pictures and household furniture of every kind, my own and my children's and servants' apparel, they carried off about 900 pounds sterling in money, not leaving a single book or paper, and having scattered or destroyed all the manuscripts and other paper I had been collecting for thirty years.

Fortunately, some of Hutchinson's invaluable research materials were saved by brave neighbors who picked them out of the streets. Some can still be seen today with mud stains on them. Hutchinson had been writing the second volume of his <u>History of Massachusetts Bay</u>, the first serious historical work by an American. The leader of the mob was later arrested, but released when Sam Adams warned that the mob might otherwise demolish the customhouse. Neither Adams nor any other prominent Whig had been with the mob that night, and they were greatly embarassed by the outcome. From that date on, Adams made sure that plenty of his hand-picked more reliable mechanics, such as Paul Revere, were on hand to prevent such excesses.

Boston's Liberty Tree became the mandatory site for the patriots' ritual demonstrations. According to the writings of Hutchinson, about one month after that eventful August 14th, Oliver was required to appear in person at noon "under liberty tree to make a public resignation" which would be pleasing to the "true-born sons of liberty." Each year thereafter, August 14th was celebrated by many of the Whigs around Boston. Hutchinson wrote of one such anniversary, in 1768:

> The anniversary of the 14th of August, the day on which the distributor of stamps had been compelled to resign, was celebrated this year with great parade. A vast concourse of people assembled at Liberty Tree, and, after rejoicing there, a procession of two or three chariots, and fifty or sixty chaises, went from thence to Roxbury, to an entertainment provided for them.

Use of a tree as a symbol of liberty was not a new idea in Boston. In 1648, Samuel Danforth had referred to a "Liberty Tree" in a poem about the Puritans' practice of governing themselves; because of the controversial poem, the Puritans had had to fortify Boston against an expected attack from the British navy. But no tree in English history caused more trouble than the Liberty Tree of Boston in the 1760s and 1770s. It was not long before trees were named for it in countless towns in all the colonies. Its fame spread throughout the English speaking world. A wealthy Whig in Cambridge, England, stipulated in his will that two friends could inherit his fortune only if they transported his body to Boston and buried him beneath its Liberty Tree.

Encouraged by news of the events in Boston, local Sons of Liberty chapters in other seaports soon burned effigies of, and destroyed property of, their own stamp masters and customs collectors. In Lebanon and other Connecticut towns, actors performed pageants featuring mock trials of stamp masters. Jared Ingersall, on his way from New Haven to Hartford to seek official sanction from the Assemby for his sale of the stamps, was stopped by about 200 Sons in Wethersfield. They forced him to resign as stamp master. The next spring, Governor Fitch, an outspoken advocate for obeying the Stamp Act, would be defeated in an election which swept the more radical towns of eastern Connecticut into power.

In Charleston, South Carolina, a wealthy Whig named Henry Laurens was mistakenly rumored to be a stamp master. He and his family were awakened in the middle of the night by a mob thumping on doors and windows, shouting the familiar "Liberty! Property! No Stamps!" Laurens told them of the condition of his sick wife. As he wrote later, "They replyed that they loved & respected me, and would not hurt me nor my property, but that they were sent over by some of my seemingly best friends to search for Stamp'd Papers which they were certain were in my custody [and] advised me to open the door to prevent worse consequences." After opening it, two intruders held cutlasses to his throat, while the rest shouted, "Lights! Lights and search!" as they dashed through the house. Laurens recognized many of them under their "disguise of soot, sailors' habits, slouch hats, etc., and to their great surprise called no less than nine of them by name."

They attempted to force Laurens to take "a Bible oath" that he had no knowledge of the stamps. Laurens refused, claiming that his word was sufficient. For this refusal, they threatened his life. Laurens responded by challenging any single one of them to a duel. They then became more moderate, and told him that they indeed did love him, and would love him more if he would agree to have no further relationship with the governor. Laurens' answer:

> In one word for all, gentlemen, I am in your power;
> you are very strong and may if you please barbicue me -
> I can but die - but you shall not by any force or means

whatsoever compel me to renounce my friendship or speak ill of men that I think well of, or to say or do a mean thing.

This speech won over the crowd. After giving Laurens shouts of approval and three cheers, they left. One man called out as he departed, "God bless your honour. Good night, colonel. We hope the poor lady will do well."

The following year, Silas Downer, one of Rhode Island's leading Sons, published an account of the Stamp Act crisis in the Providence Gazette. In it, he explained the inception and growth of radical organization in the colonies:

> Americans absolutely determined never to submit to the loss of their liberties, nor to suffer the Stamp Act to take place. They formed themselves into correspondence societies, in all the colonies, duly informing each other of the situation of their respective public affairs, and engaging, in case of necessity, to contribute all necessary assistance to each other, to the hazard of their lives and fortunes. They likewise determined to carry on all kinds of business without stamps.

Throughout the colonies, Sons of Liberty chapters were composed of sailors, mechanics, dockworkers, etc., but also some wealthy merchants and lawyers. Though in the North most of the wealthier people tended to be loyalists, in the South many of the wealthy planters and merchants were among the forces of resistance. Of the rioters, Virginia's Governor Fauquier declared, "This concourse of people I should call a mob, did I not know that it was chiefly, if not altogether, composed of gentlemen of property in the Colony." Many of the backwoods folk of the South, because they were distrustful of the wealthy landowners of the tidewater, held back. Years later, when the war came, these backwoods districts, especially in the Carolinas, would serve as good recruiting ground for Tory regiments.

Passions were so hot that, had Britain decided to use the military to enforce the Stamp Act, the war probably would have started in 1765 instead of ten years later. Colonel Israel Putnam claimed that he could muster 10,000 militia in eastern Connecticut alone, if it became necessary to fight the British. Thoughts of war were on many Americans' minds. Sons of Liberty in Connecticut and New York formed a mutual defense pact. The Sons in Providence sent a circular letter to their counterparts in all the colonies, suggesting active correspondence be initiated, and pledging aid to any colony attacked by the British. John Dickinson, a leader in Pennsylvania's Assembly, wrote privately to former Prime Minister William Pitt, predicting that Americans would not seek independence, "unless excited by the treatment they receive from Great Britain." But, he warned, if it came to war, "the strength of the colonies, their distance, the wealth that would pour into them on opening their ports to all nations, the jealousy entertained of Great Britain by some European powers, and the peculiar circumstances of that kingdom, would insure success."

But not all the resistance was violent. Local chapters of the Daughters of Liberty declared that they would accept no suitors who were not willing to resist the Stamp Act "to the last extremity." Of course, as noted earlier, this was the period of "the great debate" with pamphlets on taxation, pro and con, being written and read on both sides of the Atlantic. Most importantly, merchants throughout the colonies signed agreements not to import British goods until repeal of the Stamp Act.

Representatives from nine colonies assembled at the Stamp Act Congress in New York on October 7, 1765. The other four colonies were not represented, their governors having dissolved their Assemblies to prevent them from selecting delegates. Those delegates who did gather in New York drafted a *Declaration of Rights and Grievances*, as well as *Petitions* to the King and to each house of Parliament.

At the Stamp Act Congress, the delegates used the familiar "no taxation without representation" argument to assert that only the colonial legislatures had power to levy internal taxes upon the colonists. The issues were hotly debated for two weeks before a majority agreed with South Carolina's Christopher Gadsden, who argued that "in taxing ourselves and making laws for our own internal government, we can by no means allow our Provincial legislatures to be subordinate to any legislative power on earth."

Gadsden returned to Charleston extremely proud that delegates from nine separate and often feuding colonies had worked together toward a common goal. Though the result was only a few powerless documents, they gave the appearance of united resistance - something Benjamin Franklin had failed to achieve at Albany in 1754 on the brink of an invasion from French Canada. Gadsden declared that a united front was mandatory, if the colonists were to have any chance of successfully resisting the will of Parliament:

> There ought to be no New England men, no New York, &c., known on the continent, but all of us Americans. Nothing will save us but acting together; the province that endeavors to act separately must fall with the rest, and be branded besides with everlasting infamy.

Typical of the spirit of resistance sweeping the continent was that expressed at a Town Meeting held in Windham, Connecticut, where a resolution was passed "to keep up, establish, and maintain the spirit of liberty," and call a general meeting of the colony for that purpose. At another mass meeting, the inhabitants of New London County unanimously resolved that government originates from the consent of the people and that, if there is no other mode of relief against the Stamp Act and similar acts, they must reassume their natural rights. These principles were adopted in other towns and became the political platform of Connecticut's Whigs running for office that fall.

November 1, the day the Stamp Act was to take effect, was ushered in by tolling bells and flags flying at half staff. In Boston, a eulogy was pronounced on Liberty, dead at "age 145," a reference to the Pilgrims' landing at nearby Plymouth in 1620. Crowds in the streets shouted, "Liberty! Property! No stamps!" Posters at street corners and on the doors of public buildings threatened dire consequences to anyone who would receive or deliver a stamp, or delay business because of not having one. Printers who sold newspapers without stamps that day risked penalties, should the British decide to enforce the Stamp Act and arrest violators.

The November 1st edition of the New London Gazette appealed to "patriots" for diligence:

> We have reason to fear very interesting and terrible consequences. Shut not your eyes to your danger, O my countrymen! Do nothing to destroy or betray the rights of your posterity; do nothing to sully or shade the memory of your noble ancestors. Let all the governments and inhabitants unitedly resolve ... to sacrifice their lives and fortunes before they will part with their invaluable freedom.

The resistance movement had accomplished its objective. Though it would later prove to be somewhat misinformed about Georgia, the Pennsylvania Gazette was correct for the other colonies when it reported, on November 1, 1765:

> There is not one of the persons appointed from New Hampshire to Georgia that will execute the odious office; so that the stamps are now a commodity nobody knows what to do with, and are more abominable to meddle with than if they were infected with pestilence.

John Adams put it this way: "Our presses have groaned, our pulpits have thundered, our legislatures have resolved, our towns have voted. The Crown officers have everywhere trembled, and their little tools and creatures been afraid to speak and ashamed to be seen."

The following excerpt from a memoir of a wealthy New York City man provides a glimpse of the opinions of successful merchants who may have had Whig sympathies, but feared the social effects of protest as much as the economic effects of the Stamp Act:

In those days I was much at Mr. Wynkoop's house, and I remember one day in November, 1765, sitting with him and his father-in-law, old Nicholas Van Schoick-endinck, discussing the state of the nation. Even old Nicholas had been startled out of his customary complacency by the furious excitement occasioned by the Stamp Act.

"The Act is unconstitutional, sir," Mr. Wynkoop had just declared, somewhat dogmatically it must be confessed, and for perhaps the third time. "There can be no question about that, I think. It is not only contrary to precedent, but is destructive of British liberty, the fundamental principle of which is that Englishmen may not be taxed without their consent. We certainly never gave our assent to the Stamp Act."

"I won't say no to that," old Nicholas remarked. "And if we had done no more than protest the measure I should be well content."

"Little good protests would have done, sir. We protested before the bill was passed, and without effect. Mr. Grenville would not hear our protests and now he finds the act virtually nullified. I can't say I regret it."

"Nullified!" Old Nicholas exclaimed with some asperity. "A soft word for a nasty business. Mr. Grenville finds his law 'nullified,' you say. But in getting the law nullified we get half the windows of the Broad Way smashed too, and Governor Colden gets his chariot burned."

... [Wynkoop:] "God knows I am no friend of rioting. I have windows too. But a little rioting may be necessary, on occasion, to warn ministers that legislative lawlessness is likely to be met by popular violence."

"Tush!" he exclaimed irritably. "That's a new word, 'popular.' You young fellows have picked up a lot of precious democratical phrases, I must say. Who are 'the people' you talk so loosely about? Don't delude yourself by supposing that it was hatred of the Stamps that made them break Mr. Livingston's windows and burn Mr. Colden's chariot. They hate Mr. Livingston and Mr. Colden because they are men of substance and standing. It is not windows they aim at, but class privileges, the privilege of my class and yours. The bald fact is that a mob of mechanics and ne'er-do-wells are aiming to control the city through their committees. 'Sons of Liberty' they call themselves; sons of anarchy, in fact. I wish as much as you to preserve our liberties. But I warn you that liberty is a sword that cuts two ways, and if you can't defend your rights against ministerial oppression without stirring 'the people,' you will soon be confronted with the necessity of defending your privileges against the encroachments of the mob on the Bowling Green."

For almost six months, the American colonies waited for Great Britain's reaction to their resistance to the Stamp Act. Finally, in mid-April, 1766, word reached America that the controversial act had been repealed! Lord Grenville had just been replaced as Chancellor of the Exchequer by the more moderate Lord Rockingham, who was influenced by merchants from London and other cities hurt by the boycott. Merchants from 35 different cities showed up in London to lobby for repeal, bringing with them letters from American customers canceling orders. Such orders from Virginia and Maryland alone were said to be worth 1,500,000 pounds. Lord Dartmouth declared to the House of

Lords that there were now in England "50,000 men ripe for rebellion, for want of work," due to the American boycott.

Members of Parliament had been in a quandary as to whether to vote for repeal. To do so would be to reject the principle of Parliamentary sovereignty over the colonies. But to vote down the repeal bill would lead to permanent animosity with the Americans and the necessity to enforce an act that many felt was unenforceable. Former Prime Minister William Pitt came to the rescue with a moving speech advocating repeal in combination with a "statement of sovereignty in the strongest terms possible." Thus, the Declaratory Act was passed a few days before the repeal of the Stamp Act.

Similar in spirit to an act used to justify the subjugation of Ireland in 1719, this new act simply declared that Parliament had "full power and authority to make laws to bind the Colonies and people of America in all cases whatsoever." The vote in the House of Commons was unanimous and in the House of Lords almost so. Without this emphatic statement affirming Parliament's sovereignty, the Stamp Act would not have been repealed. Advocates of repeal had predicted that enforcement of the Stamp Act would have required use of the military; Britain would have run the risk of "lighting up a rebellion" and forcing the rebellious Americans to "fling themselves into the arms of France and Spain."

The Declaratory Act also laid to rest debate in Parliament over the constitutionality of that body levying internal taxes in the colonies. The path was now clear: Parliament could enact any new taxation it should deem necessary. During the next ten years, this act would stand as an inflexible barrier to compromise and reconciliation, as the mother country and her colonies would drift further apart with each new crisis. According to William Johnson, Connecticut's agent in London, Parliament's stance from now on would be firm. He interpreted the Declaratory Act as saying: "We have solemnly enacted our right to tax the colonies; the right of taxation is essential to our supremacy, the Americans treasonably deny it." As to further petitions of grievances, as long as "they dispute our right we cannot even hear them."

But, except for a few lawyers, Americans did not concern themselves with the Declaratory Act, because it did not specifically mention taxation. Besides, they were too preoccupied with rejoicing over the Stamp Act's repeal.

Arrival of the news brought an immediate calling out of the Sons of Liberty throughout the colonies - not to riot, but to frolic. Huge feasts, with drinking, dancing, singing and fireworks were commonplace. In Hartford, Connecticut, however, the celebrants learned that drinking and fireworks do not mix, when "the large brick school house was blown up with twenty-four white persons, two molattos, & two negro boys" inside. In New England alone, it was estimated, over five hundred sermons were preached in thanksgiving for the repeal. In Boston, bells tolled, houses were decorated with banners, and the Liberty Tree was filled with lanterns until its branches could hold no more, illuminating effigies of the King and several members of Parliament who had worked for the repeal. A collection was taken to release the debtors from jail so that they would not miss the magnificent sight.

Many of the stamp masters were allowed to resume their original professions without any more harassment. The Massachusetts Assembly, as required by the act that repealed the Stamp Act, voted to compensate Hutchinson and Oliver for damages done by rioters, but in the same measure issued a complete pardon for all persons indicted or convicted for participation in those riots.

During the crisis, British clothing had been shunned in favor of "homespun," and sheep were saved from slaughter, as wool now became more valuable than mutton. With the repeal of the Stamp Act, the boycott also ceased. It now became a patriotic duty to buy British goods. Therefore, Philadelphia's merchants voted to give their suits of homespun to the poor, and on "the King's birthday appear in new suits of broad cloth made in England." In London, where Benjamin Franklin had lobbied "night and day" for repeal and had testified before Parliament, he now celebrated the occasion by sending to his wife and

35

daughters in Philadelphia fine satin and silk clothes made in England.

The crisis had brought the colonies together for united action, and taught the patriots an important lesson: that the mother country was helpless in the face of a determined, united America. A decade later, the British government would regret its decision to repeal, rather than enforce, the Stamp Act. In the minds of most Englishmen, the way to reason with an American was to cow him with a whip, not placate him.

Over the next ten years, the King, his ministers, and Parliament would persevere in attempts to tax the colonies, ignoring the advice of Massachusetts Governor Francis Bernard, who, on October 22, 1765, had warned that, as long as Americans and Englishmen were "so widely different in their notions of their relation to one another," a clash of arms would be inevitable.

CHAPTER THREE
THE CONFLICT BUILDS
1767-1769

"No Assembly on the continent will ever concede that Parliament has a right to tax the colonies."

> *- Roger Sherman, Connecticut*
> *Assemblyman*

With the Stamp Act repealed, pressure was put on the new Chancellor of the Exchequer, Charles Townshend, to devise some other means of raising revenue in America. Some of the colonists who had argued against the Stamp Act had claimed that it was unconstitutional because the stamps were a form of internal taxation, and only external Parliamentary taxation could be supported by the English Constitution. This was mere rhetoric, and did not reflect the true feelings of most Americans - opposition to any form of taxation by Parliament.

However, Townshend used this internal vs. external argument to persuade Parliament that his newly designed tax program would be palatable to the Americans. So, in the spring of 1767, Parliament passed what would come to be known as the "Townshend Acts." These new laws placed duties on paper, glass, lead paint, and tea. The money raised would be used to support both the British army in North America and certain officials of the colonial governments, who would now be paid by the British Parliament. The feeling was that laws enacted by Parliament would be more likely to be enforced in America if the governors and judges there were not paid (and therefore indirectly controlled) by the colonial legislatures.

The Townshend Acts also established a Board of Commissioners of the Customs, with extensive powers to oversee enforcement of all laws of trade. Boston was selected as the Board's headquarters, because of the high incidence of smuggling through that port. To assist these commissioners, the vice-admiralty courts would be utilized (without juries). The new laws also clarified the legality of Writs of Assistance. Now it would be easier to obtain one from a colonial court, so that a customs collector could legally seize ships and search buildings without specific mention of what was being sought.

The propagandists in America looked upon these new measures as renewed attempts by Parliament to enslave the colonists. But their suggested method of protest was harder to commit to this time. What the patriot leaders were advising was a ban on the importation of all British goods, except a few essentials such as newsprint and fishing supplies. South Carolina's Christopher Gadsden urged on his fellow merchants and citizens:

> Nothing but God's blessing on our own immediate prudence, union and firmness can prevent our being plunged headlong into irrecoverable ruin and distress. The only probable means of averting so horrid a train of perils as are staring us in the face is not to consume one farthing more of British manufactures than we can possibly avoid.

Initially, the call for a boycott met with very little success. Reluctant merchants claimed that it would be "an unjust burthen" and cost them too dearly. However, between the first calls for the nonimportation agreement, in late 1767, and its widespread adoption, in early 1769, key developments would win over many of these merchants.

These developments were: 1) suspension of New York's Assembly for not completely complying with the Quartering Act; 2) a Massachusetts "circular letter" and Parliament's reaction to it; 3) influential political phamphlets published during the period; 4) the arrest and trial of John Hancock for smuggling; and 5) a British threat to transport

James Otis, Jr., and Samuel Adams to England to stand trial for treason.

Although Parliament had repealed the 1765 Stamp Act, its accompanying Quartering Act was still in effect. It required colonial authorities to provide any British troops within their colony sufficient barracks, candles, fuel, bedding, cooking utensils, salt, vinegar, and liquor (either five pints of beer or cider, or a gill of rum, per man per day). Since most of the Regulars stationed in America were in New York, that colony felt unfairly burdened. New York complied with the Quartering Act in 1766, but the next year it refused to provide the required ration of salt, vinegar and liquor. So Parliament then passed a Suspension Act, suspending New York's Assembly until they should agree to furnish the provisions. The 1767 elections surprisingly resulted in an Assembly more favorable to this; therefore, the legislature was able to convene, and the necessary funds were appropriated.

Upon hearing of the suspension, Boston's Assemblymen requested their governor to call a special session of the Massachusetts legislature, to consider what action might be taken to support their sister colony. The governor refused. But Boston's Whigs were determined to do something, so at a Town Meeting they passed a resolution encouraging local manufacture and proposing a "non-consumption agreement" - a boycott of British goods. People were encouraged to again wear homespun, use folk medicines made from native herbs, drink raspberry leaf and pine needle tea, etc.

When the Massachusetts Assembly convened that fall, it asked James Otis, Jr., and Sam Adams to draft a circular letter. The letter declared that the Parliament could not legally tax the colonies, and it asked the other colonies to unite in opposition. It also criticized the payment of salaries by the British government to colonial governors and judges. The letter was sent to all the colonial legislatures.

On April 2, 1768, Virginia's House of Burgesses received its copy of the Massachusetts Circular Letter, and promptly passed even stronger resolves. They declared that only the American legislatures could tax the colonies, and called for the colonies to unite in protest against any Parliamentary measure which might restrict their rights and liberties. Virginia sent a copy of its own resolves to each colony, and to the King and Parliament as well.

Colonial Secretary Lord Hillsborough sent a letter, accompanied by a copy of the Massachusetts Circular Letter, to the governors of the twelve other colonies, instructing them as follows:

> You will exert your utmost influence to prevail upon the assembly of your province to take no notice of it, which will be treating it with the contempt it deserves. If they give any countenance to this seditious paper, it will be your duty to prevent any proceedings upon it by an immediate prorogation or dissolution.

In a separate letter, Hillsborough instructed Massachusetts' Governor Francis Bernard to:

> require of the house of representatives, in his majesty's name, to rescind the resolution which gave birth to the circular letter. If the new assembly should refuse to comply, it is the King's pleasure that you should immediately dissolve them.

The Massachusetts Assembly voted 92 to 17 not to rescind. The governor promptly dissolved it, and for nearly a year that colony had no legislature in session. During that time, election day came around and only five of the 17 men who voted for rescinding were reelected. Throughout the colonies, toasts and parades were made in honor of "the glorious 92." Connecticut's Roger Sherman declared that, "No Assembly on the continent will ever concede that Parliament has a right to tax the colonies."

Virginia, Maryland, Georgia and North Carolina all passed resolutions supporting Massachusetts' refusal to rescind their Circular Letter, and thus these four additional legislatures were also dissolved by their governors. Eventually they would be reconvened without any attempt by the governors to mention the issue again.

During this time, John Dickinson, a member of Pennsylvania's Assembly, composed a series of twelve *Letters from a Farmer in Pennsylvania to the Inhabitants of the British Colonies.* These letters were widely read on both sides of the Atlantic, and they contributed greatly to the education of the masses, so vital to the resistance movement. In these letters, Dickinson argued that Parliamentary tax laws enacted for the purpose of regulating trade were reasonable, but those enacted for the express purpose of raising revenue were not.

> Parliament unquestionably possesses a legal authority to regulate the trade of Great Britain and all her colonies. Never [before] did the British Parliament think of imposing duties in America for the purpose of raising a revenue. This I call an innovation; and a most dangerous innovation.

On July 25, 1768, at a Liberty Tree dedication ceremony in Providence, Silas Downer delivered a *Discourse* that soon afterward was published in several New England cities. In it, Downer denied Parliament's right to exercise any authority over the colonies. He was the first American to publicly state such a belief since Patrick Henry three years before (in a proposed resolve that the House of Burgesses voted down). In his *Discourse*, Downer eloquently repudiated the recent Parliamentary measures with respect to the colonies, and he advocated complete self-government for the colonies.

> The parliamentary authority of Great Britain cannot be extended over us without involving the greatest contradiction: For if we are to be controuled by their parliament, our own [legislatures] will be useless. In short, I cannot be persuaded that the parliament of Great Britain has a lawful right to make any laws whatsoever

41

to bind us, because there can be no fountain from whence such right can flow. ...

It is therefore clear that that assembly cannot pass <u>any</u> laws to bind us, but that we must be governed by our own.

Dickinson's *Letters From a Farmer* and, to a less widespread audience, Downer's *Discourse*, created sensations in the press, as did coverage of the lengthy trial of John Hancock. Hancock, the wealthy benefactor of Boston's Sons of Liberty, was the sole or part owner of twenty merchant vessels, making him an important catch for the customs collectors. His outspoken anti-British activities made Hancock a conspicuous target. In May, 1768, a customs man boarded his ship, *Liberty*, to search for taxable cargo. Hancock's crew shoved the inspector into a cabin and nailed the door shut. They then leisurely unloaded the cargo of Madeira wine and saw to it that it was taken away before they let the inspector out.

A few days later, the *Romney* man-of-war arrived in Boston Harbor, since the customs collector had requested military assistance in the execution of their duties. The presence of the *Romney* was sufficient to produce considerable tension among the inhabitants who, like Englishmen everywhere, believed that a military presence in peacetime was a clear violation of the rights of Englishmen. The ship's captain exacerbated the hard feelings when he sent out press gangs for the impressment of Americans, a common and much resented method of "recruiting." The press gangs had bloody altercations with street mobs who resisted their efforts. Adding to the volatile situation was the large number of persons thrown out of work because of the boycott. And Boston's radical Whig leaders were busy working the populace into a frenzy of hatred for the customs collectors, as noted by a Tory, Lady Ann Hulton:

The common people here ... [were fed] a number of lies raised to irritate and inflame them. They believe that the Commissioners have unlimited power given to tax even their lands, for supporting a number of bishops that are coming over & they are inspired with an enthusiastic rage for defndg their religion & liberties.

On the evening of June l0th, between 6 and 7 p.m., the customs men declared formal seizure of Hancock's *Liberty*. They painted the King's Broad Arrow on her mainmast and requested sailors and marines from the *Romney* cut Hancock's vessel loose and tow her out to the safety of the *Romney's* guns. Watching this action was an angry crowd of 800 (soon to be 2,000) men and teenage boys on the wharf. One observer provided the following account to the Boston and New York newspapers:

> This conduct provoked the people who had collected on the shore; and in the dispute the Collector, the Comptroller of his Majesty's Customs, and the Collector's son were roughly used, and pelted with stones, none of them much hurt. The noise bro't together a mix'd multitude, who followed up to the Comptroller's house, and broke some of the windows, but withdrew by the advice of some prudent gen[tle]men that interposed.
>
> Between 8 and 9 o'clock they went to one of the docks, and dragged out a large pleasure boat belonging to the Collector. This they drew along the street, with loud huzzaing all the way to the Common, where they set fire to it and burnt it to ashes; they also broke several windows of the houses of the Collector and Inspector General, which were nigh the Common. No other outrage was committed that night.

The next day, the customs officials took up residence aboard the man-of-war. The leaders of the *Liberty* Riot were not apprehended and brought to justice. Lieutenant Governor Thomas Hutchinson explains why:

> It is only natural to ask where the Justices and Sheriffs are upon these occasions. The persons who are to assist the Sheriff in the execution of his office are Sons of Liberty and determined to oppose him in everything wch shall be contrary to their schemes. Some of the Justices are great favourers of them, and those who are not are afraid and will issue out no warrants to apprehend them.

John Adams, Hancock's lawyer, made much of the fact that Hancock was now at risk of losing his property without due process of law, since the case was being tried in the vice-admiralty court without a jury. Almost a year later, the trial ended when the British dropped the case, due to insufficient evidence. But the trial, as reported in the newspapers, furnished Americans with an ongoing drama, maintaining popular interest in "the cause" (the struggle for American liberties). And it was this riot, caused by the seizure of Hancock's vessel, that convinced the British government to finally send troops to Boston to maintain order.

Letters arrived from friends in London, warning the Bostonians that four regiments of Regulars were on their way and rumored to have orders to arrest fifty patriots and send them back to England for trial. When this sensational news arrived, Samuel Adams and James Otis, Jr., requested the governor reconvene the dissolved Assembly. When the governor refused, a Boston Town Meeting resolved that all inhabitants should provide themselves with firearms and ammunition to resist the tyranny of the British Regulars. The selectmen of Boston met with the local Congregational clergy, and set aside a day for fasting and prayer. The selectmen then wrote to all the towns in the colony, giving a history of their grievances, and inviting every town to send a committee to a proposed convention, to give "sound and wholesome advice" and "prevent any sudden and unconnected measures." Delegates came from ninety-six towns.

Though the convention was intended to lay the foundation for resistance to the British army, the delegates were not yet ready for armed rebellion. However, they did pass resolutions objecting to Parliamentary taxation, and refusing to provide shelter for the British troops until Castle William should become full. Governor Bernard, as usual, exaggerated the situation and used his imagination when reporting to London about the extralegal convention, describing it as a

> wild attempt to create a revolt & take the government of this province out of the King's and into their own hands, to seize the Governor & Lieut. Govr. and take possession of the treasury and then set up their standard. Should so open and notorious an attempt to raise a rebellion remain unpunished because it was unsuccessful? Some punishment is surely due.

His suggestion was that Otis, Hancock, Samuel Adams, and Thomas Cushing be "disqualified by an Act of Parliament from sitting in the Assembly or holding any place of office." But the administration in London had other ideas. The attorney general was requested to research the possibility of enforcing an old act, from King Henry VIII's time, that would allow the Bostonians to be transported to England to stand trial for treason. Governor Bernard was asked for advice, so he had some of the leading Tories provide evidence - alleged quotes from Sam Adams, mainly - that Bernard forwarded to the attorney general in London. The talk in Boston was that Adams and the others would soon be tried. A common joke at the time was that now whenever Sam passed the ropewalkers' galleries he "shuddered at the sight of hemp." However, the attorney general decided there was not enough evidence against the rebel leaders.

News of the Bostonians' possible arrest and deportation to England, for a prejudicial trial without a jury of their peers, soon reached the other colonies. It was enough to convince George Washington, a Virginia Burgess, that it was time for Virginia to join the boycott. He stated to his neighbors at Mount Vernon, in May, 1769:

> Our lordly masters in Great Britain will be satisfied with nothing less than the deprivation of American freedom. Something should be done to maintain the liberty which we have derived from our ancestors. No man should hesitate a moment to use arms in defence of so valuable a blessing. Yet arms should be the last resource. We have proved the inefficacy of addresses to the throne and remonstrances to Parliament; how far their attention to our rights and priviledges is to be awakened by starving their trade and manufactures remains to be tried.

After consulting his friend, George Mason, Washington drafted Virginia's nonimportation resolves. However, before he had a chance to introduce them in the House of Burgesses, it was dissolved by the governor because of what would come to be known as "The Virginia Resolves of 1769." These resolves were drafted by Mason and introduced in the House of Burgesses by Washington on May 16, 1769.

They asserted the legality of the colonies' acting in concert to defend their rights, and warned the King of "the dangers that would ensue" if any person in any part of America should be seized and carried to England for trial. A copy was sent to each colonial legislature and to the King and Parliament. The next morning, the governor dissolved the House. But that did not stop the Burgesses. They met at another site to hear, debate and pass Washington's nonimportation resolves, which even included a ban on importing slaves. The resolves were sent throughout Virginia for the signature of every free man in the colony.

Delaware, Georgia and the Carolinas adopted the Virginia Resolves word for word. Soon all the colonies not yet pledged to the nonimportation agreement decided for it, and, by October 1769, they were all committed. Of course, not all merchants adhered to the agreement, but many of those who at first did not were soon persuaded by the Sons of Liberty to change their minds. Property destruction and the ritual of tarring and feathering and riding out of town on a rail, popularized during the Stamp Act riots a few years before, were revived.

This boycott was referred to as "nonintercourse," since the term "boycott" would not be coined until a later century. With respect to clothing imported from Britain, the boycott was given a boost in Charleston, South Carolina, by an unfortunate event - the death of Mary Gadsden. She was the wife of Christopher Gadsden, of Stamp Act Congress fame. Among the well-to-do planters and merchants of South Carolina, proper dress was particularly important. Because of his fame and his shocking appearance at his wife's funeral, Gadsden made the newspapers all up and down the coast. For, instead of British blackcloth, he wore a new suit of blue homespun to the funeral. He was hailed in Whig newspapers for setting "a patriot example."

During the boycott, a "buy American" campaign sprang up. Benjamin Franklin's fictional character, Poor Richard, was emulated. Instead of rum (made from dutiable molasses), he drank whiskey, "a real American drink," predicting Americans would be "a more hardy and manly race of people when our constitutions are no longer jaundiced, nor our juices vitiated by abominable West India distillations." Virginia farmers planted vineyards. Attempts were also made to develop manufacturing. Paper and other products began to be produced in the colonies for almost the first time. In Massachusetts, a newly built factory produced 80,000 shoes in 1769 for sale throughout the colonies and the West Indies. "All the country seems possessed with a madness of manufacture and economy," wrote New Hampshire's Governor Benning Wentworth. Self-sufficiency became the goal of the colonies. John Hancock offered free passage across the Atlantic to artisans in England willing to immigrate to America.

The spinning wheel became the symbol of self-sufficiency and resistance to British taxation. Homespun was worn on the most formal occasions, even by some of the wealthiest Whigs. Teenage girls discovered that they could make a social occasion out of the drudgery of spinning. One observer wrote, "I found that as these Daughters of Liberty delighted in each other's company, they had agreed to make circular visits to each of their houses and, in order to excite emulation in serving their country, had determined to convert each visit into a spinning match."

As they had during the Stamp Act crisis, British merchants again voiced their concern about this new boycott. Once again, the government bowed to their pressure. Parliament repealed all the Townshend Duties except the one on tea. Though this remaining duty could not possibly raise a significant revenue, Parliament would not vote for a total repeal, lest it imply a lack of authority to tax the colonies. As a member of Parliament put it at the time:

> The majority really wish the Duty Acts had never been made; they say they are evidently inconsistent with all sound commercial and political principles ... but they think the national honour concern'd in supporting them, considering the manner in which the execution of them has been oppos'd. They cannot bear the denial of the right of Parliament to make them, tho' they acknowledge they ought not to have been made.

Benjamin Franklin, back in London again, had lobbied for a complete repeal of all the Townshend Duties. He had written to the Duke of Grafton, the new prime minister, expressing his fears of the consequences a partial repeal would have. Franklin argued that it would not afford America

> a thorough redress of grievances. This may inflame matters still more in that country; further rash measures there may create more resentment here, that may produce ... attempts to dissolve their constitutions; more troops may be sent over; your ministerial writers will re-

vile the Americans in newspapers, treating them as miscreants, rogues, dastards, rebels, &c ... Mutual provocation will go on to complete the separation; and instead of that cordial affection that once and so long existed, implacable malice and mutual hatred will take place. ...

I hope this all may prove false prophecy.

When news of the repeal reached America, the boycott dissolved, and the continent breathed a sigh of relief that the conflict, for the most part, was over. The Sons of Liberty wished to continue the boycott until the duty on tea was also repealed, but the merchants refused. They had sold out their stock and could not remain in business without ordering replacement goods from Britain.

CHAPTER FOUR
ONLY ILL CAN COME FROM
A PEACETIME ARMY, 1770

"The people seemed to be leaving the soldiers, and turning from them, when there came down a number from Jackson's Corner, huzzaing and crying, 'Damn them! They dare not fire. We are not afraid of them!'"

- George Hewes, eyewitness of the "Boston Massacre"

Ironically, on the very day that Parlaiment voted for repeal, 3,000 miles away the crisis that the Townshend Duties had helped create came to its tragic climax. It occurred in Boston on that same March 5, 1770, and would quickly come to be known as the "Boston Massacre."

Since the arrival of the British Regulars, seventeen months earlier, tensions had been mounting. The citizens of Boston resented the fact that General Gage, "to overawe the people," had ordered his troops to find quarters in town, instead of in the barracks at Castle William, the fortress on Castle Island out in the the harbor.

The soldiers had nothing to do except practice their drilling and marching, much to the displeasure of the townspeople, especially the clergy. As recorded in the <u>Boston</u> <u>Journal</u> <u>of</u> <u>Occurrences</u>, a Sam Adams creation distributed throughout the colonies, the Regulars even drilled on the Sabbath: "This being the Lord's day, the minds of serious people at public worship were greatly disturbed with drums beating and fifes playing, unheard of before [on the Sabbath] in this land."

Also scandalous was the soldiers' practice of singing, even on the Sabbath day. Many of the songs were vulgar. When townspeople taunted the soldiers, they retaliated by singing a song making fun of ignorant New England farmers - Yankee "doodles."

What was more disturbing to the Bostonians and people throughout the colonies who read about it, was the army's policy of administering public floggings to maintain discipline.

Some of the soldiers were lucky enough to find part-time jobs to supplement their inadequate military pay; others resorted to stealing from shops and mugging people on the streets. Officers attempted to curb these activities by punishing offenders with floggings, often on Boston Common. Typically, the soldier would receive hundreds of lashes on his bare back from the cat-o'-nine-tails, which was a whip made of nine knotted hemp cords attached to a wooden handle. Afterwards, salt water would be thrown on the wounds to prevent infection. Sometimes the victim would die before the specified number was applied. These revolting spectacles only hardened the people's animosity toward the army and the government that sent it here.

Though taught to despise the colonists, many of the soldiers did not relish the idea of suppressing fellow Englishmen. Some secretly sided with the colonists in their dispute with Parliament. For the typical private, forced into the army against his will, the lure of a better life in America was a great temptation. Desertions were frequent, especially when winter brought an easy escape route. One citizen noted in early 1770, after the Charles River froze over: "The ice having opened new passages out of town for the soldiers, desertions are more numerous than ever, notwithstanding all the care of the officers, and vigilance of the military guards, which almost surround the town." If a deserter was captured, he received the standard penalty for desertion: death.

Such executions, however, were infrequent, because very few deserters were captured; the inhabitants were reluctant to inform on them. In fact, often the soldiers made their escape only through the efforts of Americans who were willing to risk being caught and tried as accessories to the crime.

Drilling on the Sabbath, swearing, and looting were not the soldiers' only faults, according to the patriots. Because of their boredom and the tension, they often drank excessively. Sam Adams' Journal frequently published stories, usually from the imagination of its editor, of the soldiers beating young boys and raping women and girls. Typical was the following story, published in June, 1769:

> A woman going to the south market for a fish stopped at the shop of Mr. Chase, under Liberty Tree, appearing to be faint. They got some water, but on raising her up, she died instantly. A jury of inquest was summoned, and upon examination she appeared to be one Sarah Johnson, of Bridgewater, on whom it appeared by evidence and several marks, that violence had been perpetrated by soldiers unknown, which probably was the cause of her death.

Stories of such incidents, whether true or not, aroused the people's hatred of the troops to a fever pitch. Thomas Hutchinson, commenting on the Journal, wrote, "This paper had a very great effect. A story of a fictitious quarrel incensed the lower part of the people, and brought on a real quarrel." Fights between citizens and soldiers became frequent.

The Bostonians knew that the Regulars were under strict orders to never fire upon the citizens, except on the order of an officer, or unless they were absolutely positive that their very lives were in danger. It soon became apparent to the patriots that throwing a rock would bruise a soldier, but not endanger his life; therefore, he could not fire upon his assailants. If the soldier fought back, or even spoke threateningly to his tormentors, they would bring him before a patriot judge, who would give the soldier the standard lecture:

> What brought you here, who sent for you, and by what authority do you mount guard? It is contrary to the laws of the province, and you should be taken up for so offending.

The judge would then sentence the soldier to a heavy fine. These fines soon depleted the regimental funds allocated to pay such fines. After that, offending soldiers could be sentenced to work off the fines as indentured servants.

Six weeks before the "massacre" in Boston, a clash known as the "Battle of Golden Hill" took place in the city of New York. Many of the soldiers, in their off-duty hours, sought employment and were willing to work for lower wages than the local laborers. This took away jobs from the city's laborers, some of the most active participants in resisting British authority, whether it be a Stamp Act riot or a rumble with His Majesty's forces in arms. For four days in a row in January, 1770, they held off repeated attempts by some soldiers to cut down the Liberty Pole. But finally the troops succeeded, and sawed it into sections, which they then piled in front of the Sons of Liberty headquarters. The Sons then erected another pole, and persuaded the city's employers not to hire the soldiers anymore.

The soldiers, angered by the loss of their part-time jobs, posted throughout the city a handbill which denounced the Sons, calling them "murderers and thieves," and challenging them to a fight. Three soldiers were caught posting this handbill, and were taken, after a struggle, to the mayor's office. Soldiers wielding cutlasses and bayonets came to rescue them . The Sons met them with clubs and planks of wood quickly torn from nearby fences, carts and sleighs. Many on both sides were wounded, and one New Yorker was killed. He could justifiably be regarded as the first American martyr of the Revolution. However, this New York event would soon be overshadowed by Boston's "massacre."

Although many minor incidents had been occurring ever since the Regulars came to Boston in November of 1768, the situation really began to heat up on March 2, 1770. A ropemaker, busy running an outdoor ropemaking machine called a "ropewalk," hailed a passing soldier, and asked him if he wanted work. "Yes," answered the soldier. "Then go and clean my shithouse!" came the mocking reply from the ropemaker, followed by jeers and laughter. After exchanging curses and threats, the soldier left, promising to return with his mates. When he returned with about forty soldiers, a crowd was waiting for them with clubs. After a furious fight, patriot reinforcements arrived, but the soldiers managed to make their escape when a justice of the peace persuaded the crowd not to pursue them.

The next night, March 3rd, another fight occurred between the two groups. Also, an employee of the ropemaking firm, upon arriving at the house where he boarded, complained to his landlord that soldiers were harassing him. The landlord asked a soldier, lurking in the street outside, what he was doing. The soldier replied, "I'm pumping shit," referring to the now famous job offer of the day before. After an argument, the landlord beat the soldier with a stick until he fled to his barracks.

Rumors circulated the next two days, March 4th and 5th, that the soldiers were going to avenge the landlord in a larger riot. Lt. Colonel Carr sent a formal complaint to Lt. Governor Hutchinson (Governor Shirley, having by now grown weary of the crisis, had retired to England). Carr wrote to Hutchinson about the ropewalk altercation and the many abuses that the soldiers had been subjected to since they'd come to Boston. Hutchinson referred the complaint to the Council, but they could not decide what to do about the dangerously escalating situation.

On the evening of March 5th, as on the previous nights, groups of citizens armed with clubs roamed Boston's streets looking for trouble. A minor skirmish broke out in front of the British barracks, but it ended when officers interceded. Later, just before 9 p.m., an officer crossing King Street was recognized by a barber's apprentice. The boy called out, "There goes a mean fellow who hath not paid my master for dressing his hair."

The nearby customs house was being guarded by a lone sentry, Private Hugh White, who had been the target that evening of stones thrown by local toughs. The frustrated sentry, upon hearing this boy accuse the passing officer, walked over and took out his frustration by hitting the boy over the head with the butt of his musket, although not hard enough to knock the boy down. The crowd in the street surged toward the sentry, one of them yelling, "You damned rascally scoundrel, lobster son of a bitch!" But they backed off when he warned them, "If you come near me, I'll blow your brains out."

Someone then rang the bells in a nearby church, which brought many others into the streets. Asking where the fire was, they were told that there was no fire, but "the Regulars are cutting and slashing everyone." Differing speculations were offered to guess why the bells were ringing, including, "They are cutting down the Liberty Tree."

Meanwhile, about two hundred townsmen eager for a riot were listening to a fiery speech given by "a tall gentleman in a red cloak and white wig" (probably the extremist, Will Molineaux). The lone sentry was frightened by someone yelling out, "Knock him down!" So he shouted, "Stand off!" Then, as loud as he could, "TURN OUT, MAIN GUARD!"

At the Main Guard, Captain Thomas Preston had been watching the scene through his window. Though he was going against orders by not first obtaining authorization from a town magistrate (required before calling out the troops to quell a civil disturbance), Preston decided he had no choice but to try to rescue the sentry. With difficulty, he made his way through the crowd. Two of the seven soldiers accompanying Preston had been beaten up in the ropewalk riot two days earlier. Arranging themselves in an arc on the steps of the customs house, they loaded and primed their muskets, then pointed them, bayonets outward, toward the mob. This raised the fury of the crowd, and they soon began pelting the soldiers with snowballs filled with bits of ice and coal.

A merchant, Richard Palmes, trying to head off a tragedy, warned Captain Preston, "If you fire, you must die for it." Preston assured the man that he had no intention of firing upon the mob. Then, according to later court testimony by one member of the mob,

The people seemed to be leaving the soldiers, and

turning from them, when there came down a number from Jackson's Corner, huzzaing and crying, "Damn them! They dare not fire. We are not afraid of them!"

One of these people, a stout man with a cordwood stick, threw himself in and made a blow at the officer. I saw the officer try to fend off the stroke; whether it struck him or not, I do not know. The stout man then turned around, and struck the Grenadier's gun at the captain's right hand, and immediately fell in with his club, and knocked his gun away, and struck him over the head; the blow came either on the soldier's cheek or hat. This stout man held the bayonet with his left hand, and twitched it and cried, "Kill the dogs, knock them over!" This was the general cry; the people then crowded in.

At this point, a club, thrown by someone in the crowd, struck and knocked down a soldier. The furious and frightened man rose, shouted "Damn you, fire!" to his fellow soldiers, and pulled the trigger of his musket. An attempt by a Bostonian to seek revenge with a club was stopped by a thrust of a bayonet, which, although it missed its mark, forced the attacker to retreat.

After the single shot was fired, hitting no one, the crowd instinctively fell back, leaving an open space in front of the soldiers. This open space was portrayed in all contemporary illustrations of the incident, giving the false impression that the mob kept its distance from the soldiers, and therefore was not threatening.

In that moment, while the mob fell back, the contagion of panic, caused by the firing of the single musket and the clubbing of the soldier, had its effect on the other seven soldiers under Preston's command. They began firing, one by one, killing four and mortally wounding another. The shock of the crowd gave the soldiers enough time to quickly reload, to prevent being rushed by the crowd. Much of the crowd quickly dispersed, once they realized that the soldiers had reloaded.

The first of the five to be killed was Crispus Attacks, a Black man, who had twenty years earlier been a runaway slave from Framingham, Massachusetts, and was employed at the time of his death as a sailor. According to court testimony, Attacks was the "stout man" who had assaulted Captain Preston.

Preston marched his seven soldiers and the sentry back to the Main Guard, then immediately turned out the entire guard. He placed them in "street firings," a formation used for defense against rioters. The town drums beat, calling out the militia, and cries of "To arms!" and "Town-born! Turn out!" were heard in all directions. Soon the crowd had swelled from about two hundred, before the incident, to more than a thousand. Preston, thoroughly alarmed, had his own drummer alert the entire Boston garrison.

Several citizens went to see Hutchinson, and told him that, unless he "went out immediately, the whole town would be in arms and the most bloody scene would follow that had ever been known in America." He promptly arrived at the scene and promised the crowd a full investigation, and prosecution of those suspected of guilt. Then he urged them all to go home to bed. Most of the crowd left, but only after the soldiers took Hutchinson's suggestion and returned to their barracks. He immediately began collecting evidence and, by 3 a.m., had a warrant served for Captain Preston's arrest. Preston was joined in jail a few hours later by the other eight soldiers.

At 11 a.m., a Town Meeting commenced, with Sam Adams as moderator. John Tudor, a Boston merchant who was there, recorded the following account of what happened:

> Tuesday A.M. the inhabitants mett at Faneuil Hall & after som pertinent speches chose a committee of 15 gentlem'n to waite on the Lev't. Governor in Council to request the immediate removeal of the troops. The message was in these words. That it is the unanimous opinion of this Meeting, that the inhabitants & soldiery can no longer live together in safety; that nothing can ra-

tonaly be expected to restore the peace of the town & prevent blood & carnage but the removal of the troops. His Honor's reply was that it was not in his power to remove the troops &c &c.

The above reply was not satisfactory to the inhabitants, as but one rigiment should be removed to the Castle barracks. In the afternoon the town adjourned to Dr Sewill's Meetinghouse, for Fanieul Hall was not larg enough to hold the people, their being at least 3,000, som supos'd near 4,000, when they chose a committee to waite on the Lev't. Governor to let him & the Council know that nothing less will satisfy the people than a total & immediate removal of the troops oute of the town.

His Honor laid before the Council the vote of the town. The Council thereon expressed themselves to be unanimously of opinion that it was absolutely necessary for his Majesty service, the good order of the town &c that the troops should be immeditly removed oute of the town.

His Honor communicated this advice of the Council to Col. Dalrymple & desir'd he would order the troops down to Castle William. After the Col. had seen the vote of the Council he gave his word & honor to the town's committee that both the rigiments should be remov'd without delay. The com'te read their report as above, which was received with a shoute & clap of hands, which made the Meetinghouse ring. ...

And all was quiet again, as the soldiers was all moved of to the Castle.

On March 8th, four of the five victims were buried (the fifth died a few days later). Estimates of the number of mourners at the common grave ranged up to 20,000. Boston's propaganda machine made the most of the incident. An engraving of the British soldiers shooting unarmed, non-threatening citizens, seemingly innocently passing by in the street, was made by Paul Revere, adapted from a drawing by Henry Pelham. Revere's inflammatory engraving was printed in newspapers throughout the colonies and Britain. Hutchinson and a patriot committee each wrote their own biased account of the incident and had it rushed to influential officials and printers in London.

Sam Adams and others launched a new anti-military propaganda campaign, to keep public opinion running strongly against the soldiers. Statements from ninety-six eyewitnesses were recorded and solemnly sworn to before justices of the peace. These were attached to a twenty-two page report compiled by the Boston selectmen, and published as *A Short Narrative of the Horrid Massacre in Boston*.

All but one of the 96 were unanimous in their description of the incident. The one among them who had anything faintly favorable to say for the soldiers was labeled a liar in vicious newspaper editorials. The other 95 declared they had been on peaceful errands that night - on their way to visit friends, attend a church meeting, etc. - when they were attacked by soldiers who, they claimed, had for several days threatened a massacre.

Although the Boston selectmen distributed the pamphlet in the towns surrounding Boston, they did not do so inside Boston, for they didn't want to be accused of influencing prospective jurors. Nevertheless, the pamphlet had the intended effect. Even some of the town's clergy joined in the public outcry for revenge. "If I was to be one of the jury upon his trial," said the Reverend Chauncy, "I would bring Captain Preston in guilty, evidence or no evidence."

Sam Adams was not the only person interested in documenting the incident. In New York, General Thomas Gage, Commander-in-Chief of all British troops in North America, wrote to Lieutenant Colonel Dalrymple, commander of the Boston garrison:

> It is absolutely necessary everything relating to the
> unhappy affair of the 5th of March should appear as full
> as it is possible upon Captain Preston's tryal. Not only

what happened on the said night, but also every insult and attack made upon the troops previous thereto with the pains taken by the military to prevent quarrels between the soldiers and the inhabitants.

But Captain Preston and the eight other Regulars accused of murder would need someone to defend them. None of Boston's Tory attorneys, fearing the wrath of the mob, would agree to do it. In desperation, a friend of Preston visited some of Boston's leading Whig attorneys, and convinced them that refusing to provide a fair trial to the soldiers would alienate the moderate Whigs. So three patriot lawyers, including John Adams and Josiah Quincy, Jr., agreed to handle the soldiers' defense.

The public was shocked. Quincy received a letter from his father:

> My Dear Son, I am under great affliction at hearing the bitterest reproaches uttered against you, for having become an advocate for those criminals who are charged with the murder of their fellow citizens. Good God! Is it possible? I will not believe it.

John Adams held a deep reverence for the law, and felt he had no choice when asked to defend the hated Regulars.

> I had no hesitation in answering: that counsel ought to be the very last thing that an accused person should want in a free country; that the bar ought to be independent and impartial at all times and in every circumstance; and that persons whose lives were at stake ought to have the counsel they prefer.
> ... [However, the case] compelled me to differ in opinion from all my friends, to set at defiance all their advice, their remonstrances, their raillery, their ridicule, their censure, their sarcasm, without acquiring one

symptom of pity from my enemies.

Sam Adams repeatedly pressed Hutchinson to start the trial, but he stalled, waiting for passions to cool. Finally, in October, upon the request of Captain Preston, jury selection began, and the trial commenced soon afterward. John Adams automatically rejected all jury candidates selected by the town of Boston, assuming they were prejudiced against the soldiers. The jury ended up being packed with men who lived outside the town and were somewhat sympathetic to the soldiers. In less than three hours, Preston's trial was over. Since half the witnesses swore they heard Preston give the order to fire, and the other half swore they did not hear him give the order, he was found not guilty. Captain Preston immediately resigned his commission and returned to England without even thanking Adams and the others for saving his life.

The separate trial of the eight soldiers took many days. The prosecution's case was exploded when the defense had Dr. Jon Jeffries take the witness stand. One of the five men killed by the soldiers had lived for several days before expiring. In court, Jeffries testified that the victim, Patrick Carr, described the incident to him:

> I asked him if he thought the soldiers would have been hurt if they had not fired. He said he really thought they would, for he heard many voices cry out "Kill them." I asked him then whether he thought they fired in self-defense. He said he really thought they did fire to defend themselves, that he did not blame the man, whoever he was, who shot him.

The prosecutors had had some powerful witnesses, but none could equal the emotional impact of these words from the grave. Two of the soldiers were found guilty of murder in self-defense (manslaughter) and received a branding on the thumb and suspended sentences. The other six were found not guilty, since only seven shots had been fired and the jury would not convict a total of eight people, not knowing which five of the six other soldiers had fired.

The decisions were very unpopular, but Adams and Quincy were not blamed for them personally. They resumed their legal practices and their political writings. John Adams did not, as he had feared before the trial, lose all his clients and have to resort to farming. In fact, to his surprise and displeasure (so he wrote in his journal) he was soon elected to the legislature.

* * * * *

In an effort to keep the resistance movement alive, the story of the "massacre" was milked for all it was worth by Sam Adams and the radical press throughout the colonies. The propaganda success of the press can not be overstated. The vast majority of newspapers in the colonies were Whig in politics, though some less radical than others. Most Tory printers were terrorized by the Sons of Liberty into retirement or neutrality, although there were a few that continued to publish even during the coming war. As one Tory expressed it, in a letter to a relation in England:

> Our printers, by interest or threats, are restrained from publishing what should be generally known. The people hear nothing but what their ringleaders chuse they should hear; which is the principal reason for all the disturbances and commotions that have been raised here.

The most significant accomplishment of the radical press was the uniting of the country people behind the leadership of the seaports. After the repeal of the Stamp Act, British taxation fell almost entirely on the trading towns along the seaboard. The country people never saw the customs collectors, admiralty judges, and British troops who were living reminders of British "tyranny." To convince the vast majority of Americans - farmers - that they had a stake in the struggle, the propagandists had to make them believe they would all inevitably be taxed into paupery if Parliament was not resisted. Alexander Hamilton, a young student at King's College (later Columbia University), put it to them this way:

> Perhaps before long your tables, chairs, and platters, and dishes, and knives, and forks, and every thing else would be taxed. Nay, I don't know but they would find means to tax you for every child you got, and for every kiss your daughters received from their sweethearts; and, God knows, that would soon ruin you.

To support these arguments, printers merely had to point out that the Declaratory Act could be used as the justification for turning America into another Ireland.

Governors were powerless to curb the radical press. Since the Zenger case in 1745, the colonists had enjoyed the legal guarantee of freedom of the press. In some cases, they enjoyed the protection of powerful politicians. When the printer of the Massachusetts Spy was ordered to appear before the legislature to answer charges of printing a seditious article, he relied upon his friendship with Sam Adams and other prominent Whig Assemblymen, for he only sent a message without making an appearance. The message: he was "too busy in his office and should not attend."

And the threat of mob violence was usually enough to dissuade any sheriff or judge from taking action against a printer. During the Stamp Act crisis, Governor Bernard's effort to have the editors of the Boston Gazette indicted for libel was stopped by the grand jury's refusal to cooperate, fearing the mob. The power of government in the colonies was waning, in favor of mob rule as manipulated by the patriots.

CHAPTER FIVE
AFTER A CALM, MORE CONFLICT
1771-1773

"It was now evening, and I immediately dressed myself in the costume of an Indian, equipped with a small hatchet ..."

> *- George Hewes, participant in the*
> *"Boston Tea Party"*

In the spring of 1770, news of the repeal of all the Townshend Duties except that on tea quickly ended the boycott of British goods. Although customs officials continued to pursue smugglers, their annoying regulations were somewhat relaxed from what they had been. In New York City, the soldiers and citizens managed to avoid each other. Boston was quiet, with the Regulars now at Castle William in the harbor. The period from mid-1770 to mid-1773 would see a return to normalcy, albeit a wary one, in Britain's relations with her American colonies. Looking back, one American recalled this relatively peaceful time: "We all the time nourished the conviction that the controversy with Britain was definitely closed."

Moderate Whigs abandoned radicals such as Sam Adams and Christopher Gadsden. They were tired of the mob rule that had tried to enforce the boycott. Leading Whig merchants were accused of having secretly sold banned British goods during the just completed boycott. Old jealousies came out in the open once again. New York papers called Boston "the common sewer of America." A Boston paper referred to Rhode Island as that "filthy, nasty colony." Governor Hutchinson happily wrote, in 1773, that the prior attempt at "union between the colonies is pretty well broke."

Although other leading patriots stopped their outspoken ways, Samuel Adams could not. He used his new position as Clerk of the Massachusetts Assembly to introduce many anti-British resolutions. Between mid-1770 and the end of 1772, Adams wrote forty articles for the <u>Boston Gazette</u>, stating the fundamentals of American liberties, and describing how Parliament had transgressed them. Through these means and the ongoing letter writing campaign of his Boston Committee of Correspondence, Adams strived to "keep the attention of his fellow citizens awake to their grievances; and not suffer them to be at rest, till the cause of their just complaints are removed." He refused to give up the struggle, promising that, "Where there is a spark of patriotick fire we will enkindle it."

During this three year period of relative calm, the gradual process that was the real revolution - the changing of American minds about their allegiance to Britain - was kept from dying out completely by a few incidents which occurred in Rhode Island and Massachusetts. The first event was "the *Gaspee* Affair."

Lieutenant William Dudington was the commander of the British schooner, *Gaspee*, which was used for stopping illicit trade centered at the ports of Providence and Newport, Rhode Island, two hotbeds of smuggling activity. Dudington was not only very successful in this pursuit, but also very rude and haughty in his dealings with the suspects. In March, 1772, some Providence merchants complained about Dudington to their patriot deputy governor. He consulted the colony's chief justice, who gave the following opinion:

> Any person who should come into the colony and exercise any authority by force of arms, without showing his commission to the governor, and if a custom house officer without being sworn into his office, is guilty of a trespass, if not piracy.

Of course, Rhode Island's patriot governor had refused to commission the customs collectors; so, according to the chief justice's logic, they were "pirates." Therefore, the deputy governor sent a sheriff aboard the *Gaspee* to determine by what orders Dudington was acting. Dudington referred the problem to his superior, the admiral, who sent a letter to the deputy governor, warning him that anyone who attempts to interfere with Dudington's mission will "hang as pirates."

Feeling more confident now, Lieutenant Dudington began illegal seizures, detained vessels without cause, and pillaged farms along the shoreline, stealing livestock to feed his crew and cutting down fruit trees for firewood. He was described in the <u>Newport Mercury</u> and the <u>Virginia Gazette</u> as "piratical."

The deputy governor and admiral exchanged further letters. The admiral told him not to interfere with naval officers, nor attempt to send sheriffs onto British war vessels, and that he had no authority to ask naval officers to show orders. The deputy governor, in turn, wrote back, declaring that he would send his sheriffs wherever he pleased, and he would not receive "instructions for the administration of his government from the King's admiral stationed in America." And, like his earlier correspondence, he allowed these letters to be published in the newspapers.

The controversy soon reached its climax. On June 9, 1772, the *Gaspee* ran aground on a sandbar, a few miles from Providence. The schooner would not be able to free itself until high tide, at three o'clock the next morning. When word of this accident reached Providence, John Brown, a prominent merchant, had eight longboats with muffled oars made ready. Soon after sunset, a man went openly through the streets beating a drum and informing all who could hear that the *Gaspee* was aground offshore, it would not float until 3 a.m., and all who wished to destroy her should meet at Sabin's tavern.

A considerable number of the most respectable citizens, mainly merchants and shipmasters, assembled there during the evening hours, busying themselves molding bullets and cleaning their guns. When the clock struck midnight, they set out in the longboats. Expecting the worst, they made sure to bring along a surgeon.

The Rhode Islanders approached the *Gaspee* along her bow, so she could not fire her cannon at them. Lieutenant Dudington, seeing the dim shapes surrounding the schooner, hailed, "Who comes there?"

Abraham Whipple answered, "I am sheriff of the County of Kent, God damn you; I have got a warrant to apprehend you, God damn you; so surrender, God damn you!"

After a pause, a reply came from the ship. "I will admit no sheriff at this hour of the night."

A shout rose from the longboats, and the Rhode Islanders began climbing aboard the schooner. Dudington ordered his men, only a few of whom had as yet been roused from sleep, to resist with pistols. While aiming a blow with his sword, Dudington's arm was smashed by a club. An instant later, he received a bullet in the groin. A patriot named Bucklin exclaimed, "I have killed the rascal!"

Lieutenant Dudington gasped, "Good God, I'm done for," and collapsed. By the time he awoke, after two surgeons had treated him below decks, his papers and belongings were floating in Narragansett Bay. Whipple, holding a spike over Dudington's head, exclaimed, "Stand aside, let me dispatch this piratical dog!" After he begged for his life to be spared, Dudington was put ashore on an island. He was almost naked, but had the comfort of a few of his men, who carried him in a blanket. The *Gaspee* was then set on fire and burned to the water's edge. The next day, one of the patriots paraded through the streets wearing Lieutenant Dudington's gold-laced hat.

The governor was obliged to issue a proclamation offering a reward for the discovery of any persons who participated in the "atrocious crime." Of course, no witnesses came forward to testify. The British, surprisingly, took no action other than appointing a commission, composed of Rhode Island's governor and some colonial judges, to investigate the crime. The commission would not submit its testimony to the Rhode Island Superior Court until the following spring, at which time the court would declare that there was no evidence on which anyone could be arrested. That would end the investigation, and the British government would take no further steps in the case, preoccupied at the time by threats of war with Spain.

This was a great encouragement to the revolutionary movement. The Sons of Liberty regarded it a test case, as did the governor of Massachusetts. In a private letter, he wrote of "The *Gaspee* Affair:"

> If the nation shows no resentment against that colony for so high an affront to the mother country, they say they are safe & they may venture upon further measures which are necessary to obtain & secure their independence without any danger of ever being called to acc't for it.

* * * * *

In Boston, a new controversy arose that summer of 1772 when patriots learned that Governor Hutchinson and the Superior Court judges were now being paid by the Crown. The Assembly voted to pay the judges higher salaries if they would reject the Crown's salaries. All the judges complied except Chief Justice Andrew Oliver, who was the governor's brother-in-law. The Assembly then tried to impeach Hutchinson and Oliver for thus "accepting bribes" from the King, but Hutchinson adjourned the Assembly, preventing the impeachment vote from taking place.

While this controversy was going on in Boston, the patriot leaders were also concerned by the ministry's announcement that anyone arrested for involvement in the *Gaspee* incident would be sent to England for trial. Of course, this brought protests from several colonial legislatures, since it was a denial of the traditional American freedom of trial by one's peers. The fear was that soon any outspoken patriot would meet the same fate, especially if governors and judges started being paid by the Crown.

To safeguard themselves against such developments, a Boston Town Meeting, moderated by Sam Adams, voted that Committees of Correspondence be formed in every town in Massachusetts, so that information and orders could be quickly disseminated. One Tory described this communication network as "the foulest, subtlest, and most venomous serpent ever issued from the egg of sedition."

When Virginia's House of Burgesses learned of Massachusetts' town committees, it voted to form an official Committee of Correspondence for the colony of Virginia, and invited the other colonies to do the same. Its members were instructed "to keep up and maintain correspondence and communication with our sister colonies ... to obtain the most early and authentic intelligence of acts and resolutions of the Parliament, or proceedings of administration, as may relate to or affect the British colonies in America." Soon every colony would have an official committee. In some areas, they were known as District Committees or Committees of Safety, but they all served the same purpose: to gather and quickly disseminate information and orders. These were models of revolutionary organization, and would play a vital role over the next decade.

Hutchinson and Oliver were soon embroiled in yet another controversy, thanks to Benjamin Franklin, who was still in London in the spring of 1773. A copy of some letters the governor and lieutenant governor had written several years before, addressed to a former member of Parliament and calling for "an abridgement of what are called English liberties," was secretly obtained by Franklin. He mailed the copy to Thomas Cushing, Speaker of the Massachusetts Assembly, with instructions to show them to the leading Whigs, but not to copy or publish them. In his cover letter to Cushing, Franklin gave his opinion that this "correspondence laid the foundation of most if not all our present grievances." Despite his instructions to keep them secret, Franklin probably knew that Boston's Whigs would publish excerpts from these volatile letters in the newspapers. Clerk Sam Adams read them aloud to the Assembly, and received permission to publish them.

Before submitting the text to leading radical newspapers in several colonies, Adams deleted some mild passages and inserted outrageous words of his own invention, so readers would be misled to see a more evil purpose than was actually intended by Hutchinson and Oliver.

The Boston Committee of Correspondence, headed by Sam Adams, sent copies of the doctored letters to all the important towns in the colony. In a circular letter accompanying them, the committee declared that the circumstances which allowed the letters to become publicly known were proof that God, who had watched over and protected New England since 1620, had "wonderfully interposed to bring to light the plot that had been laid for us by our malicious and invidious enemies." Hutchinson and Oliver thus became members of that long list of "Hell-inspired men who remain on record as monuments of divine vengeance."

The Massachusetts Assembly, still fuming over the letters, sent a petition to Parliament requesting that the governor and chief justice be removed from office. However, the only person removed from office was Benjamin Franklin, who, because of the scandal, lost his job as Deputy Postmaster for the Colonies. When Franklin read Massachusetts' petition to the House of Lords, Attorney General Alexander Wedderburn used the occasion to turn the debate against the American agent. An excerpt from Wedderburn's scathing rebuke of Franklin:

> Men will watch him with a jealous eye; they will hide their papers from him. Having hitherto aspired after fame by his writing, he will henceforth esteem it a libel to be called a "man of letters." I ask, my Lords, whether the revengeful temper, attributed by poetic fiction only to the bloodyminded African, is not surpassed by the coolness and apathy of the wily New Englander.

In London's Tory newspapers, Franklin was described as "a skunk, or American pole cat." Nearly two years later, when he would sail for America, these same newspapers would claim that Franklin was planning to put himself at the head of the rebels, and "try whether he cannot do more mischief with the sword than the pen." Of course, the whole episode created a sensation in the American press, too. The infamous letters were published with Wedderburn's speech in a single pamphlet. Philadelphia's Dr. Benjamin Rush observed that, "As a result of this humiliation, Franklin is a very popular character in every part of America." Almost two years later, a Bostonian diarist would note in his journal:

> In the afternoon bought the famous Oration of Mr Wedderburn versus Franklin. This I had of Mills & Hicks, who are Tory printers; for the printers are divided into parties as well as the rest. This business of printing is at present much the most thriving of any; for all sorts of political writings are bought up with amazing avidity.

Governor Hutchinson looked upon participation of the masses in political life as disgusting and unnatural. He wanted the colony to be one where the plain people took orders from a few privileged persons appointed by the Crown. He abhorred the New England custom of holding Town Meetings, where nearly every man could speak his mind. Hutchinson especially disliked Boston Town Meetings, since Sam Adams always made sure they were packed with Whigs and members of "the mob." In a letter to his superior in London, Hutchinson wrote that the Tories "decline attending Town Meetings where they are sure of being out-voted by men of the lowest order, all being admitted. Ignorant though they be, yet the heads of Boston Town Meeting influence all public measures."

In 1774, after retiring from the governor's seat, Hutchinson would have a personal audience with King George III, who would observe, "I see they threatened to pitch and feather you." Hutchinson would reply, "'Tar and feather,' may it please your Majesty."

* * * * *

Despite these incidents, the revolutionary movement appeared to be stalled. In early 1773, Sam Adams confided to a trusted friend, "I wish we could arouse the continent." Then a new development brought on another crisis. The London based East India Company was on the verge of bankruptcy. It suffered from internal corruption, but the chief problem was reduced markets - not only in America, but at home in England, too. Like their American counterparts, greedy British merchants also smuggled cheap Dutch tea, rather than pay the Townshend Duty on East India Company tea. Seven years' supply was stockpiled, with no buyers in sight.

The East India Company's directors (many of whom were members of Parliament) appealed to Parliament for a repeal of the duty on tea, so that the American markets might expand to their full potential. Instead, Parliament passed the Tea Act of 1773, which kept the duty, but eliminated the requirement that the East India Company pay export taxes to the British government prior to shipping the tea to America. This meant that, despite the retained three pence per pound tax, East India tea could now be sold cheaper than smuggled Dutch tea. The Tea Act further stipulated that in America the tea could only be sold through a few consignees, to be selected from among the politically influential Tory merchants in Boston, New York, Philadelphia, and Charleston.

This new arrangement was to take effect when the first large shipments arrived in November, 1773. But news of the Tea Act reached America in August, giving the colonists time to discuss what appeared to be yet another attempt by Parliament to force them to acknowledge Parliament's right to tax them. Even before the measure was introduced into Parliament, Benjamin Franklin, in London, had got wind of what would be proposed. He wrote bitterly of it to Thomas Cushing, Speaker of the Massachusetts Assembly:

> It was thought at the beginning of the session that the American duty would be taken off tea. But now the wise scheme is to take off so much duty here as will make the tea cheaper in America than foreigners can supply us, and to confine the duty there to keep up the exercise of the right. They have no idea that any people can act from any other principle but that of interest; and

they believe that a 3-pence on a pound of tea is sufficient
to overcome all the patriotism of an American.

It did not take the propagandists long to convince the populace that smuggled Dutch tea would be forced off the market if Americans bought British tea and gave the East India Company a monopoly. Their price would not likely remain low for long. And, in the meantime, Parliament would have slyly tricked America into paying the last surviving Townshend Duty. The patriots realized that Americans were too addicted to tea to give it up. An editorial written by "A True Whig" admitted, "The greater part of the People are so very fond of it, that they had rather part with any enjoyment in life." And, if Parliament could restrict who could sell tea, what was to prevent them from doing the same for sugar, cotton, lead, wool, etc.?

Committees of Correspondence and patriot newspapers worked upon the passions of the people in arguing that the tea ships must be opposed. In Philadelphia, John Dickinson and Charles Thomson urged the colonists to resist the landing of the cargo. They claimed that new duties would surely follow if Americans accepted this one. Also, if such a company, whose reputation for exploitation in India and China was well known, could gain a monopolistic foothold in America, it would soon trade in other goods and drive many Americans out of business, not just those who smuggled Dutch tea.

Actually, the veteran American propagandists were not the first ones to alert Americans about this new Tea Act. American merchants in London at the time it was debated and passed in Parliament wrote home to warn their brethren of the possible consequences of the new scheme. They reported that several American shipmasters had been approached by the East India Company to freight the tea to America, and they flatly refused. But the Company would surely find others that were willing. One letter to a New Yorker was passed on by the recipient to a friend in Philadelphia, who passed it on to the publick printer there. Thus, the Pennsylvania Journal reported that Lord North, "being a great schemer," had devised upon the plan of the East India Company's sending this article to America, hoping thereby to outwit us, and to establish that [Townshend] Act effectually, which will for ever after be pleaded as precedent for every imposition the Parliament of Great Britain shall think proper to saddle us with.

It is much to be wished that the Americans will convince Lord North that they are not yet ready to have the yoke of slavery rivited about their necks, and send back the tea whence it came.

More letters arrived, expressing the same opinion, that Parliament had adopted the plan for the hidden purpose of forcing the colonists to accept the duty on tea and, implicitly, Parliament's right to tax them. One correspondent in London wrote, "I have told several of the Company that the tea and ships will all be burnt, as I think you will never suffer an Act of Parliament to be so crowded down your throats; for if you do, it is all over with you."

In New York City, the dormant chapter of the Sons of Liberty reawakened, and a broadside signed "The Mohawks" warned that any persons helping to land or store the tea would receive "an unwelcome visit, in which they shall be treated as they deserve."

In Philadelphia, 700 people met at the State House and adopted resolutions condemning the Tea Act as a plot to enforce the Townshend Duty on tea. Those assisting in the landing of the tea were to be considered "enemies of their country," and the consignees were called upon to resign. A few days later, the Delaware River pilots, who guided ship captains up the tricky river channel, were warned by "The Committee for Tarring and Feathering" that whoever of them dared to bring the tea ship in would receive "the modern mode of punishment" as an appropriate award: "What think you of a halter around your neck, then gallons of liquid tar decanted on your pate - with the feathers of a dozen live geese laid over that to enliven your appearance?"

Before the ships arrived, the consignees at New York and Philadelphia resigned their commissions. When the ships arrived, large crowds (8,000 in Philadelphia) intimidated the governors and customs collectors, so they would not seize the cargo. Pennsylvania's Governor Penn, explaining his inaction to Colonial Secretary Lord Dartmouth, wrote that the Tea Act was generally considered a private matter between the East India Company and the consignees - a matter "in which the Government had no immediate concern."

At a mass meeting in Charleston, South Carolina, the consignees of that port were also pressured into resigning. When the tea ships had spent 20 days in the harbor without the duty being paid, the customs collectors legally seized the cargo and brought it ashore. The patriots allowed them to store it in government warehouses, fearing that, if they used force to prevent it, the southern colonies might be punished by Parliament's taking away their bounty on indigo and the privilege of exporting rice under license to southern Europe. The tea would remain in the government warehouses, untouched, until 1776, when it would be auctioned to raise money for the war.

By December 2, 1773, of the four cities where the tea was destined, Boston was the only one remaining whose consignees had not yet resigned. What was keeping Boston's Sons of Liberty? The governor's determination, for one. Thomas Hutchinson had suffered since 1765 at the hands of Sam Adams and his mob. During the Stamp Act crisis of that year, his house had been destroyed. First as lieutenant governor, then as governor, he had been constantly harassed by the patriot dominated legislature and press. In recent months, his personal correspondence had been stolen and used to smear his character. Now the Assembly, led by Clerk Sam Adams, had petitioned the Crown for his removal from office. Weary of such abuse, Hutchinson had secretly written to his superiors in London, requesting a leave of absence. His request had been granted, but he postponed acting upon it until after the tea crisis, so that he could have a chance to finally triumph over Adams and his fellow radicals.

Boston's consignees, encouraged by the governor, braced themselves to weather the storm (which included a riotous mob breaking into one of their houses, smashing windows, damaging the furniture and slightly injuring the inhabitants). But they still refused to resign. These same sons and friends of the governor had been notorious violators of the nonimportation agreement a few years before, and were thus largely responsible for Boston being ridiculed at that time by New York and Philadelphia merchants who had honored the boycott. Now Josiah Quincy, Jr., just returned from a stay in the southern colonies, was reporting that patriots there were still saying that "Bostonians are better at resolving what to do than doing what they resolved." When Philadelphians learned, in late November, that Boston's consignees still had not resigned, they sent a letter to the <u>Boston</u> <u>Gazette</u> stating, "You have failed us [before] in the importation of tea, and we fear you will suffer this to be landed."

As each of the tea ships arrived in Boston's outer harbor, it dropped anchor beneath the protective guns of British warships. As long as they stayed there, Governor Hutchinson would have the option of using Regulars to unload the cargo onto Castle Island, from whence the consignees could pay the duty and secretly sell the tea to willing merchants. To prevent this, the Boston Committee of Correspondence wrote to each tea ship's captain, demanding that he bring his vessel "up to town." After the captains honored this request, Admiral John Montagu's hands were tied; he would not be able to protect the ships or any Regulars that the governor might order to unload the tea, for he would not "endanger the lives of innocent people by firing upon the Town."

Before the tea ships began arriving, a man the governor termed "a lawyer and high Son of Liberty" advised a Boston Town Meeting not to meddle with the tea, lest the town be held responsible for the consequences once the news reached London. So Boston's patriot leaders decided to hold a public meeting open to people both "in Boston and without." Soon Dr. Joseph Warren's posters were plastered all over Boston and its surrounding towns, calling people to the meeting. "Friends! Brethren! Countrymen! The Hour of Destruction or Manly Opposition to the Machinations of Tyranny stares you in the Face."

The meeting was convened on November 29th, at 9 a.m., in Faneuil Hall, but soon moved to Old South Church to accomodate the crowd of over 5,000. Seemingly unanimous resolutions were passed, declaring that the tea should "never be landed in this province, or one farthing of duty" be paid. Twenty-five volunteers, armed with muskets and bayonets, were sent to Griffin's Wharf, ostensibly to protect the tea ships from mobs, but actually to prevent the tea from being landed. Each night thereafter, at every half hour, they would cry out, "All is well!" Admiral Montagu, observing them, wrote that they were "like sentinels in a garrison."

Alarmed by the size of the gathering, the consignees within a few hours moved to Castle William, the island fortress out in the harbor, where the Regulars were barracked. Later that day, they were joined there by the governor.

At an equally large public meeting the next day, Captain Rotch, master of the only ship yet to arrive, was pressured into promising to bring the tea aboard his ship back to London. But the consignees would not allow him to do so. They knew that the Navigation Act of 1712 prohibited tea imported from England from being returned, on pain of confiscation. Besides, the ship could not leave the harbor without a written clearance from the customs collector or the governor. So the tea remained aboard Rotch's ship and the other two vessels that arrived a few days later.

But it would not remain on the ships for long. According to revenue laws, twenty days after registering with customs, if the duty was not paid, the ships and cargo must both be seized by customs for nonpayment of the duty. There was no doubt in anyone's mind that once that happened, placing the tea safely out of patriot reach, the consignees would gladly pay the duty and begin secretly selling it. And they would find buyers, for there was a shortage of Dutch tea in the Boston area at the time. If the tea could be sold, Boston's reputation would be ruined and it "would have revived and confirmed a jealousy which would have effectively prevented that union of the colonies" so desirable for continued resistance to Parliament.

Lest the 25 armed patriots standing guard at Griffin's Wharf prove to be an insufficient deterrent to the landing of the tea, every few days broadsides were posted around town, warning that anyone attempting such an act would be treated "as wretches unworthy to live and will be made the first victims of our just resentment." One of these broadsides described what experienced fighters Americans are, and it boastfully suggested that the Regulars be allowed to land the tea without opposition, then "we can bush fight them and cut off their officers very easily, and in this way we can subdue them with very little loss." On December 7th, the Essex Gazette reported that the people in and around Boston, "if opposed in their proceedings with respect to the tea, are determined upon hazarding a brush." The report advised all those willing to help to be prepared. As early as December first, Boston's John Andrews was noting that pistols in the stores "are all bought up with a full determination to repel force by force."

The Boston Committee of Correspondence assigned six persons as postriders, to quickly notify nearby towns of any attempt to land the tea by force. The tolling of bells would be the signal for the riders to arouse the countryside. The network of committees kept the whole colony informed of daily progress in the crisis. Towns as far away as Connecticut pledged their lives, if necessary, to prevent the tea's landing.

On December 13th, Captain Rotch was summoned to a joint meeting of five towns' committees, where he was asked if he still intended to abide by his promise to return the tea to England. He replied that the governor had instructed Admiral Montagu to blockade the harbor to prevent it, and he could not pass the blockade without a clearance from customs.

So, the next day, escorted by Sam Adams and a few others, Rotch and the captain of another of the tea ships went to the customs house to request the necessary clearance. The collector there just happened to be the same one that had been handled roughly by a mob in the *Liberty* riot when John Hancock was arrested five years earlier. It must have been with a feeling of satisfaction that he refused to grant the clearance.

Two days later, on the morning of December 16th, the day before expiration of the twenty day period for Rotch to unload his cargo, more than 5,000 people from as far away as Worcester and Maine crowded the rainy streets on their way to Old South Church for what most expected would be the decisive public meeting on the tea crisis. There Rotch was once more asked to live up to his promise. Again he explained that he could not. He then agreed to ride the seven miles to the governor's residence in Milton, to again seek a clearance. The meeting adjourned until 3 o'clock in the afternoon, to give Rotch time to report back.

Governor Hutchinson by now was convinced that Adams and his "crew" would have to back down. He therefore refused to grant the clearance, and confidently waited for the morning, when the customs collectors, assisted by the Regulars, could legally seize the cargo and begin secretly selling it. Adams would be discredited, and Hutchinson could retire to England in triumph.

The meeting reconvened at 3 p.m., but Rotch had not yet returned. Sam Adams, Joseph Warren, Thomas Young, and Josiah Quincy, Jr., kept the crowd, by now up to 7,000, occupied by giving speeches and proposing resolutions condemning the use of tea, dutied or undutied, as "improper and pernicious." By 5 o'clock, two hours past Rotch's expected return, the crowd seemed unwilling to wait any longer and clamored for action. A vote was taken to dissolve the meeting. The moderates, apprehensive about what might follow, pleaded for the meeting to continue until Rotch arrived with the governor's answer. An hour's extension was granted.

The last orator was Josiah Quincy, Jr., the young patriot lawyer who had, with John Adams, three years before defended the British soldiers tried for the Boston "massacre." Quincy sensed the tension in the air and suspected violence would result if Rotch failed to convince Hutchinson to grant the clearance so the tea could be returned to England. He now emotionally preached caution, lest radical mob action result in serious consequences. Some of Quincy's words:

Look to the end. Whoever supposes that shouts and hosannas will terminate the trials of the day entertain a childish fancy. We must be grossly ignorant of the importance and value of the prize for which we contend; we must be equally ignorant of the powers of those who have combined against us; we must be blind to hope we shall end this controversy without the sharpest - the sharpest conflicts. Let us weigh and consider, before we advance to those measures which must bring on the most trying and terrible struggle this country ever saw.

But Quincy's words of caution came too late - the plan for radical action had already been hatched, probably twenty days earlier at a meeting of the North End Caucus, whose leaders were the most influential radical Whigs, including the Adamses, Doctors Warren and Young, Paul Revere, and Will Molineaux. Quincy's pleading words fell on deaf ears. A shout of approval was the response when someone called out, "Who knows how tea will mingle with salt water!"

By 5:45, with darkness falling, a few candles dimly lit up the packed Old South Church. Suddenly Rotch pulled up, reined in his lathered horse, and made his way through the questioning crowd to the pulpit. There, to a hushed crowd, he announced the governor's refusal. Immediately, cries of "A mob! A mob!" went up, and the meeting leaders moved quickly to restore order. Dr. Thomas Young spoke up in defense of Captain Rotch, pointing out that he had made every effort to comply with the people's demands, short of sacrificing his property and perhaps his life by running the blockade. Young asked that Rotch's person and property be left unharmed. Young then turned to him and asked two final questions: Would he risk running the blockade; and, if not, did he intend to unload the tea. Rotch, just twenty-three years old, looked almost as if he would cry, as he answered "No" to both questions.

Then Sam Adams stepped up to the pulpit and had a very few

words to say, which ended with "... as for me, I shall go home, set down and make myself as easy as I can, for this meeting can do nothing further to save the country." As if on a pre-arranged signal, a war-whoop came from the balcony, answered by another at the door. Shouts rang out: "Boston Harbor a tea-pot tonight!" "Mohawks, get your axes, and pay no taxes!" The tumult was so loud that John Andrews, drinking smuggled tea in his kitchen three blocks away, later recalled, "You'd have thought that the inhabitants of the infernal regions had broke loose."

One of the participants, George Hewes, later wrote down what then happened:

> The meeting was immediately dissolved, many of them crying out, "Let every man do his duty, and be true to his country" and there was a general huzza for Griffin's Wharf. It was now evening, and I immediately dressed myself in the costume of an Indian, equipped with a small hatchet.
>
> After having painted my face and hands with coal dust in the shop of a blacksmith, I repaired to Griffin's Wharf, where the ships lay that contained the tea. When I first appeared in the street, after being thus disguised, I fell in with many who were dressed, equipped, and painted as I was ... When we arrived at the wharf, there were three of our number who assumed an authority to direct our operations, to which we readily submitted. They divided us into three parties, for the purpose of boarding the three ships.
>
> The commander of the division to which I belonged, as soon as we were on board the ship, appointed me boatswain, and ordered me to go to the captain and demand of him the keys to the hatches and a dozen candles. The captain promptly replied and delivered the articles; but requested me at the same time to do no

damage to the ship or rigging. We then were ordered by our commander to open the hatches, and take out all the chests of tea and throw them overboard, and we immediately proceeded to execute his orders; first cutting and splitting the chests with our tomahawks, so as to thoroughly expose them to the effects of the water. In about three hours from the time we went on board, we had thus broken and thrown overboard every tea chest to be found in the ship, while those in the other ships were disposing of the tea in the same way, at the same time.

We were surrounded by British armed ships, but no attempt was made to resist us. We then quietly retired to our several places of residence, without having any conversation with each other or taking any measures to discover who were our associates. ... [afterwards] the stillest night ensued that Boston had enjoyed for many months.

During the time we were throwing tea overboard, there were several attempts made by some to carry off small quantities of it for their family use. One Captain O'Connor, whom I well knew, came on board for that purpose, and when he supposed he was not noticed, filled his pockets, and also the lining of his coat. But I detected him, and gave information to the captain of what he was doing. We were ordered to take him into custody, and just as he was stepping from the vessel I seized him by the skirt of his coat, and in attempting to pull him back, I tore it off; but springing forward, by a rapid effort, he made his escape. He had, however, to run a gauntlet through the crowd upon the wharf; each one, as he passed, giving him a kick or a stroke.

The next morning, very considerable quantities of it were floating upon the surface of the water; and to prevent the possibility of any of its being saved for use, a number of small boats were manned by sailors and citizens, who, by beating it with oars and paddles, so thoroughly drenched it as to render its entire destruction inevitable.

Admiral Montagu stayed in his quarters at the Coffin House near Griffin's Wharf and watched the proceedings, waiting for a request to use his marines to stop the destruction. But Governor Hutchinson sent no such request. As the "Indians" marched back, their raid accomplished, they passed by the Coffin House. From an open second story window, Montagu yelled down to them, "Well, boys, you've had a fine pleasant evening for your Indian caper, haven't you? But mind, you've got to pay the fiddler yet." The fiddler's bill would surely come when Parliament learned what the Bostonians had done this time.

CHAPTER SIX
BOSTON SUFFERS IN THE
COMMON CAUSE OF AMERICA
1774

"The die is now cast. The colonies must either submit or triumph."

- King George III

The famous Boston Tory, Peter Oliver, wrote about the tea in his book, Origin & Progress of the American Revolution, published in 1781: "Whether it suited the constitution of a fish is not said; but it is said that some inhabitants of Boston would not eat of fish caught in their harbor because they had drank of the East India Tea."

The identity of the "Indians" was a well-known secret. Governor Hutchinson suggested to the Council, the upper house of the legislature, that it offer a reward for information leading to the arrest and conviction of those responsible. The Council refused. Of the several thousands that witnessed the event, only one was willing to testify - and then only on condition that the trial take place in England, which could not be had. Hutchinson, therefore, decided not to seek prosecution.

The Tories were shocked by what everyone called the "Boston Tea Party." Daniel Leonard declared the incident "more disgraceful to the annals of America than that of witchcraft." However, the Whigs saw it as legitimate resistance to tyranny, within the definition laid down by the English philosopher, John Locke. The Virginia Gazette pronounced it a "glorious illegality" by "a band of virtuous patriots ... an act of absolute moral and political necessity, and therefore exempt from even good laws."

85

Similar, but less publicized, "tea parties" occurred in the months to come. On April 22, 1774, tea secretly landed in Boston was dumped into the harbor by Sons of Liberty, again disguised as Indians. On December 22, 1774, fire destroyed tea stored in Greenwich, New Jersey. On October 14 of the same year, in Annapolis, Maryland, Anthony Stewart, owner of the ship *Peggy Stewart*, was caught paying duty on some tea that comprised a small part of his cargo just arrived from England. In a letter to a relation in England, a Marylander described what came to be known as "The *Peggy Stewart* Tea Party:"

> In my last I advised you of a vessel being arrived here from London, having tea on board. You will see the fate of it in the news-papers. The people from the country met here; some insisted on hanging Mr Anthony Stewart, the gentleman who paid the duty of the tea; others were for tarring and feathering him, and a great many were for destroying his house, &c. and with difficulty they were appeased with the burning of the vessel and tea [by Stewart himself].

Patriots began insisting upon the complete elimination of tea from the American diet. Smugglers were warned not to import tea of any origin whatever, so Americans could be certain that they were not drinking dutied British tea. The Sons of Liberty reacted violently whenever they caught anyone selling tea, regardless of whether it was British tea or smuggled Dutch tea. They did such a thorough job that, in 1774, a traveler observed, "You may ride for days, nay weeks, and never get a drop." Daughters of Liberty took solemn oaths to never drink another cup of the brew, and whole chests were burned upon village commons, thus sacrificing "the obnoxious drug at the Shrine of Liberty." Raspberry leaf were used to make an inferior "patriot tea." Coffee beans from South America were tried, as Americans began to be weaned from the tea cup to the coffee cup, to which their devotion has remained steadfast ever since.

Massachusetts voted funds to have Benjamin Franklin act as their agent in London, as he was doing for Pennsylvania, to lobby on their behalf amongst the members of Parliament and the ministry. Clerk Sam Adams provided Franklin with the following instructions from the Massachusetts Assembly:

> It will be in vain for any to expect that the people of this country will now be contented with a partial and temporary relief; or that they will be amused by court promises while they see not the least relaxation of grievances. Colonies begin to communicate freely. There is a common affection among them; and shortly the whole continent will be as united in sentiment and in their measures of opposition to tyranny as the inhabitants of this province. Their old good-will and affection for the parent country are not totally lost; if she returns to her former moderation and good humor, their affection will revive. They wish for nothing more than a permanent union with her upon the condition of equal liberty. This is all they have been contending for; and nothing short of this will or ought to satisfy them.

But in England, both the people and Parliament were becoming less open-minded about the situation in Boston. Letters arriving from Boston exaggerated the situation, and London newspapers published wild stories about official committees of tarring and feathering in the Massachusetts Assembly, with the governor as one of the designated victims. The press aroused the national pride, until the zeal of the English people to maintain supremacy over "our subjects in the American colonies" became equal to that of the King and his ministers. One citizen, writing to the editor of a London newspaper, suggested the Massachusetts charter be annulled and that half the colony be given to New York and the other half to Nova Scotia. Another suggested "about one hundred of these puritanical rebels in Boston" ought to be hung. The next cargo, accompanied by several thousand Regulars, should be "gunpowder tea." "There is not a more obnoxious character here presently," wrote one observer, "than that of a friend to America." Virginia's agent in London, Arthur Lee, expressed concern for the lives of "active Americans here."

Even some of the pro-American Whigs in Parliament were convinced that something must be done. As Lord North said, the dispute was no longer over taxation, but whether Britain still possessed any authority at all over the "haughty American Republicans. We must master them, or totally leave them to themselves and treat them as aliens." Boston's "Tea Party" had brought ten years of political crisis to a head. King George III declared, "The die is now cast. The colonies must either submit or triumph." General Thomas Gage, Commander-in-Chief of all British forces in North America, was in London at the time, having been called home for consultations. He told the King:

> I am willing to go back at a day's notice, if coercive measures are adopted. They will be lyons, while we are lambs; but, if we take the resolute part, they will undoubtedly prove very meek.

The general feeling now was that the lenient policy that repealed the Stamp Act and most of the Townshend Duties had been the wrong approach for the mother country to take with her rebellious colonies. Alluding to the repeal of the Stamp Act, King George III wrote, "All men seem now to feel that the fatal compliance in 1766 has encouraged the Americans [toward] that thorough independency which one state has of another, but which is quite subversive of the obedience which a colony owes to its mother country." As one member of Parliament put it, "The leading question is the dependence or independence of America." And an editorialist, writing in a newspaper, put it this way:

> Is it not rather a duty incumbent on the parent when

every lenient measure, every soothing expedient has been tried in vain, to bring [the children] back to their allegiance by a gentle correction? "<u>Spare the rod and spoil the child</u>" is an adage perfectly applicable in the present instance.

Instead of bloody reprisals against the Bostonians, Prime Minister Lord North opted for the more moderate strategy of starving them into submission. This was the purpose of the Boston Port Act, passed by Parliament on March 25, 1774. It provided that the port be closed to all shipping until the citizens paid the East India Company for the destroyed tea, and compensated the consignees for damages suffered at the hands of the mob.

When the bill was introduced in Parliament, most of the pro-American Whigs were quiet, and offered little opposition. Even they agreed that the destruction of property was a criminal act that could not be condoned. As the Whig leader, Edmund Burke, explained, there was in Parliament "a general notion that <u>some</u> <u>Act</u> of power was become necessary, and that the hands of government ought to be strengthened." An agent for the Massachusetts Council petitioned to be heard on behalf of Boston. The House of Commons voted 170 to 40 to not hear him. One member of Parliament, the former governor of West Florida, warned his fellow members "that the effect of the present Bill must be productive of a General Confederation, to resist the power of this country." His warning was not heeded, and several months later his prophecy would come true with the formation of the first Continental Congress.

Several London merchants who traded mainly with Boston merchants were confident that the Bostonians would pay for the damages. A delegation of these London merchants met with Lord North one week before the bill was to be voted on. They offered to be answerable to 16,000 pounds (far more than the tea was worth), if North would give them six months to procure the money from the town of Boston. If they failed, North could then close the port. North asked these merchants if they would be willing to also be answerable for Boston's conduct if more tea were sent there. But they considered this condition absurd and not something they could agree to. So North told them to return to their counting-houses and leave politics to his direction. A similar offer by London's mayor was also rejected.

In the few months between the Tea Party and the arrival of news of the Boston Port Act, the newspapers in and around Boston were full of letters, some advocating the tea be paid for, others agreeing with a London merchant who advised, "Stand your ground, be not intimidated, and the day is yours." Benjamin Franklin wrote from London to the Boston Committee of Correspondence, strongly suggesting immediate repayment as the only way of gaining the opinion of Europe, in case Great Britain should use military force against the colonies. Sam Adams made sure the letter was never made public, for it would have greatly encouraged the moderates and conservatives who favored repayment. Adams told one confidant, "Franklin is a great philosopher, but a poor politician."

Once the news of the Boston Port Act's passage arrived, however, the demand for repayment took on the appearance of ransom, and even many of the moderates felt that "the revenge of the ministry was too severe." The issue of repayment came to a head at a Boston Town Meeting on June 17, 1774. John Adams presided as moderator in place of his cousin Sam, who was busy at the legislature in Salem. Many were in favor of repayment, and it looked like a majority might vote for it, until one patriot insinuated that anyone favoring repayment was in effect endorsing the Port Act. He declared that the debate would show "our friends from our foes." The moderates quickly clammed up and acquiesced with the patriots in voting against repayment.

General Gage returned to America as the retired Thomas Hutchinson's replacement. Gage, as both royal governor of Massachusetts and Commander-in-Chief of all British forces in North America, was given the task of enforcing the Boston Port Act. The day he arrived, the Boston Committee of Correspondence sent Paul Revere riding off to

New York and Philadelphia with a plea for united action by all the colonies. Without it, Boston, a town that lived by the traffic and fish of the sea, would surely be forced to submit. Revere carried what the Bostonians hoped would be a very persuasive letter.

> This attack, though made immediately upon us, is doubtless designed for every other colony who will not surrender their sacred rights and liberties into the hands of an infamous ministry. Now, therefore, is the time when all should be united in opposition to this violation of the liberties of all.

The Boston Committee of Correspondence also attempted to start a new nonintercourse agreement. Merchants throughout Massachusetts were put under pressure by local chapters of the Sons of Liberty to sign a Solemn League and Covenant, written by Dr. Joseph Warren, pledging to give up the buying or selling of British goods. This attempt met with little success outside Massachusetts, and eventually the idea was dropped in favor of a gathering of delegates from all the colonies, similar to the Stamp Act Congress of 1765.

When the Virginia House of Burgesses indicated it would vote on resolves to support Boston, the royal governor dissolved that assembly. The burgesses then moved to the Raleigh Tavern, where they resolved to renew the "Virginia Association" (the Nonintercourse Agreement of 1769). They also passed the following resolve, written by Thomas Jefferson:

> An attack, made on one of our sister colonies, to compel submission to arbitrary taxes, is an attack made on all British America, and threatens ruin to the rights of all, unless the united wisdom of the whole be applied. And for this purpose it is recommended to the committees of correspondence, that they communicate with their several corresponding committees on the expedi-

ency of appointing deputies from the several colonies of British America, to meet in general congress.

In other colonies, the radicals wanted to join the boycott, while conservatives wanted Boston to pay for the tea. The logical compromise was to propose a continental congress, letting all the colonies jointly decide what to do. New York's moderate Committee of Correspondence called for a continental congress that excluded delegates from Boston; their aim was to have a congress that would recommend Boston pay for the tea, rather than commit the entire continent to the sacrifices of yet another boycott. Pennsylvania's Assembly also called for a congress, but at the same time suggested Massachusetts pay for the tea.

June 1, 1774 - the day the Boston Port Act was due to take effect - was acknowledged by demonstrations throughout the colonies. In Virginia, the House of Burgesses declared it a day of fasting and prayer. In Philadelphia, flags were flown at half-mast, and shops were closed for the day. In Connecticut, two weeks before, one thousand citizens had gathered on Farmington Common to raise a liberty pole, burn a copy of the Boston Port Act, and pass resolves denouncing "the present ministry" as "pimps and parasites instigated by the devil" to enslave the colonies.

In Boston, all water traffic came to a halt, except the Charlestown ferry, which was only allowed to carry passengers without baggage. "Our wharfs," wrote John Andrews, "are entirely deserted; not a topsail to be seen, save the ships of war." Thomas Young wrote from Boston to a friend in New York, "At length, the perfect crisis of American politics seems arrived. A very few months must decide whether we and our posterity shall be slaves or freemen."

Throughout the colonies, Committees of Correspondence arranged for transportation of food to Boston. In Britain, Tories who expected to read about famine in Boston, instead found the Boston Whigs "insulting us with the plenty they enjoyed, boasting that their sheep and their flour, their fish and their rice came faster than they could use them." The magnitude of the support provided by the other colonies was, according to Governor Gage, "beyond the conception of most people, and foreseen by none." Typical was a donation from the village of Durham, New Hampshire, accompanied by this letter to Boston's Committee of Correspondence:

> We take pleasure in transmitting to you a few cattle, with a small sum of money. Soon you will receive the donations of a number in Lee, a parish lately set off from this town, and in a few days those of Dover, Newmarket and other adjacent towns.
>
> This is considered by us, not as a gift or an act of charity, but of justice, as a small part of what we are in duty bound to communicate to those truly noble and patriotic advocates of American freedom who are bravely standing in the gap between us and slavery, defending the common interests of a whole continent and gloriously struggling in the cause of Liberty.

The patriots' cause was no longer local or provincial, wrote a New Yorker, but now continental in scope. The citizens of Arundel County, Maryland, resolved, "That the town of Boston is now suffering in the common cause of America."

Philadelphia's William Goddard rode through the middle and northern colonies, pointing out to local Committees of Correspondence the need for some means of communication that would be safe from the British authorities. By late summer of 1774, a new continental postal system, run by the colonists themselves, would be in operation.

Governor Gage reported to the Secretary of War, Lord Barrington, on conditions in America, July 18, 1774:

> The seditious here have raised a flame in every colony, which your speeches, writings, & protests in England have greatly encouraged. They depend for sup-

port on their former measures of a general union, non importation, assistance of their friends in England, clamors of merchants, manufacturers &ca, and in the mean time hope to support the people by contributions, and prevent their suffering from the shutting up the port.

During the summer, news arrived from London of the passage of several more acts, which, together with the Boston Port Act, would be known in England as "The Coercive Acts," and in America as "The Intolerable Acts." These were the Massachusetts Government Act, an Act for the Impartial Administration of Justice, a new Quartering Act, and the Quebec Act.

The Massachusetts Government Act changed that colony's charter, something that had been considered in Parliament for the past several years. Members of the Council (the upper chamber of the bicameral legislature), heretofore annually elected by the General Assembly (the lower chamber), would now, as was already done in most colonies, be appointed by the Crown. Judges, sheriffs and all executive officials would now be appointed and paid by the Crown, instead of by the Massachusetts legislature. Town Meetings would be prohibited, except for an annual one limited to only discussing the coming year's budget. Juries would now be selected by the sheriffs. The past selection of jurors by the people, Parliament felt, had contributed greatly to riot and rebellion, as explained in a pamphlet published in London:

> Juries were packed. They were nominated at the Town Meeting by the heads of a party. A jury, for instance, was summoned to inquire into riots. Among these impartial and respectable jurors one was returned [selected] who was a principal in the very riot into which it was the business of the very jury to inquire.

The Act for the Impartial Administration of Justice provided that soldiers who killed rioters could be tried in another colony or in England, rather than in local courts where the judge and jury might not be fair because of fear of retribution by the mob.

The new Quartering Act authorized the military to seize barns and unoccupied buildings to house, or "quarter," troops in towns that did not provide adequate, conveniently located barracks. Gage would now be able to move the regiments from Castle Island to Boston.

The Quebec Act was associated by Americans with the other Coercive Acts, although it had been in the planning stages for several years and the British did not consider it one of the Coercive Acts. It was enacted to finally answer the question of how Britain would govern the former French colony of Canada, acquired at the end of the last war. The Quebec Act promised that Roman Catholics (95% of all Canadians) would be guaranteed freedom to practice their religion without fear of persecution. They would also be eligible for civil service jobs, since the Quebec Act toned down the loyalty oath enough to make it palatable to the former French colonists.

In addition, the Quebec Act extended Canada's southern and western boundaries to include the Ohio and Illinois valleys, and declared a prohibition on all whites, except Canadian trappers and fur traders, from entering those valleys. The earlier promise of a colonial Assembly (expected to be dominated by, if not limited to, the English speaking minority) was deemed "inexpedient." Instead, the form of government would be a governor and advisory Council, all appointed by the Crown. This was acceptable to the French-Canadians, as was the continuance of the old French civil law, which had no habeus corpus or trial by jury. Britain could now feel confident that Canada would not join the other colonies, should the "American problem" deteriorate into armed rebellion.

Americans were particularly concerned about the Quebec Act. In Pennsylvania, newspapers published scenarios of the future, depicting the British government sending a "horde of Popish slaves" against the Protestant colonies to the south in an effort to establish a "universal despotism in the British Empire." In New York, Alexander Hamilton declared that the act would bring millions of Roman Catholics from

Europe, until the Protestant colonies found themselves surrounded by "a nation of Papists and slaves." As descendants of the Puritans, New England's farmers now had a seemingly more compelling reason to join the radicals from the seaport towns. As one colonist put it, "the Quebec Bill, that open and avowed design of subjugating America, has alarmed the most inattentive, and given us but one mind." A Connecticut soldier later recalled that the Quebec Act produced "a real fear of Popery" and stimulated timorous people "to send their sons to join the military ranks."

The Quebec Act, or rather the clergy's reaction to it, destroyed General Gage's last hope of preventing Boston and backwoods New England from uniting. As he expressed it in a letter to Colonial Secretary Lord Dartmouth, Americans were beginning to view Britain as a foreign, despotic and "Papist" power. Americans wondered if a government without an Assembly, habeus corpus, and trial by jury was what Britain had in mind for all her colonies, and if their stubbornly won Protestantism was also in danger.

Gage explained to Dartmouth that the propagandists had the people believing that the Coercive Acts would "lead to others which are to divide their lands into lordships and tax them so much per acre; and that the Quebec Act has been made use of to persuade them that their religion is to be changed."

Gage was not the only one making such observations. An Englishman visiting the colonies that winter of 1774-75 wrote home to his brother:

> The leading men, I mean those called patriots, have taken every measure to keep up the spirit of the people. Mankind in general are very jealous of any innovation in their religion; of this the leaders have taken the advantage, and impressed on the minds of the people a belief that the Romish is going to be established in America by an act of Parliament; that they have begun with Canada, and intend to introduce it among the rest of the colonies.

This the lowest class verily believe, and the more substantial yeomanry are so prejudiced by party, that anything asserted by a Whig they take it for granted is so, without enquiring any further about the matter.

I have been frequently in the country, and had many opportunities of conversing with the country people; they say "we had sooner die than be made slaves; it is a pity the King of England was turned Papist," and a great deal of such stuff. When I assured them to the contrary, they seemed surprized at my talking in that manner, and were quite enraged. "What (said they), do you know better than the newspapers? Are we not to believe what they tell us?"

In their churches the Gospel is laid aside for politics, and nothing is more common than their offering up prayers for the destruction of the navy and army.

Of most concern to General Gage in Boston was his duty as governor to execute the new Massachusetts Government Act. But he faced a determined people. Only once did Gage send Regulars to stop a Town Meeting. In Salem, the citizens barred the doors to the meetinghouse when the Regulars arrived, and defiantly carried on their meeting inside. The British officers, remembering their orders against harming any citizens, swallowed their pride and ordered their men to turn around and march back to Boston.

Throughout Massachusetts, "Liberty Boys" (members of the secret Sons of Liberty) used violence to force all the new Crown-appointed Council members to resign. Peter Oliver, forced to resign as president of the new Council, had seen Boston's mob violence at its worst during the Stamp Act crisis. Now, having witnessed some of the recent terror in the countryside, he wrote, "I never knew what mobbing was before. I am sick enough of confusion & uproar. I long for an asylum, some blessed place of refuge."

The Act for the Imparial Administration of Justice was known in

Massachusetts as the "Murder Act." The patriot press claimed that, under its provisions, "every inhabitant in Massachusetts" was "exposed to the lawless violence of a soldiery to be destroyed as wild & savage beasts of the forests" because each one of them "who ravishes our wives and deflowers our daughters, can evade punishment by being tried in Britain, where no evidence can pursue him." To prevent the Act's execution, propagandists aroused the rage of the mobs against the judges and sheriffs. In Berkshire County, a mob forced the judges from their seats and boarded up the Pittsfield courthouse. In Worcester, an armed mob of 5,000 compelled the judges, sheriffs, and lawyers to march up and down while reading thirty times a pledge to refrain from "all judicial proceedings on account of the unconstitutional act of the British Parliament respecting the administration of justice in this province." In a similar way, the courts at Taunton, Springfield, Plymouth, and Great Barrington were also mobbed. So many sheriffs and judges fled to Boston that some called it the "Asylum for Magistrates."

Councillors, judges and sheriffs were not the only ones persecuted during the hot summer of 1774. Tories all over Massachusetts, and to a lesser degree the rest of New England, were driven from their homes. One rural Whig boasted that, "it is more dangerous being a Tory here than at Boston, even if no troops were there." Tory merchants were boycotted by local Whigs and anyone who feared the wrath of the mob.

One man named Moses Dunbar, who had bought some cattle from a Tory, was for that "offence" put into the belly of an ox that had just been dressed by the butcher, and he was carried like that in a cart for four miles. As if that was not enough, the mob relieved him of four head of cattle and one horse. Three years later, while a captain in a Tory regiment, he would be captured and found guilty of treason by Connecticut's Superior Court. Moses Dunbar became, and still is, the only person ever executed in Connecticut for a political crime. The sentence was carried out on a hilltop which later became the site of Trinity College, the first college founded in America by the Anglican or Episcopalian Church (the Church of England).

Between mid-June and mid-August, delegates to the first Continental Congress were chosen in twelve colonies (Georgia would not send delegates until the second Congress, held in the spring of 1775). Benjamin Franklin headed up a group that traveled to Canada in an effort to entice that colony to send delegates, too, but the Canadians declined the invitation. Their refusal was not surprising, considering the way their neighbors to the south had reacted to the Quebec Act's recognition of their religion.

In some colonies, the delegates were selected by patriot Committees of Correspondence, while in other colonies the patriot-controlled Assemblies made the selections. One exception was South Carolina, where deputies selected from the various counties combined with a large number of townspeople at Charleston in a public meeting on July 6th, and there elected that colony's delegates. Four weeks later, the Assembly confirmed the July 6th meeting's selections and allocated funds for their expenses. The Assembly secretly met two hours earlier than posted, to prevent the governor from dissolving the session to prevent the vote from taking place.

New York was the only other colony where some semblance of a popular election was used for the selection process. A resident of the city of New York, where the vote took place amongst the inhabitants, explained why the loyalists there voted, instead of trying to prevent the election from taking place:

> The colonies labored under grievances which wanted redressing. To redress which and to form a happy, perpetual, and lasting allegiance between Great Britain and America, were the reasons which induced the New York loyalists so readily to the delegation. The republicans wanted members chosen out of their own faction. This the loyalists opposed and a kind of compromise took place.
>
> With such a delegation, the New York loyalists thought themselves safe. A redress of grievances and a

firm union between Great Britain and America upon constitutional principles was their only aim. To this purport they also verbally instructed their delegates.

In Massachusetts, with General Gage as governor, one would suppose that the Assembly would secretly assign the selection process to the Committee of Correspondence. But Sam Adams was determined, perhaps to spite the new governor, that the Assembly should choose the colony's delegates to the Continental Congress. On June 17th, as a meeting of the Assembly was about to start, Samuel Adams, as Clerk of the Assembly, ordered the doorkeeper to let no one enter or leave the room once the meeting commenced.

However, as soon as a Tory Assemblyman figured out what was about to be voted on, he feigned illness and rushed past the doorkeeper. Adams then walked to the door, locked it, and put the key in his pocket. When the Tory reached the governor's house, he warned Gage of what he suspected the Assembly was about to do. Gage immediately wrote a proclamation dissolving the session. The messenger arrived with the proclamation, but beat on the door in vain, while the Assembly voted in a slate of delegates, and funds for their expenses.

Many delegates wrote that, on their way to Philadelphia, they were feasted, praised, and encouraged by the people in the colonies through which they passed. John Adams described the scene he encountered as he approached New Haven:

> Seven miles out of town, at a tavern, we met a great number of carriages and of horsemen who had come out to meet us. As we came into the town, all the bells in town were set to ringing and the people, men, women and children were crowding at the doors and windows as if it was to see a coronation. At nine o'clock the cannon were fired, about a dozen guns.
>
> These expressions of respect to us are intended as demonstrations of the sympathy of this people with the

Massachusetts Bay and its capital, and to show their ex-
pectations from the Congress, and their determination to
carry into execution whatever shall be agreed upon.

The British government, for the most part, felt confident that the
Coercive Acts would solve "the American problem." Even news of
the formation of a continental congress was not taken seriously. Thomas Hutchinson, former governor of Massachusetts, was now in
England. There he noted that, "nobody seems to give themselves the
least concern about the consequences of the projected Congress, supposing it can do no hurt to the Kingdom." Others felt that even
though it was "undoubtedly illegal, some good may arise out of it."
Colonial Secretary Lord Dartmouth thought it would be "wise to over-
look the irregularity of the proceedings" if the rebel congress should
help to cool things down by authoring petitions full of "fine words."

When the Massachusetts delegation reached Philadelphia, they
found the composition of the Congress, in John Adams' words, was
"one third Tories, another Whigs, and the rest mongrels." Friendly
Whigs, or "patriots," there cautioned him that the other colonies' delegates were suspicious of Boston's hot-headed radicals. John Adams
recorded one of their warnings in his journal: "You must not utter the
word independence, nor give the least hint or insinuation of the idea,
either in Congress or any private conversation, for independence is unpopular in all the Middle and South ... No man dares speak of it."

Along with political radicalism, the Yankee delegates, as Congregationalists, brought with them a reputation for religious intolerance.
Taking advantage of this, the shrewd Sam Adams started his subtle
campaign to solidify a political alliance between the New England and
Virginia delegates by moving that Philadelphia's Anglican minister,
Jacob Duche, deliver the opening prayer. Adams explained his motive
in a letter to Dr. Joseph Warren, remarking that, since "many of our
warmest friends are members of the Church of England, I thought it
prudent." A delegate from Pennsylvania thought it a "masterly stroke
of policy" on Adams' part. Duche responded with a moving prayer

"for America, for the Congress, for the Province of Massachusetts Bay, and especially the town of Boston." John Adams observed that the prayer "had an excellent effect upon everybody here."

The conservatives were prepared to resist the arguments put forth by the radical "pumpkin gentry" from New England, who would be vulnerable to attack because of the strong prejudice in the other, more aristocratic, colonies against "the New England leveling spirit." However, the conservatives were thrown off balance by the shrewdness of the Yankees, who were strangely quiet during most of the debates. Realizing that direct opposition to proposals of accomodation would quickly brand them as proponents of independence, they pursued their interest "out of doors," meeting with radical and moderate delegates in the evenings, at dinner and in the City Tavern. It was around these tables, rather than on the floor of Carpenter's Hall, that John and Sam Adams put forth their ideas. John wrote:

> We have been obliged to act with great delicacy and caution. We have been obliged to keep ourselves out of sight, and to feel pulses and sound depths, to insinuate our sentiments, designs, and desires by means of other persons, sometimes of one province, sometimes of another.

The result was that those delegates espousing the most radical position were not the Yankees, whom everyone expected to advocate their "damned republicanism," but rather the Southerners. South Carolina's Christopher Gadsden urged that General Gage's troops be attacked before reinforcements arrived from Britain. Virginia's Richard Henry Lee proposed a new nonimportation and nonexportation agreement. Subtly advocating independence, Patrick Henry argued that the empire was already dissolved, and the colonies were in a "state of nature." Together with a few other aristocratic planters who supported the radical faction, these Southerners gave the revolutionary movement a respectability that the New Englanders could not provide.

The conservatives, led by Pennsylvania's Joseph Galloway, attempted to grab the leadership at the outset, fearing that if the radicals steered Congress's course the only possible destination would be independence. Galloway believed that if he could persuade Congress to open negotiations with Great Britain, it would eventually lead to reconciliation. He was aware that the great majority of Americans wished to remain united with England, and if they could be convinced that they'd retain their colonial freedoms then they would stop following the radicals on the road to revolution.

So Galloway proposed a reorganization of the empire as a means of permanently resolving the crisis between Britain and her colonies. His "Plan of Union," as he called it, provided for a Grand Council, similar to the Continental Congress, which would have jurisdiction over matters that jointly affected all the colonies, though each colony would continue to exercise authority over its own internal affairs. The Grand Council would have a president-general, appointed by the Crown, who would have veto power over bills passed by that body. Bills affecting both Britain and one or more colonies, after passage in either the Parliament or the Grand Council, could be vetoed by the other body.

The problems with Galloway's Plan were that: 1) it would postpone decisive action; 2) there was a good chance that Parliament would reject it; and 3) in the meantime, the Coercive Acts would still be in effect and taking their toll in Massachusetts.

The radicals opposing the Plan were led by Patrick Henry. Henry argued that, if it should be accepted by Parliament, "We shall liberate our constituents from a corrupt House of Commons, but throw them into the arms of an American legislature that may be bribed by that nation which avows in the face of the world that bribery is a part of her system of government." Gadsden, Henry, Lee and the Adamses were convinced that Britain had a depraved society, corrupt in religion, politics and morals. Although they would bide their time and wait for the mood of Congress to change before espousing it, these men wanted total independence, unlike the majority of delegates, who desired reconciliation.

After several days of heated debate, Congress voted six colonies to five, with one abstention, to postpone further debate on the Plan. When it was brought up again a few weeks later, the disposition of the members had hardened, and they voted that all reference to the Plan be expunged from the record of their proceedings. The conservatives' best chance for reconciliation had stalled and died. They had failed to control the nature of Congressional measures to resist Parliament, and would never again be a serious threat to the radicals' control of the revolution.

Whatever chance Galloway's Plan of Union had of passage was dashed when Paul Revere arrived from Boston with a copy of the "Suffolk Resolves." Galloway, ever suspicious of Bostonians, suspected a plot. In a pamphlet published six years later, when he was a loyalist refugee in London, he charged (accurately, as Adams' letters would prove) that

> continued expresses were employed between Philadelphia and Boston. Whatever these patriots in Congress wished to have done by their colleagues without [that is, outside Congress] to induce General Gage to give them a pretence for violent opposition, or to promote their measure in Congress, Mr. Adams advised and directed to be done; and when done, it was dispatched by express to Congress.
>
> By one of these expresses came the inflammatory resolves of the county of Suffolk, which contained a complete declaration of war against Great Britain.

On September 9, 1774, delegates from each town in Suffolk County (Boston and its environs) had met and adopted resolutions drawn up by Dr. Joseph Warren. They resolved that, to the Coercive Acts "no obedience is due from this province, but that they be rejected as the attempts of a wicked administration to enslave America." They also resolved: to withhold collected taxes from the current government of

Massachusetts; to cancel all commissions of militia officers who were paid by the Crown; to boycott British goods; and "that all the inhabitants use their utmost diligence to acquaint themselves with the art of war as soon as possible." Not wanting to risk losing the support of the moderates in Congress, Dr. Warren slyly put forth the Quebec Act as the justification for these preparations for war:

> 10. That the late act of Parliament for establishing the Roman Catholic religion and the French laws in that extensive country, now called Canada, is dangerous in an extreme degree to the Protestant religion and to the civil rights and liberties of all America; and, therefore, as men and Protestant Christians we are indispensably obliged to take all proper measures for our security.

These Resolves were a major test, because the citizens of Suffolk County had asked Congress for guidance. Congress was faced with a choice: it must pass a resolution either condemning or approving the Resolves. Any resolution endorsing them could be interpreted as support for suspension of civil government, and open armed resistance to British authority. Joseph Warren's master stroke had the desired effect on Congress, as his Suffolk Resolves were "read with great applause" before the Congress by its secretary. Perhaps just as effective as the nineteen Resolves was Dr. Warren's moving preamble, excerpted here:

> ... Great Britain, which scourged and exiled our fugitive parents from their native shores, now pursues us, their guiltless children, with unrelenting severity. If a boundless extent of continent, swarming with millions, will tamely submit to live, move, and have their being at the arbitrary will of a licentious minister, they will basely yield to voluntary slavery, and future generations shall load their memories with incessant execrations. On the other hand, if we arrest the hand which would ransack

our pockets, if we disarm the parricide who points the dagger to our bosoms, if we nobly defeat that fatal edict which proclaims a power to frame laws for us in all cases whatsoever, posterity will acknowledge that virtue which preserved them free and happy.

After pledging continued support to the besieged town of Boston, Congress passed a resolution to "most thoroughly approve" the Suffolk Resolves and "earnestly recommend to their brethren a perseverence" to those resolves. A few days later, after the Galloway Plan had been narrowly defeated, the radical faction was stong enough to have another resolution passed, stating that, if "the late acts of Parliament shall be attempted to be carried into execution by force, all America ought to support them in their opposition." Galloway and James Duane attempted to have their opposition to this resolution entered into the Congressional minutes. When their request was denied, the two men each supplied the other with a certificate stating that he had given no support to the seditious resolution.

The other results of the first Continental Congress were:

. A *Declaration of Rights* listing America's grievances since 1763. Through James Duane's efforts, its language was kept moderate, so as not to jeopardize chances for reconciliation with Great Britain.

. An *Address to the Inhabitants of Great Britain* providing an historical review of the colonial grievances, couched in terms of "slavery and oppression," and suggesting that the people of Britain had been "extremely negligent in the appointment of her rulers." It declared that Americans "will never submit to be hewers of wood or drawers of water for any ministry." It also suggested that if the ministry continues to be allowed to tax America at its pleasure, it would soon take oppressive measures against inhabitants of England itself.

. An *Address to the King* assuring him that repeal of obnoxious laws would remove all the grievances. As usual, loyalty to the King was sworn to, while blame for the crisis was placed on the ministry: "... as your majesty enjoys the signal distinction of reigning over freemen, we apprehend that the language of freemen cannot be displeasing. Your royal indignation, we hope, will rather fall upon those dangerous and designing men."

. Authorization of a boycott of trade with Britain, to be enforced by "Committees of Safety" to be formed in "every county, city and town." This new boycott was called "The Continental Association for Nonintercourse." December 1, 1774, was set as the date when the colonies were to stop importing British goods; and on September 10, 1775, American products would stop being sold to Great Britain. The boycott, or "nonintercourse," would stop as soon as the Coercive Acts and all other offensive acts passed since 1763 were repealed. Persons violating the Association were to be "stigmatized" by having their names published, a practice which amounted to "inviting the vengeance of an outrageous and lawless mob."

The first Continental Congress adjourned on October 26, 1774, the delegates agreeing to reconvene on May 10, 1775, if by then the offensive acts have not yet been repealed. The radicals must have been surprised at the results of the Congress. The Association for Nonintercourse was a hard-line approach to the crisis, which many felt would surely bring England to her senses. Like many of the other delegates, John Adams expected that a second Congress in May would not be necessary. "It is not likely," he wrote before leaving Philadelphia, "that I shall ever see this part of the world again."

Loyalists must have been even more surprised at the results, after assuming that the delegates would merely send petitions to the British government. The Reverend Samuel Seabury, in a pamphlet entitled *Free Thoughts on the Proceedings of Congress*, objected to these new committees. "If I must be enslaved, let it be by a King at least, and not by a parcel of upstart, lawless Committee-men." Seabury later became the first Anglican bishop in America.

The moderates in Congress now faced a dilemma, since they were implicated in the creation of two truly revolutionary institutions - the Association for Nonintercourse, and the Committees of Safety. This dilemma is illustrated by the following excerpt from the memoirs of a wealthy New York merchant, who wrote about his Congressman friend, Jeremiah Wynkoop.

It was to keep New York from violent measures of all sorts that Mr. Wynkoop had consented to serve on the Committee of 51; it was for that reason he had gone to Philadelphia. "I am very glad you went to Philadelphia," I said.

"What else could I have done?" he exclaimed. "I have asked myself that a dozen times without finding any answer. But about the Association, I don't know. You say it is a measure of the New Englanders, and among the moderates of Philadelphia it was commonly thought to be perhaps too vigorous. I was opposed to it. I voted against it. And having done so, perhaps I was ill advised to sign it. I don't know."

I was about to make some reply, when old Nicholas came into the room. "Fine doings!" old Nicholas growled. "The New Englanders had their way, as I expected. I warned you against meddling with treason. ..."

[Wynkoop:] "I cannot think so, sir. The Association is a voluntary agreement not to do certain things; not to import or to export certain goods after a certain date. No law that I know of compels me to import or to export."

[Nicholas:] "No law requires you to import or to export, very true. But does any law require me not to import or export? Certainly no law of the British Parliament or of New York province obliges me. But suppose I exercise my lawful privilege of importing after the date

108

fixed? What then? Will not your committees seize my goods, and sell them at public auction for the benefit of the starving mechanics of Boston? I tell you your Association erects a government unknown to the law; a government which aims to exert compulsion on all citizens. When I am given a coat of tar for violating the Association, will you still say it is a <u>voluntary</u> Association?

* * * * *

By the summer of 1774, ten years of debating and pamphleteering had boiled down to one direct and simple issue: Was the Parliament supreme over the colonies, or not? In England, both Tories and Whigs agreed that the supremacy of Parliament must be maintained, though they differed in what that entailed. However, American Whigs vehemently denied that supremacy.

The colonies' original charters spoke only of the colonists and the King, without any mention of Parliament; all authority to tax them and regulate their internal affairs rested with the King. The King had given them permission to emigrate, given them title to the lands, and granted their charters. Both King James, in 1621, and later Charles I, had declared the colonies distinct states outside the jurisdiction of Parliament. Therefore, the patriots argued, through these charters the colonies were autonomous governments owing loyalty only to King George III, who, if he did his duty, would protect them from foreign countries and from Parliament.

Their opponents in Parliament refuted this logic by simply pointing to the "glorious English Revolution" of 1688, when Parliament became the ruling power in Britain and the Crown took a back seat. They claimed that charters granted prior to 1688 were now void, because after that date only Parliament could grant charters. During the almost ninety years since then, Parliament had gradually become even more powerful. To an Englishman in 1774, the idea that there was any part of the British Empire to which the whole power of Parliament did not extend was simply absurd.

It may have seemed absurd to Englishmen, but to most Americans independence from Parliament (but not from England) was natural, just, and necessary. With each new, progressively more militant and tyrannical measure Parliament enacted, Americans became more convinced that they would ultimately be forced to defend their liberties with their lives. By supporting the Suffolk Resolves, Congress justified fighting a defensive war. The Coercive Acts convinced Americans that a revolution was being launched by Parliament against a British heritage of freedoms. If it should come to war, Americans who resisted Parliament would not be traitors, but "patriots" fighting a counter-revolution to restore centuries old freedoms. From the patriot perspective, the traitors would be those who sided with Parliament. Thus, the Tories, or "loyalists" as they liked to call themselves, were viewed by the patriots as "traitors to America's cause."

Parliament had done its best to peaceably force its will upon America, without success. All that remained was for it to try a military solution or give up. America now waited for the British military to make the first move and start the war that seemed unavoidable. Led by their Continental Congress, they were determined to make a spirited defense of their liberties. In this respect, the latter half of 1774 and first half of 1775 was perhaps the purest moment of the Revolution.

CHAPTER SEVEN
A WAR OF NERVES
SEPTEMBER 1774 - MARCH 1775

"The man was cleaning a gun. I asked him what he was going to kill, as he was so old I should not think he could take sight at any game; he said there was a flock of redcoats in Boston, which he expected would be here soon ... I asked him how old he was; he said, 'Seventy-seven, and never was killed yet.'"

- John Howe, British spy, traveling the countryside west of Boston

On August 31, 1774, while the delegates to the Continental Congress were arriving in Philadelphia, a dress rehearsal for war - the "Powder Alarm" - was taking place in New England. Massachusetts' governor, General Gage, was informed by a Tory that, at a powder house six miles northwest of Boston, the colony's largest store of gunpowder was being dispensed among the rebels. So at 4:30 a.m. the next morning, 260 British Regulars marched through Boston's streets to the wharf, and were rowed by sailors in landing barges across the harbor and up the Mystic River. They landed while the people of Cambridge were still asleep, and safely returned to Boston with the remaining 250 barrels of powder.

The expedition had met with no resistance. However, that night signal bonfires burned on the surrounding hilltops. Postriders, seeing the bonfires, incorrectly assumed that Boston was being bombarded by the British warships in the harbor. They therefore set off on their horses to spread the alarm throughout New England.

By morning, 3,000 patriots were on Cambridge Common, just outside Boston, and thousands were on their way from all directions. One exaggerated report, which arrived by boat later that day, claimed that an estimated 100,000 men were marching in Connecticut. No one recorded the actual number that eventually reached the Boston area, though Reverend Ezra Stiles estimated that one-third of all the militia in New England had set out for Boston before being called back.

Two days later, two militia from the Connecticut Light Horse rode slowly across the narrow neck of land leading to the peninsula of Boston. They passed, unchallenged, by the British cannon in place on "the Neck," then walked their horses through town. Satisfied that there had been no bombardment, they rode back to report the false alarm.

Paul Revere noted in a letter soon after this incident that the British "troops have the horrors amazingly." Gage quickly threw up earthen fortifications across the Neck. When asked to explain this threatening action, he claimed it was to keep his Regulars from deserting. No one believed him, just as he did not believe the militia commanders' assertion that their sudden interest in drilling was due to anxiety about another war with France.

Writing home to Secretary of War Lord Barrington, Gage urged him to press the government to repeal the Coercive Acts, to provide time enough to raise the large army that he was convinced would be needed to put down the rebellion. Until such a force arrived, Gage was determined to continue his policy of nonprovocation. He refused to institute martial law; he imposed no curfews or travel restrictions; he censored neither the radical press nor the public meetings that constantly ridiculed him and encouraged armed revolt. In addition, he forbade his troops to bear arms while off duty, and he punished any soldier about whom Bostonians made a complaint. The Tories and his own troops were disgusted with these measures and bitterly referred to Gage as "the Old Woman" because of his reluctance to take action against the rebels. But the governor defended his policies, claiming that they were both diplomatically and militarily sound:

I have been at pains to prevent anything of consequence taking its rise from trifles and idle quarrels, and when the cause of Boston became the general concern of America, endeavoured so to manage, that Administration might have an opening to negotiate if anything conciliatory should present itself.

If force is to be used at length, it must be a considerable one, and foreign troops must be hired, for to begin with small numbers will encourage resistance, and not terrify; and will in the end cost more blood and treasure. An army on such a service should be large enough to make considerable detachments to disarm and take in the counties, procure forage carriages, etc., and keep up communications, without which little progress could be made in a country where all are enemies.

One month after the incident in Cambridge, acting in his capacity as governor, Gage summoned the members recently elected to the next session of the Massachusetts Assembly to meet on October 5th, 1774. But before that day arrived, he learned that the Continental Congress in Philadelphia had just approved the Suffolk Resolves. Furious, he issued a proclamation suspending the convening of the Assembly. Its members, however, met in spite of the proclamation. With no governor present to swear them in, they passed a resolution declaring the formation of a temporary government. They called themselves "the Provincial Congress of Massachusetts Bay" and moved the meeting place to Concord, a village 18 miles west of Boston, considered a "safe" distance from Gage's troops. The following spring, New York, Pennsylvania, Virginia and South Carolina would likewise form such Provincial Congresses. New extralegal governments would not be necessary in Connecticut and Rhode Island, which already had patriot governors, or in the other six colonies, which would gradually come under patriot control.

The Massachusetts Provincial Congress set to work immediately to complete a process started as a result of a Worcester County convention, which on September 21, 1774, resolved that all militia officers should immediately resign, and the militia of the various towns should elect new officers. This weeded out nearly all the Tory officers, since, in most cases, they were either not re-elected or were pressured by mobs into resigning.

One-third of each town's militia was assigned to be ready "to meet at one minute's warning, equipt with arms and ammunition" - hence, the term "minutemen." This was not a new term, as some militia, in letters home during the attack on Crown Point in 1756, had referred to themselves as "minnit men."

The Provincial Congress also voted to raise 15,000 pounds on bills of credit and use it to purchase blankets, tents, powder, cannon, flour, spoons, etc., to be stored at Worcester, Concord and Salem. And each town was ordered to provide to its own militia, "as soon as may be, double the quantity of powder, balls, and flints that they were before by law obliged to provide." A Committee of Safety for the whole colony was formed, and authorized to call out the militia, if necessary, to resist any attempt by Gage "to carry into execution by force the late Acts of Parliament."

Gage issued a proclamation ordering all "His Majesty's liege subjects" to disobey the Provincial Congress, but the people (except for Tories) took no notice. Drilling of militia continued on every village common; the Provincial Congress recommended it be done "three times a week and oftener as opportunity may offer." It was said that "in most towns they have a deserter from his Majesty's forces by way of a drill sergeant." Abigail Adams wrote to her husband, John, then in Philadelphia at the Congress: "The maxim, 'In time of peace, prepare for war,' if this can be called a time of peace, resounds throughout the country." Captain Thomas Pickering, of Salem, began writing his *Easy Plan of Discipline for a Militia*, prescribing a simplified version of the British army drill. It provided detailed instructions on how to "take good sight at the object you would hit," a step the British army's manual of arms omitted.

The British scoffed at the idea of an army of citizen soldiers. Surely they would not stand up to a professional army, if it should come to a fight. One officer in Boston wrote home to London about the ludicrous sight of "barbers and tailors strutting about in their Sunday wigs, muskets on their shoulders, struggling to put on a martial countenance."

Meanwhile, Governor Gage was receiving disturbing news from other colonies. New Hampshire's governor reported from Portsmouth that, on December 13th, "One Paul Revere arrived express from a Committee in Boston to another Committee in this town." The message he carried was a warning that the British were planning to reinforce the garrison at Portsmouth's Fort William and Mary. The next day, the fort was assaulted by 400 men led by John Sullivan, resulting in several cannon, 97 barrels of gunpowder, and 1,500 muskets being taken by the rebels. Some cannon were also seized at New Castle on the Piscataqua River.

From Rhode Island, came a report that Fort Island in Newport had been attacked, and its cannon taken to Providence, "to prevent their falling into the hands of the King." Virginia's governor wrote that the militia there were arming and drilling in every county, the courts were abolished, and the royal government was "entirely disregarded, if not wholly overturned."

Whereas, in late August, Gage had written to Lord Barrington that the other colonies "will never venture so far as to rise to assist New England," one month later he told a different story:

> I write to your lordship by a private ship, fearing the post may be examined, for there seems no respect for anything.
>
> Affairs here are worse than even in the time of the Stamp Act. I don't mean in Boston, but throughout the country. The New England provinces, except part of New Hampshire, are, I may say, in arms; and the question is not now whether you shall quell disturbances in Boston, but whether those provinces shall be conquered.

I find it is the general resolution of all the Continent to support the Massachusetts Bay in their opposition to the late acts. You supposed in England that the Port Bill regarded Boston alone, as well as the Acts for regulating their government, but they have contrived to get the rest of their brethren in every province to be as violent in their defense as themselves. From appearances no people are more determined for a civil war.

Gage sent a copy of the resolves of the Massachusetts Provincial Congress, and his own request for 20,000 more Regulars, to the King. While waiting for these reinforcements, he bought all the blankets, canvas, and other camp supplies he could find. At the same time, the patriots tried to persuade merchants not to sell to him. In several colonies, patriot controlled Assemblies began investigating the possibility of purchasing munitions from Europe. France and Spain openly refused to honor England's request that they not sell munitions to the Americans. The Dutch agreed to the request, but secretly sold to American agents gunpowder hidden in wine bottles.

Upon request, Gage sent 300 muskets to loyalists in Marshfield, New Hampshire. He also dispatched two disguised soldiers to scout the roads to Worcester. One of them, Private John Howe, noted in his journal a conversation he had with a backwoodsman:

The man was cleaning a gun. I asked him what he was going to kill, as he was so old I should not think he could take sight at any game; he said there was a flock of redcoats at Boston, which he expected would be here soon; he meant to try and hit some of them, as he expected they would be very good marks. I asked the old man how he expected to fight; he said, "Open field fighting, or any other way to kill them redcoats!" I asked him how old he was; he said, "Seventy-seven, and never was killed yet. Old woman put in the bullet pouch a handful of buckshot, as I understand the English like an assortment of plums!"

Cannon balls and half-barrels of gunpowder were now being carried out of Boston, concealed in wagonloads of manure, or in butcher's carts. On March 18, 1775, the British seized 13,425 musket cartridges and 300 pounds of ball, which were being smuggled out in candle boxes. British Lieutenant Frederick Mackenzie noted in his journal:

> The people are evidently making every preparation for resistance. They are taking every means to provide themselves with arms. A soldier of the 4th Regiment who was tried a few days ago for disposing of his arms [for rum] to the townspeople has been found guilty and sentenced to receive 500 lashes.

Two days later, the soldier died. Vengeance was also inflicted upon Americans caught buying arms from British soldiers. On March 8th, Thomas Ditson, a farmer who was caught buying a gun from a private, was stripped, tarred and feathered, then paraded in a cart through the streets of Boston while the soldiers sang "Yankee Doodle."

Supplies were not all that disappeared from Boston that winter. The British troops themselves were being enticed to desert by handbills, such as one that read:

> Friends and Brothers: You may have liberty and by a little industry may obtain propety. March up either singly or in companys. The country people are determined to protect you and screen you.

To many of the soldiers, the thought of having to kill fellow English subjects was a repulsive one. The unpromising, harsh army life made civilian life in America seem particularly attractive. Many were willing to take the risk of being caught and hung for desertion. Dozens deserted, including one soldier who traveled all the way to South Carolina before he wrote home to his father:

> The hospitable kindness I received from the country people, on my way from Boston to this place, is beyond my description. Before I knew these people, I was shocked at the thought of being sent out to cut their throats, and resolved not to turn human butcher, for it is no better to destroy friends and countrymen.
>
> I intend accepting a plot of land that is offered me, some distance from this town, where the gentlemen have proposed to build me a house, give me some tools, and lend me some negroes to settle. Whatever you may think of negroes, I assure you they live better than the greatest part of the poor in England do at present.
>
> Be assured, if the army moves up the country, they will soon want a number of recruits, as all the men know they can change a life of beggary, as well as slavery, for liberty, and have a portion of land forever.

The Secretary of War, Lord Barrington, thought it futile to take military action. He urged the immediate withdrawal of all troops from Boston. With the troops gone, he reasoned, the propagandists would no longer be able to rely on the real or threatened "violence of persecution" to animate the otherwise peaceful colonists, and the rebellion would fade. Barrington favored a naval blockade, which, he believed, would reduce the colony into submission without shedding a drop of blood.

But no one paid heed to Barrington's advice. The King and a majority in Parliament were determined that Massachusetts must be forced by military means to submit to Parliamentary authority. Prime Minister Lord North told Massachusetts' agent, Josiah Quincy, Jr., that if he were to yield on the question of Parliamentary supremacy, "he should expect to have his head brought to the block by the general clamor of the people, and he should deserve it." Quincy wrote home to his wife in December, 1774: "Let me tell you one very serious truth: <u>your countrymen must seal their course with blood</u>. I see every day more reason to confirm my opinion."

In Parliament's House of Lords, Lord Sandwich stated:

> Suppose the colonies do abound in men, what does that signify? They are raw, undisciplined, cowardly men. Believe me, my Lords, the very sound of a cannon would carry them off as fast as their feet could carry them.

About the same time that Lord Sandwich spoke those sentiments aloud, they were echoed in a letter, written by Captain Evelyn, one of General Gage's officers, and published in a British newspaper:

> As to what you hear of their taking up arms to resist the force of England, it is mere bullying, and will go no further than words. Whenever it comes to blows, he that can run fastest will think himself best off. ... they are a mere mob, without order or discipline, and very awkward at handling their arms.

In the House of Commons, Richard Rigby declared, "The Americans will not fight. They will never oppose General Gage with force of arms." The British attitude was colored by class prejudice that held courage to be a consequence of good breeding.

The ambitious Lord Richard Howe, an admiral, had plans of his own to lead a commission to America to settle the dispute before events reached the point of armed conflict. He asked his sister, an accomplished chess player, to pry useful information out of Benjamin Franklin, who was known to have a weakness for both chess and beautiful women. Although she did not gain any information, she later introduced him to her brother. Franklin agreed to join Admiral Howe in the peace mission. On January 27th, Colonial Secretary Lord Dartmouth had written a letter to General Gage, instructing him to initiate military action against the rebels; the letter was held up during the negotiations and did not sail from England until March 10th. By then, it was clear that the negotiations would be fruitless. Franklin's proposals differed little from the unpalatable demands put forth earlier by the Continental Congress. Franklin expressed his disappointment in his journal, observing that Admiral Howe seemed to think "I had powers or instructions from the Congress to make concessions that would be more satisfactory." On March 21st, with Britain resolved to pursue a military solution, Franklin's work was finished; he sailed for America.

The King was firmly against accepting the demands of a rebel congress, writing that it would "look like the mother country being more afraid of the continuance of the dispute than the colonies, and I cannot think it likely to make them more reasonable." He viewed Gage's idea of suspending the Coercive Acts to gain time for better military preparations as "absurd." The King felt that the time had arrived when "blows must decide." Any surrender to American views of Parliamentary authority was simply out of the question. He wrote to Prime Minister Lord North, stating, "I am clear there must always be one tax to keep up the right, and as such, I approve of the tea duty." From the start, the attitude of King George III had been consistent and would continue to be: he insisted on America's submission to Parliamentary authority. Since the King rarely made his views public, Americans were slow to realize this, and clung to their old allegiance to him. They were reluctant to give it up even after the war had started.

On February 1, 1775, Lord Chatham (William Pitt) introduced a "Provisional Bill for Settling the Troubles in America." It would preserve Parliamentary control of trade and navigation, but recognize the Continental Congress as a legal body competent to raise money for imperial defense. The bill would repeal the Quebec Act, the Coercive Acts, and the duty on tea. The sanctity of colonial charters would be guaranteed, and judges would not be Crown-appointed when the colonies were on good behavior. If passed, this bill would have prevented the war, but it was soundly defeated, as was his motion to remove the troops from Boston.

The only concession made was a resolve that if any colony raised what Parliament considered to be that colony's share of the cost of imperial defense, and also raised revenue for the salaries of its Crown-appointed judges and officials, Parliament would exempt that colony from revenue acts. Benjamin Franklin predicted that this resolve, known as "Lord North's Conciliatory Offer," would be rejected by the colonies, because it left ultimate power over colonial taxation to Parliament, and it did nothing about the Coercive Acts. Instead of granting them exemption from Parliamentary taxation, the offer would simply convert the American legislatures into tax gatherers for the British Parliament. An indignant American wrote that, "An armed robber who demands my money might as well pretend he makes a concession, by suffering me to take it out of my own pocket, rather than search there for it himself."

As usual with Parliamentary measures, the timing of the offer was bad. In New York, perhaps the only colony other than Georgia where it might have had a good chance of acceptance, the offer would arrive the day after news of Lexington and Concord reached the city. By then, public opinion was turning rapidly away from those in favor of conciliation; and the radical faction was gaining more popularity with the onset of the war.

On March 30th, Parliament passed the New England Restraining Act, forbidding all the colonies except Georgia, North Carolina and New York from fishing off Newfoundland and Nova Scotia, and prohibiting them from trading with any non-British country. To thus deprive New Englanders of their ability to catch whales and codfish would be like not allowing Virginians to grow tobacco. A New Yorker, in a letter to a friend in England, warned that the new act "calls home as many men as your little army, reinforced at Boston, will consist of; and it drives these seamen to the sword for revenge." However, the war would start before news of this new act would reach New England in May; otherwise, there might have been a conflict known as The Great Codfish War.

In Boston, master propagandist Sam Adams was again, as in 1768-1770, using actual incidents, embellished generously by his imagination, to describe in the newspapers the alleged actions of the British troops. Lt. John Barker's own journal provides perhaps a truer picture of the life of a British soldier in Boston during this period:

> 1775, Jany. 1st. Nothing remarkable but the drunkenness among the soldiers, which is now got to a very great pitch; owing to the cheapness of the liquor, a man may get drunk for a copper or two. Still a hard frost.
>
> 12th. The frost is broke up and today it rains and thaws. Gaming having got to a very great length among many of the officers, the Genl. lately expressed his disapprobation of a club they have instituted for that purpose. But I don't believe he will succeed, as it's very rare seeing a person alter who is once entered into this way, unless it is by being incapable of continuing it, which I dare say will be the case of many of them before the winter is over.

The same officer described a riot which occurred in Boston later that same month of January, between British soldiers and patriots assigned by the Boston Committee of Safety to watch for any movement of troops or Tories.

> 21st. Last night there was a riot in King Street in consequence of an officer having been insulted by the watchmen, which has frequently happened, as those people assume they may do it with impunity. The contrary, however, they experienced last night. A number of officers as well as townsmen were assembled, and in consequence of the watch having brandished their hooks and other weapons, several officers drew their swords,

and wounds were given on both sides, some officers slightly; one of the watch lost a nose, another a thumb, besides many others by the points of swords.

Boston's John Andrews, in a letter of the same date, gives a quite different telling of the same incident.

> Last evening a number of drunken officers attacked the town house watch between eleven and 12 o'clock, when the assistance of the new Boston watch was called, and a general battle ensued; some wounded on both sides. A party from the main guard was brought up with their captain together with another party from the Governor's. Had it not been for the prudence of two officers that were sober, the captain of the main guard would have acted a second tragedy to the 5th March, as he was much disguised with liquor and would have ordered the guard to fire on the watch had he not been restrained.
>
> This afternoon there was a general squabble between the butchers in the market and a number of soldiers. It first began by a soldier's tripping up the heals of a fisherman who was walking through the market with a piece of beef in his hands. A guard from the 47th barracks appered and carried off the soldiers, together with one butcher who was most active, the officer taking him by the collar. He was able to have crushed the officer, but was advised to be quiet. ... the officer dismissed him after finding upon deliberation that [the soldier's] conduct was not justified - and seemed to be much afraid lest the butcher take advantage of him by law or complaint.

Although it was a time of many incidents, each one of which might be the spark needed to set off a war, it was also a time of psychological warfare. Bostonians were not the only ones who attempted to instill fear in the minds of the British soldiers, who were appehensive about the fabled sharpshooting backwoodsmen they would be matched up against, if it came to a war. Again, from the letters of John Andrews, this one dated October 1, 1774:

> It's common for the soldiers to fire at the bottom of the Common. A countryman stood by a few days ago, and laughed very heartily at a whole regiment's firing, and not one being able to hit it. The officer observed him, and asked why he laughed.
>
> Says he, "I laugh to see how awkward they fire. Why I'll be bount I hit it ten times running."
>
> "Ah! Will you?" replied the officer. "Come try."
>
> He accordingly loaded, and asked the officer where he should fire. He replied, "To the right" - when he pulled the tricker, and drove the ball as near the right as possible. The officer was amazed - and said he could not do it again, as that was only by chance.
>
> He loaded again. "Where shall I fire?"
>
> "To the left" - when he performed as well as before. "Come! Once more," says the officer.
>
> He prepared the third time. "Where shall I fire naow?"
>
> "In the center." He took aim, and the ball went as exact in the middle as possible. The officers as well as soldiers stared, and thought the Devil was in the man.
>
> "Why," says the countryman, "I'll tell you naow. I have got a boy at home that will toss up an apple and shoot out all the seeds as it's coming down."

The winter dragged on, and tensions did not lessen. The Regulars and the patriots were each tired of drilling, and were itching for Gage to make the first move. Both for exercise and to learn the local roads, the Regulars often marched into the nearby countryside. Gage also had another reason for these marches into the countryside, as Lt. Frederick Mackenzie noted in his journal:

> This practice is conducive to the health of the troops; and may enable the General to send regiments or detachments to particular parts of the country without occasioning so much alarm as would otherwise take place.

Not to be intimidated, the patriots used these occasions for more psychological warfare, as related in a letter which a visitor from England wrote home:

> The troops for these two months past have marched from five to ten miles into the country; I have been the different routs they took, and saw the effigies of soldiers in their regimentals hanging by the road side. You may judge of the effect this will have on the army, who wish for nothing so much as a skirmish with the Yankeys, to revenge the many affronts already offered them.

In late February, Tories informed General Gage that the rebel Provincial Congress was storing cannon at Salem, a few miles northeast of Boston. So Gage planned a secret expedition. Rather than send a regiment from Boston, which would be easily noticed, he would send the 64th Regiment, stationed out in the harbor at Castle William. They would leave Castle Island in boats on a Sunday morning, land at Marblehead, then march to Salem to seize and bring back the cannon.

Gage's secretary, who happened to be father-in-law of the patriot bookseller, Henry Knox, unsuspectingly let slip in conversation the possibility of an expedition to Salem. Knox lost no time in passing the knowledge on to Paul Revere, a member of the town watch.

Revere and a few other watchmen rowed over to a point in the harbor from which they could watch for activity on Castle Island, but they were discovered, taken to the fortress, and, in Revere's words, "detained there till 10 o'clock Monday, lest we should send an express to our brethren at Marblehead and Salem." Although Revere was not able to ride to Salem with a warning, the patriots there would discover the British march soon enough.

William Gavitt wrote the following account of what happened when the British arrived at Salem.

On Sunday, 26 Feb'y, 1775, my father came home from church rather sooner than usual, which attracted my notice, and said to my mother, "The reg'lars are come and are marching as fast as they can towards the Northfields bridge."

Colonel David Mason had received tidings of the approach of the British troops and ran into the North Church and cried out, at the top of his voice, "The reg'lars are coming after the guns and are now near Malloon's Mills!" One David Boyce, a Quaker who lived near the church, was instantly out with his team to assist in carrying the guns out of reach of the troops.

The northern leaf of the draw was hoisted when the troops approached the bridge, which prevented them from going any further. Their commander, Col. Leslie, then remarked that he should be obliged to fire upon the people on the northern side of the bridge if they did not lower the leaf. [Salem's] Captain Felt told him if the troops did fire they would all be dead men.

A man cried out, as loud as possible, "Soldiers, red-jackets, lobstercoats, cowards: <u>damnation to your government</u>!" The inhabitants rebuked him for it and requested nothing should be done to irritate the troops. Colonel Leslie now spoke to Mr. Barnard, probably observing by his dress that he was a clergyman, and said, "I will get over this bridge before I return to Boston, if I stay here till next autumn."

Turning to Captain Felt, he said, "By God! I will not be defeated; to which Captain Felt replied, "You must acknowledge you have already been baffled."

The British colonel and the townspeople spent the next two tense hours in angry debate and futile negotiations. Salem's William Gavitt continues his account of the standoff:

> Colonel Leslie then promised, if they would allow him to pass over the bridge, he would march but fifty rods and return immediately without troubling or disturbing anything. Captain Felt was at first unwilling to allow the troops to pass over on any terms, but at length consented. The troops then passed over and marched the distance agreed upon without violating their pledge, then wheeled and marched back again.
>
> A nurse named Sarah Tarrant, in one of the houses, placed herself at the open window and called out to them: "Go home and tell your master he has sent you on a fool's errand and broken the peace of the Sabbath. What, do you think we were born in the woods, to be frightened by owls?" One of the soldiers pointed his musket at her, and she exclaimed, "Fire, if you have the courage, but I doubt it."

The British detachment returned to Boston empty-handed, having failed to seize a single cannon from the rebels in Salem.

One week later, the fifth anniversary of the Boston Massacre would be recognized. On the fourth anniversary, the previous year, John Hancock had delivered a fiery anti-British speech (written by Joseph Warren) at the commemoration ceremony in the Old South Church. This time, many British soldiers attended, eager to see whether this year's speaker would dare do the same. A British officer recorded the church scene in his journal:

> March 6th. This day an oration was delivered by Dr. Warren, a notorious Whig. It was known for some days that this was to be delivered; accordingly, a great number of officers assembled at it, when after he had finished a most seditious, inflammatory harangue, [Sam Adams] stood up and made a short speech in the same strain, at the end of which some of the officers cried out, "Fie! Fie!" which, being mistaken for the cry of fire, an alarm immediately ensued, which filled the people with such consternation that they were getting out as fast as they could by the doors and windows.
>
> It was imagined that there would have been a riot, which if there had would in all probability have proved fatal to Hancock, Adams, Warren and the rest of those villains, as they were all up in the pulpit together, and the meeting was crowded with officers and seamen in such a manner that they could not have escaped; however, it luckily did not turn out so. It would indeed have been a pity for them to have made their exit that way, as I hope we shall have the pleasure before long of seeing them do it by the hands of the hangman.

One of Gage's officers, Major John Pitcairn, expressed his opinions to Lord Sandwich in a letter dated March 4, 1775:

> Orders are anxiously expected from England to chastise those very bad people. The General had some of the Great Whigs, as they are called here, telling them that if there was a single man of the King's Troops killed in any of their towns he would burn it to the ground.
>
> I am satisfied that one active campaign, a smart ac-

tion, and burning two or three of their towns, will set everything to rights. Nothing now, I am afraid, but this will ever convince those foolish bad people that England is in earnest. What a sad misfortune it was to this country, the repealing of the Stamp Act; every friend to government here asserts in the strongest terms that this had been the cause of all their misfortunes.

While Major Pitcairn was writing that letter, the orders he anxiously hoped for were on their way across the Atlantic Ocean. On April 2nd, Gage received strong orders from Secretary of War Lord Dartmouth: act now to stop the rebels' stockpiling of munitions; arrest Adams, Hancock and Cushing; and enforce the Coercive Acts. Gage was also informed that the long awaited reinforcements were on their way. Without the assurance of reinforcements, Gage had been reluctant to take any of these steps with barely 3,000 troops. Now he could attempt to follow those orders, confident that the reinforcements, if needed, were on the way.

Thomas Gage had done his best "to avoid any bloody crisis as long as possible." But it now appeared that events were spinning out of his control. He must do his duty; he could not extend the peace by appeasement and inaction any longer.

CHAPTER EIGHT
THE INEVITABLE CLASH
APRIL 1775

*"The rebels, you know, have of a long time been making prepara-
tions as if to frighten us, though we always imagined they were too
great cowards ever to do it."*

- *A British officer, after returning
from Lexington and Concord*

Finally, it was time for the conciliatory posture of the royal governor, General Thomas Gage, to come to an end. His hand was being
forced both by the rebels' accelerated preparations for war and by new
instructions he received from London. On April 14th, Gage received
another letter from Colonial Secretary Lord Dartmouth, who had
earlier urged him to take "a more active and determined part."
Dartmouth pressed the issue again:

> It seems to be your idea that matters are come to
> such a state that conquest of the people of the three gov-
> ernments of Massachusetts Bay, Connecticut, and Rhode
> Island cannot be effected with less force than 20,000
> men. I am unwilling to believe that matters are as yet
> come to that issue. I think that a smaller force now, if
> put to the test, would be able to encounter them with
> greater probability of success than might be expected
> from a greater army.

Dartmouth's implication was for Gage to act offensively right away.

Dartmouth believed that "a single action" could decide the contest, before the rebels had a chance to prepare themselves.

> Any effort of the people, unprepared to encounter with a regular force, cannot be very formidable, and though such a proceeding should be, according to your own idea of it, a signal for hostilities, yet it will surely be better than the conflict be brought upon such ground in a riper state of rebellion.

The Massachusetts Provincial Congress was taking bolder steps now, as it called for the establishment of a New England army of 30,000 men, 18,000 of whom would be raised within Massachusetts. Several of its members were sent to the other New England Assemblies, to urge them to help form this new army.

From his informer in the Provincial Congress, Doctor Benjamin Church, Gage learned of stockpiles of rebel military supplies at Concord, 18 miles west of Boston, and at Worcester, thirty miles beyond Concord. Gage felt compelled to raid at least one of these sites, and possibly both. So he sent two soldiers, an officer and a private, on a trip to Worcester, disguised as country gunsmiths looking for work.

On April 7th, their second day out of Boston, they stopped at a tavern in Watertown for some breakfast. When Lieutenant Colonel Francis Smith asked the Negro serving girl, "Where could we two find employment?" she shocked him by replying, "Smith, you will find employment enough for you and all Gage's men in a few months!" When Smith complained to the keeper about the "saucy wench," he was told she "had recently come from Boston, where she had been much with the soldiers." Frustrated that he was found out already, Smith decided to return to Boston, but told Private John Howe to continue on, promising him a corporal's commission if he should complete the mission. That night, Howe noted in his journal, "The last I saw of Smith he was running through barbary bushes to keep out of sight of the road."

On his return trip to Boston from Worcester, Private Howe circled north through Concord. After hearing his report, Gage asked him how many men he thought would be needed to destroy the stores at Worcester and return safely to Boston. The private bravely answered the general, "If they should march 10,000 Regulars and a train of artillery to Worcester, not one of them would get back alive." Having conversed with "the inhabitants," during the course of the trip, he judged them "determined to be free or die." He then told the general that Concord, being much closer than Worcester, might be a different matter. However, he warned Gage about "a very bad place" he had passed on his return, on the road between Concord and Lexington, a perfect place for an ambush.

Gage therefore gave up on Worcester and set Concord as his objective. He now knew the exact location of the stores hidden at Concord. He also learned from Dr. Church that Sam Adams and John Hancock, while their rebel Provincial Congress was in session at Concord, were lodging at the Reverend Jonas Clark's parsonage, in nearby Lexington. So he included their arrest in the marching orders. Gage was also concerned that the Provincial Congress might alert the countryside as soon as they learned the troops approaching. The useful Dr. Church, who was one of the leading Whigs both in the Provincial Congress and its Committee of Safety, assured the British commander that "a recess at this time could easily be brought about" so that "a sudden blow" could be taken without the rebel leadership taking action to counteract it. So, on April 15, 1775, the Provincial Congress adjourned for a one month recess. Their last act before adjourning was to advise the inhabitants of Boston to evacuate the city.

Gage planned the expedition to Concord for Tuesday, the 18th. By leaving in the evening, the troops could march during the night, while the rebels slept. Hopefully, by the time the rebels reacted, it would be late afternoon and the troops would be nearly back to Boston. Gage picked Lieutenant Colonel Francis Smith to command 750 elite troops: Grenadiers and Light Infantry, no line infantry. They would silently assemble on Boston Common, then march as quietly as possible to Boston's north shore. From there, they would be transported in longboats, with muffled oars, across the Charles River to the Cambridge shore, where they would land at the inconspicuous location of Phipp's farm. This would make the journey to Concord shorter and less noticeable to the inhabitants than going out across Boston Neck.

For two days, these select troops were relieved of their regular duties, so they could practice "new evolutions" to ready themselves for the expected combat. The town watchmen, observing this, became suspicious of an imminent march into the countryside. The obvious choice would be the supplies at Concord and/or the Whig leaders at Lexington, who were due to leave on the 19th for the Continental Congress in Philadelphia. Paul Revere later recalled:

> In the fall of 1774 and winter of 1775, I was one of upwards of thirty, chiefly mechanics, who formed ourselves into a committee for the purpose of watching the movements of the British soldiers.
>
> In the winter, towards the spring, we frequently took turns, two and two, to watch the soldiers by patrolling the streets at night. The Saturday night preceding the 19th of April, about 12 o'clock at night, the boats belonging to the transports were all launched and carried under the sterns of the man-of-war. We likewise found that the Grenadiers and Light Infantry were all taken off duty.
>
> From these movements we expected something serious was about to be transacted. On Tuesday evening, the 18th, it was observed that a number of soldiers were marching toward the bottom of the Common.

Later, a British deserter gave the following account of the secret expedition's start:

> They took every imaginable precaution to prevent a discovery. Their meat was dressed on board a transport

ship in the harbor. Their men were not apprised of the design till, just as it was time to march, they were waked up by the sergeants putting their hands on them and whispering gently to them, and were even conducted by a back way out of the barracks without the knowledge of their comrades and without the observation of the sentries.

They walked through the street with the utmost silence. It being about ten o'clock, no sound was heard but of their feet. A dog, happening to bark, was instantly killed with a bayonet. They proceeded to the beach under the new powder house, the most unfrequented part of the town, and there embarked on board the boats, which had their oars muffled to prevent a noise.

General Thomas Gage selected a subordinate general, Lord Hugh Percy, to command a reserve force of about 1,000, ready in Boston. Percy would join Colonel Smith in the morning if Smith sent back word that the reserve was needed. But, Gage added, this would probably not be necessary, because he "did not think the damned rebels would take up arms against His Majesty's Troops." Percy agreed. Although a Whig, and in Boston less than a year, he had already come to the conclusion that "the people here are a set of sly, artful, hypocritical rascals, cruel and cowards."

At dusk that evening, Percy was walking home from headquarters when he came, unrecognized, upon a group of Bostonians talking on the Common. He heard one of them say, "The British have marched, but they will miss their aim." "What aim?" Percy blurted out. "Why, the cannon at Concord," answered the man, surprised that the question needed asking. Percy quickly went back to headquarters to relate the conversation. Gage, surprised and upset, declared that "his confidence had been betrayed, for he had communicated his design to one person only." The next day, Gage sent his American wife home to England.

Some historians conjecture that it was she who leaked the plans to her countryman Dr. Joseph Warren. Gage decided not to abort his carefully made plans, but to proceed as scheduled, hoping the plans were not yet known outside the city.

The soldiers were rowed across the Charles River by sailors from the British navy. The heavily loaded boats sank deep into the water, barely keeping afloat. For this reason, they could not go close in when they approached the Cambridge shore. The men dropped overboard into the shallow water and waded the rest of the way to shore. Lieutenant John Barker described in his journal the landing at Phipp's farm on Cambridge Marsh:

> After getting over the marsh, where we were wet up to the knees, we were halted in a dirty road and stood there till two o'clock in the morning waiting for provisions [navy hard biscuit] to be brought from the boats and to be divided, and which most of the men threw away, having carried some [better army rations] with them. At two o'clock we began our march by wading through a very long ford up to our middles.

The two hour wait at Phipp's farm probably cost Colonel Smith the element of surprise so important to the expedition. Striving to maintain the mission's secrecy, he ordered the troops to wade the streams, rather than risk too much noise from boots marching on the bridges' wooden planks. Smith's force would be joined by inconspicuously small parties sent out the previous day to stop all riders on the roads to Concord.

While the troops were being rowed across the Charles River, Paul Revere and William Dawes were setting out to warn the countryside. Dawes would go on horseback across Boston Neck. Revere would go across the Charles River, then on horseback by a different route. Though they would both make it to Lexington to warn Adams and Hancock, neither Revere nor Dawes would reach Concord. Here is how Revere, many years later, remembered his ride to Lexington:

About 10 o'clock, Dr. Warren sent in great haste for me and begged that I would immediately set off for Lexington, where Messrs. Hancock and Adams were, and acquaint them of the movement, and that it was thought they were the objects.

When I got to Dr. Warren's house, I found he had sent an express by land to Lexington - a Mr. William Dawes. The Sunday before, by desire of Dr. Warren, I had been to Lexington, to Messrs. Hancock and Adams, who were at the Rev. Mr. Clark's. I returned at night through Charlestown; there I agreed with a Colonel Conant and some other gentlemen that if the British went out by water, we would show two lantherns in the North Church steeple; and if by land, one, as a signal; for we were apprehensive it would be difficult to cross the Charles River or get over Boston Neck. I left Dr. Warren, called upon a friend and desired him to make the signals.

I then went home, took my boots and surtout, went to the north part of the town, where I had kept a boat; two friends rowed me across Charles River, a little to the eastward of where the *Somerset* man-of-war lay. It was then young flood, the ship was winding, and the moon was rising. They landed me on the Charlestown side. When I got into town, I met Colonel Conant and several others; they said they had seen our signals. I told them what was acting, and went to get me a horse; I got a horse of Deacon Larkin. While the horse was preparing, Richard Devens, Esq., who was one of the Committee of Safety, came and told me that he came down the road from Lexington after sundown that evening; that he met ten British officers, all well mounted, and armed,

137

going up the road.

I set off upon a very good horse; it was then about eleven o'clock and very pleasant. After I had passed Charlestown Neck, I saw two men on horseback under a tree. When I got near them, I discovered they were British officers. One tried to get ahead of me, and the other to take me. I turned my horse very quick and galloped towards Charlestown Neck, and then pushed for the Medford Road. The one who chased me, endeavoring to cut me off, got into a clay pond ... I got clear of him, and went through Medford, over the bridge and up to Menotomy [present day Arlington]. In Medford, I awaked the captain of the minute men; after that, I alarmed almost every house, till I got to Lexington.

Thus detoured by the necessity of eluding the British patrol, Paul Revere's route to Lexington would be further north and longer than planned. On the way, he made a point to stop at the houses of key militia captains, ministers, and physicians - people who knew all the local inhabitants and the roads, and had agreed beforehand to help spread the alarm if the British should come out. By the time the Regulars would reach Lexington at 5:20 a.m., towns in a 25 mile radius would already know of their destination, thanks to express riders and prearranged signals. In Sudbury, a dozen miles southwest of Lexington, at 3 a.m. a young boy named Faulkner would listen in fascination to the sounds of three consecutive musket shots echoing in the distance, then, after a few minutes, repeated at a greater distance. In other towns, patriots would spread the alarm by means of beacon fires on hilltops. And in Needham, a slave named Abel Benson would awaken distant neighbors by playing his trumpet.

Some of the people of Lexington had suspected something momentous was stirring, ever since the previous Sunday, when Revere had advised them of rumors circulating in Boston about an upcoming expedition to Concord. They'd had more recent warning than that, though.   Sergeant William Munroe, a Lexington minuteman, years later recalled:

> Early in the evening of the 18th of April, I was informed by Solomon Brown, who had just returned from Boston, that he had seen nine British officers on the road, traveling leisurely, sometimes before and sometimes behind him; that he had discovered, by the occasional blowing aside of their topcoats, that they were armed. On learning this, I supposed they had some design upon Hancock and Adams, who were then at the house of the Rev. Mr. Clarke, and immediately assembled a guard of eight men, with their arms, to guard the house.
>
> About midnight, Paul Revere rode up and requested admittance. I told him the family had just retired, and had requested that they might not be disturbed by any noise about the house.
>
> "Noise!" said he, "You'll have noise enough before long! The Regulars are coming out!"

The village's minutemen were soon aroused. They assembled on Lexington Common "about one o'clock," according to one of them:

> After the company had collected, we were ordered by Capt. John Parker, who commanded us, to disperse for the present, and to be ready to attend the beat of the drum; and accordingly the company went into houses near the place of parade [Lexington Common].

William Dawes, the other rider who had set out from Boston (over Boston Neck and a longer route) arrived at the Clark house a half hour after Revere. They had some food and drink there, then together "set off for Concord [and] were overtaken by a young Dr. Prescott," who was on his way home to Concord, having spent the evening courting a Lexington girl. They told him "it was probable we might be stopped before we got to Concord, but the town must be warned. The young doctor much approved of it," and joined Revere and Dawes. Dr. Prescott told them that, since he was "a high Son of Liberty" in Concord, the people there would "give more credit" to their warnings if they saw he was with them. Revere continues his account:

> We had got nearly half way. Mr. Dawes and the doctor stopped to alarm the people of a house. I was about one hundred rods ahead when I saw two men in nearly the same situation as those officers were near Charlestown. I called for the doctor and Mr. Dawes to come up. In an instant I was surrounded by four. They had placed themselves in a straight road that inclined each way; they had taken down a pair of bars on the north side of the road, and two of them were under a tree in the pasture. The doctor being foremost, he came up and we tried to get past them; but they being armed with pistols and swords, they forced us into the pasture. The doctor jumped his horse over a low stone wall and got to Concord.
>
> I observed a wood at a small distance and made for that. When I got there, out started six officers on horseback and ordered me to dismount. One of them, who appeared to have the command, examined me, where I came from and what my name was. I told him. He asked me if I was an express. I answered in the affirmative. He demanded what time I left Boston. I told him, and added that there would be five hundred Americans there [at Lexington] in a short time, for I had alarmed the country all the way up.

Revere told them about the countryside being aroused, and mentioned "five hundred" converging on Lexington for a reason. It was Revere's sly attempt to persuade these officers to notify the others leading the march from Boston. He wanted them to stay away from the village where Adams and Hancock were staying. Major Edward Mitchell, interrogating Revere, now decided he had caught enough rebels and had better locate the main British column before he and his patrol found themselves surrounded. Mitchell's patrol set out for Lexington with Revere and several other captives they'd stopped during the night. Before reaching the village, though, they heard more militia firing guns. Revere says this

> appeared to alarm them very much. The major inquired of me how far it was to Cambridge, and if there were any other road. After some consultation, the major rode up to the sergeant and asked if his horse was tired. He answered him it was - he was a sergeant of Grenadiers and had a small horse. "Then," said he, "take that man's horse." I dismounted, and the sergeant mounted my horse. They told me that they should make use of my horse for the night and rode off down the road.

Paul Revere never saw that horse again, and neither did its owner, the Charlestown man who had lent it to him when he began his ride that night. Left alone, Revere walked "across the burying-ground and some pastures and came to the Rev. Mr. Clark's house." He was very concerned to find John Hancock and Sam Adams still there. After much argument, they finally agreed to set out in a chaise down the Woburn Road. Adams was willing and anxious to flee, but Hancock for a while had other ideas, as his fiancee, Miss Dorothy ("Dolly") Quincy, who was also at the Clark house, later recalled:

> Mr. H. was all night cleaning his gun and sword, and was determined to fight with the men who had collected. It was not till break of day that Mr. H. could be per-

141

suaded that it was improper for him to expose himself against such a powerful force.

The cold, wet, miserable march was not long under way when Colonel Smith, dissatisfied with the slow progress, dispatched Major John Pitcairn, his second in command, to go ahead with six companies of Light Infantry as an advance corps to secure the two bridges in Concord. Pitcairn took precautions to prevent warnings of his approach from reaching Concord and Lexington. By ordering a small advance guard to act as flankers, Pitcairn was able to capture all but one of Captain Parker's Lexington scouts.

That one, Solomon Brown, avoided capture, although he did not see the flankers waiting in the shadows of the trees along the sides of the road. While Brown was riding out toward Boston from Lexington, his horse suddenly stopped and refused to proceed any farther. Finally, after trying in vain to prod the horse on, Brown realized that it probably smelled the British. So he quickly turned around and galloped back to Lexington to alert Captain Parker.

Eventually, Major Pitcairn, leading the British vanguard, was met by a British party coming from Lexington. This was Major Mitchell's patrol that had captured, then released, Paul Revere. As the British Lieutenant William Sutherland recalled, they "told us the whole country was alarmed" and his patrol "had galloped for their lives."

According to another officer, Richard Pope, "This information was soon after confirmed by firing of alarum guns. The bells rang, and were answered by all the villages round." Mitchell told Pitcairn that 500 rebels stood ready at Lexington to oppose him. Pitcairn therefore slowed his march to allow Colonel Smith and the main body to draw closer.

Mitchell rode on to inform the colonel. After listening to Mitchell's account, Smith dispatched a messenger back to Boston, to ask General Gage to immediately send out Lord Percy and the reinforcements. Paul Revere's ruse about the "500 men" had slowed the British advance, giving the militia more valuable time.

Three miles away, in Woburn, 23-three-year-old Sylvanus Wood heard the signal muskets and the ringing of church bells, and sleepily concluded that "there was some difficulty" at Lexington:

> I immediately arose, took my gun, and with Robert Douglass went in haste to Lexington. When I arrived there, I inquired of Captain Parker the news. Parker told me he did not know what to believe, for a man had come up about half an hour before and informed him that the British troops were not on the road. But while we were talking, a messenger [Solomon Brown] came up and told the captain that the British troops were within half a mile. Parker immediately turned to his drummer, William Diamond, and ordered him to beat "To arms."

Parker asked Wood and Douglass if they would join his company, then forming on Lexington Common. Continuing Wood's account, as the men gathered, Captain Parker called out to them:

> "Every man of you who is equipped, follow me. And those of you who are not equipped, go into the meeting-house and furnish yourselves from the magazine and immediately join the company."
>
> Parker led those of us who were equipped to the north end of Lexington Common, near the Bedford Road, and formed us in single file. I was stationed about in the center of the company. While we were standing, I left my place and went from one end of the company to the other and counted every man who was paraded, and the whole number was thirty-eight and no more. Just as I had finished and got back to my place, I perceived the British troops had arrived on the spot between the meetinghouse and Buckman's [Tavern].

According to two of his men, as the British approached, Captain Parker instructed the militia: "Stand your ground. Don't fire unless fired upon, but if they mean to have a war, let it begin here." Looking back, this might seem to have been an unreasonably bold stance to take with only three dozen men, facing 200 trained Regulars (Pitcairn's vanguard), especially since the ground offered no cover. In his deposition, taken a few days later, Captain Parker would state that he ordered the militia "to meet upon the Common to consult what to do, and concluded not to be discovered nor meddle or make with said Regular troops."

Perhaps, in his deposition, Parker was recalling what he'd said the first time the company assembled, before he'd dismissed them to the houses around the Common, and before he perhaps had a talk with the influential Reverend Clark. Reverend Clark, widely known as "a superior Wigg," had advocated military resistance to Gage's troops in numerous political essays and sermons. We do know that Hancock walked from the parsonage to the Common to see the militia. It is reasonable to assume that both Adams and Clark accompanied him, and the three of them consulted Captain Parker. The revolutionary movement could certainly have used some more martyrs to wake up the other colonies, as the victims of the Boston Massacre had done five years earlier. By the time the British arrived, Parker had his men lined up in two rows on the Common, directly in the path the British would have to take to reach Concord. According to one minuteman, when one of the men grumbled, "There are so few of us, it's foolish to stand here," Parker firmly declared, "The first man who offers to run shall be shot!"

Major Pitcairn's vanguard reached Lexington Common at 5:20 a.m. and formed a battle line. An officer shouted, "Damn them, we will have them!" and the Regulars rushed forward, all yelling, "Huzzah! Huzzah! Huzzah!" so loud that it was difficult for orders on either side to be heard. Pitcairn rode quickly to the front to try to gain control of his men. It should be remembered that Pitcairn was a major in the Marines. None of the soldiers or subordinate officers under him were Marines.

Pitcairn decided these foolhardy "peasants" blocking his path to Concord must be disarmed and sent home, to avoid an incident. So he rode toward the 38 Americans lined up at the north end of the Common, reined in his horse, and shouted at them, "Ye villains, ye rebels, disperse! Lay down your arms!"

A resident named Willard, who viewed the scene from a window, recalled, "upon that the Regulars ran till they came within about eight or nine rods [44 to 49 yards] of the militia, at which time the militia dispersed." Captain Parker ordered his men to disperse, but he did not order them to lay down their arms. The men began dispersing, taking their guns with them. Their muskets were their main provider of meat, and would be very costly to replace - not something to give up to the British, who were not likely to return them.

This irritated Major Pitcairn, who shouted, "Lay down your arms, damn you! Why don't ye lay down your arms?" He then gave orders to his men: "Soldiers, don't fire, keep your ranks, form and surround them." Immediately, a detachment of Light Infantry ran forward to cut off their escape, and force them to give up their guns. According to the British Lieutenant William Sutherland, as the Regulars were moving toward the militia "some of the villains were got over the hedge, fired at us, and it was then and not before that the soldiers fired."

This, of course, differs from the American accounts. Elijah Sanderson contends that it was Pitcairn who had yelled, "Damn them, we will have them!" and immediately afterward, "the Regulars shouted aloud, ran and fired upon the Lexington company." Thomas Fessenden claimed that, while Pitcairn was trying to gain control of his troops, another mounted officer "about two rods behind him fired a pistol."

No one was killed by these first few shots, and several of the minutemen testified that they thought the British muskets were "probably charged only with powder" and not ball. According to Sylvanus Wood, "Just at this time, Captain Parker ordered every man to take care of himself. The company immediately dispersed, and while the

145

company was dispersing and leaping over the wall, the second platoon of the British fired and killed some of our men."

Whether they fired before, at the same time, or just after the first British fire, it is reasonable to assume that some of the first Americans to reach the stone wall had leaped over it, turned, and began firing. A British officer shouting menacing words ("Damn them, we will have them!" and "... form and surround them!") coupled with the swift movement of the Regulars would seem justification enough "to meddle with them."

The Reverend Ezra Stiles, President of Yale College, had an interview with Major John Pitcairn a few weeks later. Stiles recorded what Pitcairn told him:

> As he turned, he saw a gun in a peasant's hand from behind a wall flash in the pan without going off; and instantly or very soon 2 or 3 guns went off by which he found his horse wounded and also a man near him wounded. These guns he did not see, but believing they could not come from his own people, asserted that they came from our people; and that thus they began the attack. The impetuosity of the King's troops were such that a promiscuous, uncommanded but general fire took place, which Pitcairn could not prevent; tho' he struck his staff or sword downwards with all earnestness as a signal to forbear or stop firing.

When the first shots went off, it was like a signal for the frustrated British troops to finally "have at the dogs" who had abused and tormented them ever since they first came to Boston seven years earlier. For a few minutes, the British officers lost all control over their men. As one officer put it, "the men were so wild they could hear no orders." In the words of another, "Our men, without any orders, rushed in upon them, fired and put 'em to flight."

Parker's men were pursued with ball and bayonet. Corporal John

Munroe, of the Lexington company, described the scene:

> After the first fire of the Regulars, I thought, and so
> stated to Ebeneezer Munroe, who stood next to me on
> the left, that they had fired nothing but powder. But, on
> the second firing, Munroe said they had fired something
> more than powder, for he had received a wound in his
> arm; and now, said he, to use his own words, "I'll give
> them the guts of my gun." We then both took aim at the
> main body of British troops - the smoke preventing our
> seeing anything but the heads of some of their horses -
> and discharged our pieces.

Jonas Parker, aged cousin of the captain, stood his ground. In his
hat at his feet he had bullets, wadding for ramming them down his gun
barrel, and spare flints. When a British ball buckled his knees, he tried
to reload his gun, but, as Sergeant Munroe explains:

> The British came up, run him through with the bayo-
> net, and killed him on the spot.
>
> After I had fired the first time, I retreated about ten
> rods, and then loaded my gun a second time with two
> balls; and, on firing at the British, the strength of the
> charge took off about a foot of my gun barrel. Such was
> the general confusion, and so much firing on the part of
> the British, that it was impossible for me to know the
> number of our men who fired.
>
> The Regulars kept up a fire in all directions, as long
> as they could see a man of our company in arms. Samuel
> Hadley and John Brown were killed after they had got-
> ten off the Common. Asahel Perter of Woburn, who had
> been taken a prisoner by the British on their march to
> Lexington, attempted to make his escape, and was shot
> within a few rods of the Common. Caleb Harrington was

shot down on attempting to leave the meeting-house, where he and some others had gone, before the British came up, for the purpose of removing a quantity of powder that was stored there.

Jonathan Harrington, with a ball in his body, dragged himself from the Common almost to his doorstep, but he died before his anguished wife and children, bursting from the house, could reach him.

Elijah Sanderson witnessed one of the closing moments:

> After our militia had dispersed, I saw the British firing at Solomon Brown, who was stationed behind a wall. I saw the wall smoke with bullets hitting it. ... [Brown] fired into a solid column of them, and then retreated. He was in the cow yard. The wall saved him. He leaped it just about the time I went away.

A few British soldiers, perhaps seeing it as an opportunity to desert, had gone into some of the nearby houses and did not return to the Common when the column proceeded on to Concord. They were soon captured by the Lexington minutemen. Ebeneezer Munroe recalled, "I carried their arms into Buckman's Tavern, and they were taken by some of our men who had none of their own."

When Colonel Smith galloped up, ahead of the main body of troops not yet in Lexington, he saw that things were out of hand. Several soldiers were trying to break down the door of Buckman's Tavern, while others were pursuing fleeing minutemen in all directions. "I was desirous of putting a stop to all further slaughter of those deluded people." So Smith immediately ordered Pitcairn's drummer to beat his drum, calling the men to assemble on the Common.

Although Smith was furious with the unruly troops, and gave them a tongue-lashing, he did allow them the traditional victory volleys and cheers. According to Lieutenant Mackenzie's journal, several officers "advised Colonel Smith of giving up the idea of prosecuting his march, and to return to Boston ... [because] of the country being alarmed and assembling. But Colonel Smith determined to obey the orders he had received, and accordingly pursued his march" to Concord.

No attempt was made to search for Sam Adams and John Hancock, by now miles away in their horse-drawn chaise, on their way finally to Philadelphia and the second Continental Congress. When they heard the rattle of musket fire, the two patriot leaders stopped the horse and listened. Adams turned to Hancock and said, "It is a fine day!" Hancock replied, "Very pleasant." Evidently, Adams thought, Hancock hadn't understood, so he added, "I mean, this is a glorious day for America."

CHAPTER NINE
A COUNTRYSIDE AROUSED
APRIL 19, 1775

"The war had begun, they told me; the British had marched out into the country to Lexington, to the tune of 'Yankee Doodle' but they made them dance it back again."

- *American arriving from Maine, a*
day after Lexington and Concord

Ever since Paul Revere had ridden out to Concord the previous Sunday, the local militia had been busy hiding the munitions that the Massachusetts Provincial Congress had been stockpiling there. Now, as the British neared the town, a farmer hurriedly ploughed furrows of earth over a cannon buried that morning in his cornfield. Knowing the Regulars would be eager for plunder, a woman dropped the church silver in a barrel of soft soap. The Reverend William Emerson (whose grandson, Ralph Waldo Emerson, would later write the poem, "The Midnight Ride of Paul Revere") explains how they were informed of the imminent arrival of the redcoats:

Intelligence was brought to us at first by Dr. Samuel Prescott, who narrowly escaped the guard that were sent before on horses, purposely to prevent all posts and messengers from giving us timely information. He, by the help of a very fleet horse, crossing several walls and fences, arrived at Concord [at 2 a.m.].

... [Later] several posts were dispatched, that returning confirmed the account of the Regulars' arrival at

Lexington, and that they were on their way to Concord.

Upon this, a number of our minute men belonging to this town, and Acton and Lyncoln, with several others that were in readiness, marched out to meet them, while the alarm company were preparing to receive them in the town. Capt. Minot, who commanded them, thought it proper to take possession of the hill above the meeting-house, as the most advantagious situation. No sooner had our men gained it than we were met by the companies that were sent out to meet the troops, who informed us that they were just upon us, and that we must retreat, as their number was more than treble ours.

They "had beautiful musick" as they marched back to Concord playing their fifes and drums, one-third of a mile in front of the British column, whose own musicians, not to be outdone, also played tunes. Reverend Emerson continues his account:

We then retreated from the hill near the Liberty Pole and took a new post back of the town upon an eminence, where we formed into two battalions and waited the arrival of the enemy. Scarcely had we formed before we saw the British troops at the distance of a quarter of a mile, glittering in arms, advancing towards us with the greatest celerity. Some were for making a stand, notwithstanding the superiority of their number; but others more prudent thought best to retreat till our strength should be equal to the enemy's by recruits from neighboring towns that were continually coming to our assistance.

Accordingly, we retreated over the [North] Bridge. The troops came into the town [at 9:00 a.m.], set fire to several carriages of artillery, destroyed 60 barrels flour, rifled several houses, set a guard of 100 men at the

152

North Bridge, and sent a party to the house of Col. Barrett, where they were in expectation of finding a quantity of warlike stores. But these were happily secured just before their arrival by transportation into the woods and other by-places.

With all the militia a mile outside of town, on a hill beyond North Bridge, the British were able to search Concord for munitions. They found a supply of wooden spoons and trenchers and a few artillery gun carriages, all of which they set ablaze. When sparks jumped onto a nearby house, setting it on fire, the soldiers quickly joined the "country people" in forming a bucket brigade to extinguish the flames.

While the search and destroy mission went on for about an hour, Colonel Smith and Major Pitcairn retired to Concord's tavern. Stirring his brandy and water with his finger, Pitcairn remarked, "I hope I shall stir the damned Yankee blood so before night."

On the hill beyond North Bridge outside of town, the restless militia were now about 450 strong. Seeing the smoke of the burning gun carriages, they thought the British were setting fire to the town. Thomas Thorp recalled Concord's Captain Isaac Davis drawing his sword and saying to his company, "I haven't a man that is afraid to go. March!" There was a general determination "to march into the middle of the town for its defence, or die in the attempt."

About 100 Regulars were defending the North Bridge, nervously watching the oncoming militia. Then, according to British Lieutenant John Barker, "Capt. Laurie made his men retire to this [the Concord] side of the bridge. As soon as they were over, the three companies got one behind the other so that only the front one could fire." The idea was that after the front company fired, they would move to the rear, and the next company would fire, while the one now at the rear reloaded, etc. Using this formation, known as "street firings," Laurie planned an orderly, slow retreat to the town, since the reinforcements he had requested from the main body in town had not yet arrived.

In retrospect, Laurie's men would have benefitted more by adapting

Yankee methods and shooting from behind the nearby stone walls and trees. However, the British were trained to fight in the proper European manner - standing in the open. Lieutenant Barker explains why the reinforcements did not arrive in time to assist in, or perhaps prevent, the skirmish at the North Bridge:

> Capt. Laurie, who commanded these three companies, sent to Col. Smith begging he would send more troops, and informing him of his situation. The Col. ordered 2 or 3 companies, but put himself at their head, by which means [he] stopt 'em from being [in] time enough, for being a very fat heavy man he would not have reached the bridge in half an hour, though it was not half a mile to it.

Laurie's men hastily tried to make the bridge impassable by removing "some of the planks." The attempt was abandoned when the oncoming Americans, marching to the tune "The White Cockade," saw it and "hastened our steps toward the bridge." British fingers were tense on their "trickers" and, without orders, "three guns, one after the other," were fired at the Americans. Moments later, the front rank of the British all fired.

The first casualty, a fifer from Acton, cried out that he had been hit. This came as a shock to some, who, not having heard of the blood spilt at Lexington, assumed the British would just try to frighten them by firing powder. "God damn it!" a militia captain shouted. "They are firing ball!" Concord's Major Buttrick quickly yelled, "Fire, fellow soldiers! For God's sake, fire!" Corporal Amos Barrett explains their approach and the skirmish, which lasted only a few minutes:

> Major Buttrick said if we wair all of his mind he would drive them away from the bridge; they should not tair that up. We all said we wood go. We then warnt loded. we wair all orded to load and had stricked order

not to fire till they fir'd firs, then to fire as fast as we could. we then march'd on, 2 deep. Capt Davis had got, I be leave within 15 rods of the B when they fir'd 3 gons one after the other. I see the balls strike in the river on the right of me. as soon as they fir'd them, they fir'd on us. their balls whisled well. We then was all orded to fire.

It is straing that their warnt no more kild but they fird to high. Capt Davis was kild and mr osmore and a number wounded. We soon drove them from the bridge.

As Amos Barrett pointed out, one of the two Americans slain was the gallant Captain Isaac Davis, the bullet hitting him square in the chest and piercing his heart. His widow was later to write:

He was then thirty years of age. We had four children; the youngest about fifteen months old. They were all unwell when he left me in the morning; some of them with the canker-rash. My husband said little that morning. He seemed serious and thoughtful; but never seemed to hesitate as to the course of his duty. As he led the company from the house, he turned himself round, and seemed to have something to communicate. He only said, "Take good care of the children," and was soon out of sight.

Instead of the planned orderly retreat, the outnumbered British broke ranks, and fled back to the town, "despite," Captain Laurie reported later, "of all that could be done to prevent them." Having taken the bridge, the astonished Americans did not pursue the fleeing soldiers. Amos Barrett remembers:

We did not follow them. There was eight or ten that was wounded, and a-running and hobbling about, look-

155

ing back to see if we was after them.

We then saw the whole body [Smith's reinforcements] a-coming out of town. We then was ordered to lay behind a wall, and when they got nigh enough, Major Buttrick said he would give the word "fire." But they did not come quite so near as he expected before they halted. The commanding officer [Smith] ordered the whole battalion to halt and officers to the front.

There we lay behind the wall, about 200 of us with our guns cocked, expecting every minute to have the word, "fire." Our orders was, if we fired, to fire two or three times and then retreat. We could have killed almost every officer there was in the front, but we had no orders to fire and there wasn't a gun fired.

According to Thaddeus Blood, "They stayed about ten minutes and then marched back" to Concord. The Americans did not follow. Casualties from the skirmish at the North Bridge were about even on each side: two dead and three wounded Americans; and two dead and ten wounded British. Among the British casualties were four officers. As in other battles to come, the Americans deliberately aimed for the fancy officers' uniforms, to bring confusion to the enemy troops, who would suddenly find themselves leaderless.

The British detachment that had ventured beyond Concord to search for the hidden munitions, thought to be at Colonel Barrett's farm, did not find them. When they returned, the Americans were milling around without order, so they quickly marched past them, across North Bridge, and returned safely to their main body in town. The American officers were reluctant to attack until the British left Concord, for fear they would burn the town. Acton's Solomon Smith:

After a short time, we dispersed, and without any regularity went back over the bridge. While we were there, the detachment which had been to destroy stores at Col. Barrett's returned and passed us. It was owing to our want of order and our confused state that they were not taken prisoners. They passed two of their number who had been killed, and saw that the head of one had been split open. It was said this circumstance gave them the impression that the Americans would give no quarter.

The sight of their comrade's head split open to the skull seemed to verify their image of Americans as little more civilized than the "savages" who shared the wilderness with them. The story of the "barbarity of the rebels, who scalped and cut off the ears of some of the wounded men who fell into their hands," spread through the British army, both in America and Britain, and had an impact on the way the army would treat American prisoners during the course of the war. What actually happened in this alleged "scalping" incident was explained many years later to Concord's Nathaniel Hawthorne by his neighbor, James Russell Lowell. The "manse" he mentions was the parsonage of the Reverend William Emerson, near the North Bridge.

A youth in the service of the clergyman had been chopping wood at the manse. When he heard the shooting he ran across the field, his axe in his hand. The British had by this time retreated, the Americans were in pursuit; and the late scene of strife was thus deserted by both parties. Two soldiers lay on the ground - one was a corpse; but as the young New Englander drew nigh, the other Briton raised himself painfully upon his hands and knees and gave a ghastly stare into his face. The boy - it must have been a nervous impulse, without purpose, without thought, and betokening a sensitive and impressible nature rather than a hardened one - uplifted his axe and dealt the wounded soldier a fierce and fatal blow on the head.

The boy was Ammi White. New Hampshire's General John Stark met White in 1807 and noted that he was still "tortured" by his memory of the incident. Even then, thirty-two years later, "It worried him very much."

While Colonel Smith and his men waited in vain at Concord for the arrival of Lord Percy's reinforcements, boys and men in dozens of surrounding towns were converging on Concord, traveling by foot or horseback as fast as they could. The town of Woburn "turned out extraordinary," 256 strong. Dedham was left "almost literally without a male inhabitant before the age of seventy, and above that of sixteen." Concord's alarm guns and church bells had been heard by the nearby town of Lincoln, Lincoln's by Carlisle, and Carlisle's by Chelmsford. There a woman tried to keep her boy at home. But he refused to obey her, saying, "Mother, I hear the shoots; I'm going." All told, about 4,000 patriots took part in the fighting that day, but not more than about one-third of them were together at any one point in time. These citizen soldiers quickly used up the small amount of ammunition they brought with them, then returned home.

The roads were crowded with people going in both directions - armed militia hastening toward the Concord-Lexington road, as well as others, chiefly but not entirely women and children, fleeing the expected battle scenes. Many women stayed put and busied themselves molding bullets, making cartridges, preparing food for those going to fight, etc. In the case of the village of Pepperell, the women organized their own defense, in the absence of their menfolk. After arming themselves and electing officers, they watched the roads and, laying an ambuscade, they captured a Tory messenger trying to pass through town.

Before he went to bed the night before, General Gage had issued a written order that the relief force of about 1,000 men and two light cannon, whether needed or not, was to be paraded on Boston Common at 4 a.m. But the order had been mislaid, and shortly after 5 a.m., when Smith's request for reinforcements arrived, they were all still asleep in their barracks. It was not until 9 a.m. that they marched out of Boston, over the Neck. The Marines denied that they were late, since they had never been summoned. The summons had been addressed to their commanding officer - Major Pitcairn, who was in Concord, not Boston! Had Lord Percy left on time that morning, he would have joined Smith in Concord, and perhaps his artillery and men, added to Smith's, might have ensured a safer trip back to Boston.

After Percy marched out of Boston with the reinforcements, Gage thought about the danger Percy was in, and sent out two ammunition wagons and an escort of one officer and thirteen men, with orders to hurry and catch up with Percy's column. Percy had refused to be slowed down by taking more ammunition than the men could carry on their persons. This party was ambushed by the "alarm company" (men too old to march and fight with the militia's regular "training band"). Despite their advanced age, these were capable, experienced veterans, led by a "mulatto man" named David Lamson. They ambushed Gage's ammunition detail en route.

> Two waggons with provisions and ammunition for the Regulars, guarded by an officer and 13 men, were going to the army. ... Twelve of our men jumped from behind a stone wall, fired upon and killed two men, and wounded the officer. The guard retreated and ran into the woods, and our people took the waggons and the stores.

In their panic, six of the Regulars who ran away threw their muskets in a pond. The first person they encountered after that was a poor, starving old lady who was minding her business, picking wild roots to eat. The six soldiers threw up their hands and insisted they were her prisoners. When news reached London of this incident, Whigs in Parliament used it as ammunition in their arguments against carrying on this unnecessary war: "If one old Yankee woman can take six Grenadiers, how many soldiers will it require to conquer America?"

One of the patriots rushing to Concord was Dr. Joseph Warren. The 34-year-old Warren was chairman of Boston's Committee of Safety, and the only patriot leader still in Boston. Risking his own arrest for treason, Warren had stubbornly refused to leave, so that he could remain behind and direct the spy operations. But this morning he finally left Boston, rowing across the Charles River as Paul Revere had done the night before. Now he was on his way to Concord, or wherever the fighting was. Warren had done much to bring on this war; now that it was here, he was determined to do his part.

Also on the way to Concord, on another spying mission for Gage, was John Howe, a corporal now, once again disguised as a "countryman." On the way, he was surprised to learn of the raid on Concord, but quickly realized that it could add to his cover. From thereon, he yelled, "The Regulars are out!" as he rode. Corporal Howe safely arrived in Concord in the late morning. Colonel Smith, glad to see that Howe was dressed as a farmer, promptly turned him around and sent him back the way he came, instructing him to find Lord Percy and tell him to hurry along with the reinforcements.

Though staying in Concord provided some measure of safety (the Yankees were not likely to start a battle amidst their homes), Colonel Smith was becoming increasingly concerned about the newly arriving Americans. From his good vantage point, Concord's hilltop cemetery, Smith could see through his spyglass armed militia rushing toward Concord from all directions. So he gave up waiting for Percy at noon, and decided to make an orderly retreat over the 18 miles to Boston. Concord's Reverend Emerson observed:

> At length they quitted the town and retreated by the way they came. In the meantime, a party of our men took the back way through the Great Fields into the east quarter and placed themselves to advantage, lying in ambush behind walls, fences and buildings, ready to fire upon the enemy on their retreat.

These Concord militia waiting at Meriam's Corner were joined by many others, some of them newly arrived from towns as far as twenty miles away. It was here, where the road crossed a narrow bridge, that they started firing at the British column on their return march to Lexington. This was only the beginning of the redcoats' torment. The slowly moving column soon discovered that it was in serious trouble. This hilly terrain, where the narrow road was lined by stone walls and woods, was the "very bad place" that John Howe had told General Gage about. The British officers had difficulty keeping their panicky men from breaking ranks and running headlong toward Boston. Lt. John Barker, of the King's Own Regiment, later recalled the scene:

> We were fired on from all sides, but mostly from the rear, where people hid themselves till we had passed and then fired. The country was an amazing strong one, full of hills, woods, stone walls, &c., which the rebels did not fail to take advantage of, for they were all lined with people who kept up an incessant fire upon us, as we did too upon them but not with the same advantage, for they were so concealed there was hardly any seeing them.

Ensign Henry DeBerniere also recalled the action:

> All the hills on each side of us were covered with rebels so that they kept the road always lined and a very hot fire on us without intermission.
>
> When we arrived within a mile of Lexington our ammunition began to fail, and the light companies were so fatigued with flanking [attempting to clear rebels from stonewalls and woods ahead of the column] they were scarce able to act; and a great number of wounded, scarce able to get forward, made a great confusion.
>
> Col. Smith had received a wound through his leg; a number of officers were also wounded; so that we began

to run rather than retreat in order. The officers got to the front and presented their bayonets, and told the men if they advanced they should die. Upon this they began to form under a very heavy fire.

Another British officer noted that the rebels

always posted themselves in the houses and behind the walls by the roadside, and there waited the approach of the column, when they fired at it. Numbers of them were mounted, and when they had fastened their horses at some little distance from the road, they crept down near enough to have a shot. As soon as the column passed, they mounted again, and rode around until they got ahead of the column, and found some convenient place from whence they might fire again.

Eventually the desperate troops staggered onto Lexington Common. There they were finally met by the reinforcements from Boston. General Percy signaled his arrival by having an artillery crew fire a cannon ball through the church steeple. When Smith's men sighted the reinforcements, they let out a heartfelt cheer. Percy, in his official report to General Gage, described his rescue mission:

About 2 o'clock I met them retiring through the town of Lexington. I immediately ordered the 2 field pieces to fire at the rebels, and drew up the brigade on a height. The shot from the cannon had the desired effect and stopped the rebels for a little time, who immediately dispersed and endeavored to surround us, being very numerous.

As it began now to grow pretty late [3:45 p.m.], and we had 15 miles to retire, and only our 36 rounds, I ordered the Grenadiers and Light Infantry to move off first, and covered them with my brigade, sending out very strong flanking parties, which were absolutely necessary, as there was not a stone-wall or house, though before in appearance evacuated, from whence the rebels did not fire upon us.

As soon as they saw us begin to retire, they pressed very much upon our rear-guard, which for that reason I relieved every now and then. In this manner we retired for 15 miles under an incessant fire all round us, till we arrived at Charlestown between 7 and 8 in the even, very much fatigued with a march above 30 miles and having expended almost all our ammunition.

Many a Congregational minister led his town's minutemen in the fighting. Some, when paper for wadding the powder charges ran out, ordered pages from the hymnals of Dr. Isaac Watts, carried by some on their person or in their saddlebags, torn out and used for this purpose. A catchword of the day became "Put a little Watts into 'em, brethren."

One British soldier noted that "even women had firelocks. One was seen to fire a blunder bus between her father and her husband from their windows; there the three with an infant soon suffered the fury of the day." Lieutenant John Barker, in the front, later admitted:

We were now obliged to force almost every house in the road, for the rebels had taken possession of them and galled us exceedingly; but they suffered for their temerity, for all that were found in the houses were put to death.

On entering the home of Deacon Joseph Adams, the soldiers found no one bearing arms, only a woman who had recently given birth, and was recovering in bed. Adams had just fled the house at the insistance of his wife, who feared his life would be taken if the British found him,

163

but hers would be spared because of her condition. She relates what happened when the soldiers entered her house:

> Three of the soldiers broke into the room in which I was confined to my bed. One of the soldiers immediately opened my [bed] curtain with his bayonet fixed, pointing the same at my breast. I immediately cried out, "For the Lord's sake, do not kill me!"
>
> He replied, "Damn you!" One that stood near said, "We will not hurt the woman if she will go out of the house, but we will surely burn it."
>
> I immediately arose, threw a blanket over me, and crawled into a cornhouse near the door, with my infant in my arms. They immediately set the house on fire, in which I had left five children; but the fire was happily extinguished.

When the British reached the crossroads in Cambridge, they found hundreds of militia facing them in ranks. Some were local units, others had been circling the British column ever since Lexington, their "dispersing tho' adhering" tactics having been directed by William Heath, a militia general from Roxbury. Seeing the militia lined up in front of him, Lord Percy quickly realized that their intention was to force him to return to Boston the way he'd come that morning, and this time the bridge's planks would surely be missing, not conveniently piled on the far bank as they had been that morning, when the inhabitants had been reluctant to obey Heath's orders to burn it.

Therefore, Percy determined to go through Heath's men. Once more, the wounded soldiers slid off the gun carriages, and the two six-pounder cannon were driven forward to the front of the column. As usual, the use of artillery had the intended effect. The militia scattered, and the British marched on down the Charlestown road. Once across the "Neck" that connected the mainland to Charlestown peninsula, they came under the protection of the guns of the warships.

Later, the Provincial Congress would order the events of April 18th and 19th retraced by recording depositions from participants and witnesses. The purpose was to have a documented (albeit one-sided) account to use in negotiations with Parliament, to prove that America was not rebelling. A few weeks later, Virginia's George Washington would read and analyze a copy of these depositions, and conclude:

> If the retreat had not been as precipitate as it was, the ministerial troops must have surrendered, or been totally cut off. For they had not arrived in Charlestown, under the cover of their ships, half an hour before a powerful body of men from Marblehead and Salem was at their heels and must have intercepted their retreat.

After crossing Charlestown Neck, Percy ordered the exhausted troops to start digging in atop Bunker's Hill, where they could defend from a high position. But the Yankees, respecting the threat of the British naval guns at the mouth of the Charles River, gave up their pursuit. General Gage soon sent over fresh troops from Boston to finish, then defend the earthworks, and the expeditionary forces were ferried over to Boston and sent to their barracks to sleep for the first time in almost 48 hours.

Jeremy Lister, an ensign of the 10th Regiment of Foot, recalled what he experienced after finally reaching the safety of Bunker Hill:

> I got Mr Simes, Surgeons Mate to 43'd Reg't, to examine my arme. He extracted the ball, it having gone through the bone and lodg'd within the skin. From our long fateaguing march and loss of blood for 9 miles [and] want of provisions having not had a morcel since the day before, I begun to grow rather faint.
>
> I then proceeded through the Town to my lodgings where I arriv'd about 9 o'clock. Mrs Miller, mistress of the house, I desired to get me a dish of tea, which she

immediately set about. But Mr & Mrs Funnel, who was drove in from the country by the Rebels and lodging in the same house, came to ask me how I did. [They] pronounc'd me light headed in asking for tea, [and said] I ought instantly to go to bed. But persisting in having some tea before I left the place, it was brought.

The imagination may conceive the satisfaction I felt from that tea, notwithstanding I was interupted with a thousand questions. Till I was ask'd whether I had seen Lt Sutherland of 38th Reg't; when I reply'd I had, and supposed by that time he was dead. His wife, being just behind my chare, immediately drop'd down in swoon; which then diverted the comp'ys attention a little from me, which I was not at all sorry for, as I then got my tea with a little more quietness.

The expedition to Lexington and Concord had been disastrous for the British. They had failed to keep their march secret from the rebel minutemen, failed to capture Hancock and Adams at Lexington, and even failed to destroy much of the rebels' military stores at Concord. At the least, they could have had the satisfaction of seizing the illegal Provincial Congress's treasury - if they had recognized it. A few days earlier, the treasurer had brought the funds in a chest to a Concord inn. While searching the inn for munitions, the soldiers came upon the chest. A young woman, sitting on it, insisted that it was hers and contained private property. The soldiers, believing her, left without opening the chest.

Only a few cannon (those too heavy to quickly hide) had been found; the British had spiked them, but not permanently put them out of commission. No stores of powder or guns were found. The 500 pounds of musket balls the British discovered and threw into Concord's millpond were quickly retrieved as soon as the soldiers left the town. The British did find about 100 barrels of flour, and begin breaking them open and scattering the contents on the ground. But this was hard work, and the soldiers were tired after marching 18 miles, so they rolled most of the barrels into the millpond. The small amount of water that seeped into the cracks formed a paste with the flour it contacted. This paste effectively sealed the cracks, and about ninety percent of the flour was later salvaged.

Not only did they fail to achieve their objectives, but the British also suffered terrible casualties in their ill-fated expedition to Lexington and Concord. From their total force, including reinforcements, of about 1,750 men, 73 were killed, 174 wounded, and 25 missing. Colonel Francis Smith had indeed been fortunate to return to Boston at all. Of the 3,763 Americans who claimed to have answered the alarm, 50 were killed, 39 wounded, and 5 captured. Twenty-six towns were represented among the 94 American casualties. The physical feat performed by the British troops that day was nothing short of astounding. Heavily encumbered with equipment, in 20 hours they had marched nearly 40 miles, almost half of it while under fire from the enemy.

Lord Percy gained respect for these "rascals and cowards" who he had predicted would never fight:

> Whoever looks upon them as an irregular mob will find themselves much mistaken. They have men amongst them who know very well what they are about, having been employed as Rangers against the Indians and Canadians. And this country being much covered with wood, and hills, it is very advantageous for their method of fighting.
>
> Nor are several of their men void of a spirit of enthusiasm, as we experienced yesterday, for many of them concealed themselves in houses and advanced within 10 yards to fire at me and other officers, though they were morally certain of being put to death themselves in an instant.
>
> You may depend upon it that, as the rebels have now had time to prepare, they are determined to go through

with it. Nor will the insurrection turn out so despicable as it is perhaps imagined at home. For my part, I confess, I never believed that they would have attacked the King's troops, or have had the perseverance I found in them yesterday.

But others, such as General Gage and most of the Tories, were not convinced. Typical were the opinions of Captain William Glanville Evelyn. He wrote home to his father:

The rebels, you know, have of a long time been making preparations as if to frighten us, though we always imagined they were too great cowards ever to presume to do it. They are just now worked up to such a degree of enthusiasm and madness, that they are easily persuaded the Lord is to assist them in whatever they undertake, and that they must be invincible.

This first "battle" of the war, technically, was a skirmish, not a formal, standing battle. Nevertheless, the war had started, and the casualty figures were deadly serious. Although they may have seemed significant at the time, they would during the next eight years be dwarfed by the final totals. British army and navy losses would amount to nearly 10,000 killed in action, and 30,000 deaths from disease in camp and on board ships. Their German allies would add another 1,200 deaths from battle and 6,400 from disease. Besides these fatalities, the combined British and German forces would lose about 65,000 men to desertion. Figures are difficult to ascertain for the American loyalist regiments. On the patriot side, about 5,000 would be killed in action, 12,000 from maltreatment aboard British prison ships, and another 20,000 from smallpox, influenza, starvation and hypothermia, etc.

One of those who would die in captivity was Samuel Prescott, the young doctor who had been on his way home to Concord that night after courting his sweetheart in Lexington. After escaping from Major Mitchell's patrol, Prescott had gone on to warn the people of Concord, but he never did have a chance to marry his Lexington sweetheart. He soon enlisted in the Continental Army as a surgeon, then later went to fight at sea. Unfortunately, he would be captured, and taken to a prison ship in Halifax Harbor, where he died in 1777. His Lexington sweetheart, Lydia Mulliken, whose house was one of those the British burned on their return march to Boston, would wait in vain until the war's end in 1783 for word from Prescott. Eventually, she married another.

CHAPTER TEN
"TO ARMS!"

"Even our women and children now talk of nothing but the glory of fighting, suffering and dying for our country."

> *- Lord Dunmore, royal governor of Virginia*

"The fearful day has arrived! A civil war has actually commenced in our land. We must be prepared for the worst, and may God preserve and protect our country." With these words, James Otis, Sr., concluded an explanation of what had happened at Lexington and Concord. Otis had been speaking to James Thacher and other neighbors. Thacher later recorded his own thoughts on the occasion:

> This tragical event seems to have electrified all classes of people. The brave are fired with manly resentment, the timid overwhelmed in despair; the patriotic Whigs sorrowing over public calamities, while the Tories indulge the secret hopes that the friends of liberty are about to receive their chastisement. Expresses are hastening from town to town, in all directions through the country, spreading the melancholy tidings and inspiriting and rousing the people, "To Arms! To Arms!"

By the day after the battle, the news had spread across most of New England. Lacking hard facts, many people relating the story let their imagination run wild in describing atrocities they presumed the Regulars must have committed on their march to and from Concord, and might be still committing elsewhere at that very moment.

At Ipswich, 25 miles northeast of Boston, someone started a rumor that British soldiers were being landed from boats and were bayoneting the citizens. The inhabitants of the town frantically fled inland. According to one report of Ipswich's exodus, "A poor woman ran four or five miles up the river and stopped to take breath and nurse her child, when she found to her great horror that she had brought off the cat instead of the baby!" Within an hour of the rumor's start, word reached Beverly, ten miles away, that the entire town of Ipswich had been wiped out. And, at a town meeting in Newbury, a rider interrupted the minister's prayer by shouting "Turn out, for God's sake, or you will all be killed. The Regulars are marching on us; they are at Ipswich now, cutting and slashing all before them." In Portsmouth, the militia were notified by seven different riders to march in seven different directions.

At Harvard Yard, in Cambridge, Dr. Joseph Warren, now head of the Massachusetts Committee of Safety, quickly set up a tent to serve as committee headquarters. From there, he tried to bring some semblance of order to the chaotic scene as patriots poured into the area from all over New England, to help with the blockade of Boston. Governor Gage's informant, Doctor Benjamin Church, described the rebel forces to him as a "mass of confusion."

The true patriot, Doctor Warren, had been the only political leader to join the militia chasing the Regulars back to Charlestown. In the process, he had constantly exposed himself to enemy fire. One British bullet shot a pin out of his wig, barely missing his scull. Joseph Warren's actions as a fighter, an inspiration to the militia, and a physician aiding the wounded while under fire, won him the admiration of the militia, adding to his reputation as a leader.

By 1775, Joseph Warren had developed a skill at propaganda that was the equal of Samuel Adams. The previous fall, Warren had written the Suffolk Resolves that had persuaded the Continental Congress to authorize a military buildup for defensive purposes. He had learned how to strengthen the power of reason with an appeal to the emotions.

Like his friend and mentor, Sam Adams, Warren realized that facts were useful only as a foundation, that they have to be built upon by exaggeration and distortion. After Lexington and Concord, the Provincial Congress asked Dr. Warren to write an appeal to arms, to be sent by express riders to every town in Massachusetts. It was a masterly statement, not a single fact in it. He knew that facts would not be necessary and might even be harmful, since they might contradict the wild rumors floating about.

> The barbarous murders committed on our innocent brethren, on Wednesday, the 19th instant, have made it absolutely necessary that we immediately raise an army to defend our wives and our children from the butchering hands of an inhuman soldiery who, incensed at the obstacles they met with in their bloody progress, and enraged at being repulsed from the field of slaughter, will, without the least doubt, take the first opportunity in their power to ravage this devoted country with fire and sword. We conjure you, therefore, by all that is dear, by all that is sacred, <u>that you give all assistance possible in forming an army</u>. Our all is at stake. Death and destruction are the instant consequences of delay. Every moment is infinitely precious. An hour lost may deluge your country in blood and entail perpetual slavery upon the few of your posterity who may survive the carnage.

Country farmers could no longer consider the British soldiers a threat only to the coastal towns, for now they had ventured inland, "slaughtering" defenseless women, children and old men. Throughout New England, upon hearing the news, men dropped whatever they were doing, grabbed their muskets, and hurriedly set out "to meet the British." About 12,000 militia from Massachusetts poured into Cambridge, to be joined there by 2,300 from Connecticut, another 1,000 from Rhode Island and 1,200 from New Hampshire.

On April 22nd, the Massachusetts Provincial Congress reconvened and unanimously elected Dr. Warren as president. He replaced John Hancock, who was on his way to Philadelphia to serve in the second Continental Congress, scheduled to convene on May 10th. Next, they appointed a committee of five to take depositions "from which a full account of the transactions of the troops under General Gage, in their route to and from Concord, may be collected." The committee was instructed to be sure that the depositions consistently portrayed the Regulars as firing the first shots at Lexington Common and again at Concord's North Bridge. Many of these depositions, even some from captured British soldiers, were taken from alleged "eyewitnesses" who, in fact, had not even been at those locations when the first shots were fired.

Dr. Warren sent a copy of these depositions, and a narrative account he wrote, as well as copies of the <u>Salem Gazette</u> account on a swift, cargo-less schooner to London. Although it left four days after General Gage's official report, it arrived in London fifteen days sooner. The package was given to Arthur Lee, a Virginian, who gave it to London's pro-American alderman, John Wilkes. The <u>London Evening Post</u> published an extra, reprinting the <u>Salem Gazette</u> account and some of the depositions, shocking its readers with accounts such as:

> Women in childbed were driven by the soldiery naked
> into the streets, old men peaceably in their houses were
> shot dead, and such scenes exhibited as would disgrace
> the annals of the most uncivilized nations.

Dr. Warren also enclosed a letter he wrote, addressed "To the Inhabitants of Great Britain," appealing to them for support. "We cannot think that the honour, wisdom and valour of Britons will suffer them longer to be inactive spectators of measures which, if successful, must end in the ruin and slavery of Britain, as well as the persecuted colonies." An American sympathizer reported the reaction in London:

Administration were alarmed at the unexpected success of the Provincials. Runners were sent to every part of the city, who were authorized to deny the authenticity of the facts, and so distressed was Government that they officially requested a suspension of belief until dispatches were received from General Gage.

One group of citizens in London raised 100 pounds "to be applied to the relief of the widows, orphans, and aged parents of our beloved American fellow-subjects, who, faithful to the character of Englishmen, preferring death to slavery, were for that reason only, inhumanly murdered by the King's troops at Lexington and Concord." Other donations were added, and an article supporting the fund-raising was published in a London newspaper. For it, three printers were fined 100 pounds each, and the publisher was sentenced to a fine of 200 pounds and one year in prison for libel.

The working class of Great Britain, unrepresented in Parliament, expressed its opposition to the war by not enlisting to fight the colonists. Many of them felt that the colonists were fighting for the suppressed rights of all British citizens. Recruiting was so slow that, by the end of summer, 1775, Lord North acknowledged, "The ardor of the nation in this cause has not arisen to the pitch one could wish." With less than 200 enlistments after three full months of recruiting, the King realized he would have to hire foreign mercenaries to help him subdue the rebels.

Although the war was unpopular with many, those who had political influence - the merchants and landed gentry - saw little hope for preserving their own interests except by supporting the Administration. The merchants feared that coming to the aid of the colonies in 1775 as they had in 1765 (when they pushed for repeal of the Stamp Act) would mean that the Americans would "never rest till they have obtained a free trade with all the world." The landed gentry feared that success of republican ideas in the colonies would induce the oppressed classes back home to rise up and demand the same rights.

The Whigs in Parliament were blamed for the American rebellion. It was their support of the colonies, the Administration declared, that had encouraged rebellion. Continued opposition now made the Whigs unpopular. "Who could have imagined," wrote Lord Camden, "that the Ministry could have become popular by forcing this country into a destructive war, and advancing the power of the Crown to a state of despotism?"

The events of April 19th made King George III more certain than ever that he was correct in pursuing his policy of coercion. His private sentiments:

> No consideration could bring me to swerve from the present path which I think myself in duty bound to follow. Once these rebels have felt a smart blow, they will submit; and no situation can ever change my fixed resolution, either to bring the colonies to a due obedience to the legislature of the mother country or to cast them off!

The King decided to unleash the Iroquois of New York upon the frontier settlements. He wrote to the Indian agent, Guy Johnson, informing him that he would no longer report to Canada's Governor Carleton, who the King knew was too scrupulous and would oppose initiation of frontier warfare. "Lose no time," the King wrote to Johnson, "induce them to take up the hatchet against his majesty's rebellious subjects in America." He also looked for results from Gage in Boston, expecting that, "the next word from Boston would be of some lively action, for General Gage would wish to make sure of his revenge."

The King and others in his administration still had unrealistic opinions about the rebels' level of committment. The former governor of Massachusetts, Thomas Hutchinson, now living in London, predicted a quick end to the blockade of Boston. "Uunless fanaticism got the better of self-preservation, they must soon disperse, as it is the season for sowing their Indian corn, the chief subsistence of New England."

Returning to the Committee of Safety's headquarters at Watertown, Massachusetts, on the day of the battle, we find Colonel Joseph Palmer writing an alarm and sending it by express rider to Connecticut. The rider, Israel Bissell, a native of East Windsor, Conn., went first to Worcester. Upon arrival there about noon, his horse dropped dead. He procured another horse and headed south, reaching Norwich, Conn., at 4 p.m. the next day. He reached Lyme nine hours later, at 1 a.m. on the 21st. After having gone as far as Fairfield by the 22nd, Bissell decided the news must be spread as far and as quickly as possible. So he pressed on, reaching New York at 4 p.m. on the 23rd. From there, other riders carried this "momentous intelligence" farther south. Here is the message he carried from the Committee of Safety:

> Wednesday Morning near 11 o'clock
> To all friends of American liberty, be it known that this morning before break of day a brigade, consisting of 1000 or 1200 men, landed at Phipp's farm at Cambridge and marched to Lexington, where they found a company of our militia in arms, upon whom they fired without any provocation and killed 6 men and wounded 4 others. By an express from Boston, we find another brigade are now upon their march from Boston supposed to be about 1000. The bearer, Israel Bissell, is charged to alarm the country quite to Connecticut, and all persons are desired to furnish him with fresh horses as they may be needed.

Dispatches carried by express riders were not the only means by which the news spread to the other colonies. The Massachusetts Spy, which had just moved its printing press from Boston to Worcester on April 16th, published the following broadside. It was reprinted in dozens of newspapers throughout the colonies.

AMERICANS! forever bear in mind the BATTLE

177

OF LEXINGTON! - where British Troops, unmolested and unprovoked, wantonly and in a most inhuman manner fired upon and killed a number of our countrymen, then robbed them of their provisions, ransacked, plundered and burned their houses! Nor could the tears of defenceless women, some of whom were in the pains of childbirth, and cries of helpless babes, nor the prayers of old age confined to beds of sickness, appease their thirst for blood! - or divert them from their DESIGN of MURDER and ROBBERY!

By the 26th, the committees assigned to collect depositions and to write an official narrative had finished their work, and it was quickly copied and distributed from Maine to Georgia. Among the most frequent references, were those of British soldiers "driving into the street women in child-bed" and "killing old men in their houses unarmed." Actually, the one woman forced to flee her home, Hannah Adams, had delivered her baby 18 days before the British arrived. And the only unarmed "old men" killed were two men, 39 and 43 years old, who refused to stop drinking while all around them militia were using the tavern for shelter and firing at the British. When the soldiers scattered the militia and burst into the tavern, they did not stop to ask whether the two men were among the snipers or just harmlessly imbibing.

Americans had no way of knowing whether the version of the battle as depicted in the patriot press was truth or exaggeration. General Gage, with good reason, accused the Whigs of stopping the posts and breaking open the mail to remove letters, so that Tory and British accounts of the battle would not become known. The royal governor of North Carolina wrote that the Whig propagandists had done their work of "confirming the seditious in their evil purposes, and bringing over vast numbers of the fickle, wavering and unsteady multitude to their party."

Everywhere the news spread, the spirit of resistance flared. Meetings were held, government arms and powder supplies were seized, and people prepared for war. One colonist wrote, "Travel through whatever part of the country you will, you see the inhabitants training, making firelocks, casting mortars, shells and shot, and making saltpetre" for gunpowder. A Maryland Tory remarked, "the churlish drum and fife are the only music of the times." Virginia's royal governor reported to Lord Dartmouth that the Virginians were said to be "even madder than [those] in New England," and it was now fashionable for the burgesses to meet while wearing a frontiersman's hunting shirt and carrying a tomahawk. The governor continued, "Even our women and children now talk of nothing but the glory of fighting, suffering and dying for our country."

As Pennsylvanian Joseph Barroll put it, writing to a friend in England:

> We are ready to die free but determined not to live slaves. We ardently wish the people of England would arouse before it is too late. 'Tis not Boston, 'tis not the prov. of Masst. Bay, 'tis not the four N.E. Provinces only but 'tis the continent of America joined in the opposition. We have many and daily reports from every part of the extended continent. They all seem determined and more awake than ever. <u>Oppression will make a wise man mad</u>; you will soon be made acquainted with the spirit of the times.

The following excerpts are taken from a Virginian's letter to a relation in England, printed in a London newspaper in July of 1775:

> It would really surprise you to see the preparations making for our defence, all arming themselves, and independent companies from 100 to 150 men in every county in Virginia, well equipped and daily endeavouring to instruct themselves in the art of war, in order [to] oppose any forces that shall be sent here. There will be

many most bloody battles before the Americans will give up their liberties.

When you traded here you well knew it to be the ambition of the people of this country to endeavour who should be best dressed with the British manufactures, but they are now quite on the contrary extreme, for their glory now is to dress in their own manufacture. The example is daily followed by all ranks of people here: you may see from this how scandalous our G[overnor] has been in informing the ministry that we could not subsist more than one or two years without the assistance of the British manufactory.

Instead of our fields being planted with tobacco, they are now flourishing cotton and flax, and our pastures well stored with sheep; so I think there will not be the least danger of our suffering for want of clothes.

Until Lexington, the enemy who threatened American rights seemed to many colonists rather remote and impersonal in the form of the King's ministers and Parliament. However, General Gage's redcoats marching into the countryside transformed abstract rights - life, liberty, property - into concrete form: family, home, village. And to defend these by force of arms was now seen as a real necessity, the right and duty of every citizen, just as they had years ago defended them against the Indians and Frenchmen coming down from Canada. The Stamp Act crisis motto "Liberty, property, no stamps!" was now replaced by "Liberty or death!"

Many Tories made plans to leave the country, and some to join the British army as auxiliary troops. In Boston alone, two hundred signed up to serve in a loyalist regiment. However, Gage never did put them to use, perhaps not trusting them, but more likely realizing that untrained citizens would be more of a hindrance than a help. The majority of the Tories, however, decided to stay home, either to do what they could for their beliefs or to pursue a neutral course and try to avoid public notice. To the more ardent patriots, a loyalist was "a creature whose head is in England, whose body is in America, and who ought to have his neck stretched." Doctor James Thacher, of Massachusetts, author of A Military Journal During the American Revolutionary War, wrote of their plight:

> Liberty-poles are erected in almost every town and village; and when a disaffected Tory renders him odious by any active conduct, with the view of counteracting the public measures, he is seized by a company of armed men and conducted to the liberty-pole, under which he is compelled to sign a recantation and give bonds for his future good conduct. In some instances, individuals have been imprisoned or their names have been published in the newspapers as enemies of their country. It has indeed unfortunately happened that a few individuals have received from the rabble a coat of tar and feathers.
>
> The Tories make bitter complaints against the discipline which they receive from the hands of the Whigs. Their language is, "You make the air resound with the cry of liberty, but subject those who differ from you to the humble condition of slaves, not permitting us to act, or even think, according to the dictates of conscience." The reply is, "It is one of the first principles of a free government that the majority shall bear rule. We have undertaken the hazardous task of defending the liberties of our country. If you possess not patriotism and courage enough to unite your efforts with ours, it is our duty to put it out of your power to injure the common cause. "

Although no colonies outside of New England would send any men to join the army until the Continental Congress requested it in early summer, each colony did prepare for war by weeding Tories from its own militia organization, seizing government guns and powder sup-

181

plies, and either seizing or solidifying control of the government. In the seaport towns of Rhode Island, Connecticut and New York, patriots commandeered the cargoes of merchant ships about to set sail for the British army in Boston. Even in Georgia, where Tories dominated the government, the Whigs managed to start building a patriot militia, and they sent a shipment of rice to the New England army.

* * * * *

After April 19th, with virtually all the British military forces in America located in the cities of Boston and New York, the only remaining semblance of British sovereignty was the royal governors. And the patriots soon effectively rid themselves of all opposition from them.

In Massachusetts, General Gage was powerless as governor except within Boston itself, which became the only safe haven for Tory refugees. Connecticut was, in the spring of 1775, the only colony to have a patriot governor, Jonathan Trumbull. In Rhode Island, Governor Joseph Wanton, who in previous years had on occasion acted as a patriot to win popularity, suddenly began showing signs of loyalism. The legislature, predominantly Whig, forbade him to exercise his functions, and directed the lieutenant governor to act in his place. In New Hampshire, loyalist Governor Benning Wentworth quickly lost influence, and in the summer took refuge with the British garrison inside Portsmouth's Fort William and Mary.

In New York, the city's balanced Committee of 51 was replaced by a Whig-dominated Committee of 100, and the legislature was replaced by a Provincial Congress. Patriot leader Isaac Sears, who had led the seizure of the city's artillery and the provision ships destined for Gage's army, had the opportunity to assume one-man control of the city, supported by his faithful mob. But "King" Sears turned away from the temptation, in favor of the Committee of 100. Sears declared that he sought political change, not power.

For a decade, Isaac Sears had been cultivating a following amongst the city's poor. Like Sam Adams in Boston, Isaac Sears had given them favorable treatment while performing his duties as tax collector. Later, he was a vestryman in charge of dispensing funds to the poor. When the Liberty Pole was erected, Sears wisely chose a spot for it next to the city's poorhouse. After each of the Sons of Liberty's annual banquets to celebrate the anniversary of the repeal of the Stamp Act, he directed all leftover food and two barrels of beer be sent to the jail "to be distributed among prisoners." In these and other ways, Sears had developed a loyal mob ready to be used for radical action whenever he deemed it necessary. And, because of his renown as a courageous privateersman during the late French and Indian War, Sears was also a leader of the town's seamen and dock laborers. Together, these segments of the city's population formed a large enough mob to ensure that the governor and the Tory-dominated legislature were not able to enforce Parliament's wishes in that key city. By July, 1775, Sears was a member of New York's Provincial Congress. Disgusted with that body's inaction - he'd wanted them to authorize the arrest of Governor Tryon and the forced relocation of the city's Tories to the interior - Sears left and moved to Connecticut, where he organized a fleet of privateers.

Because of the strong loyalist faction in New York's Provincial Congress, Governor Tryon was safe until mid-summer, when his efforts to strengthen and organize the loyalist opposition were reported to the Continental Congress. A motion to order his arrest and confinement was voted down as being an infringement on the authority of the New York Provincial Congress. So the Congress subtly solved the problem by passing a resolution recommending that conventions, congresses and committees of safety from Georgia to New Hampshire imprison any persons who endanger the public safety. A "friend of government" set off for New York on a swift horse to warn the governor that this resolution passed. He arrived at the governor's mansion before a copy of the resolution reached the New York Provincial Congress. Governor Tryon lost no time in seeking refuge on a British man-of-war in New York's harbor.

In New Jersey, the legislature was replaced by a Provincial Congress. In January, 1776, it ordered loyalist Governor William Franklin (Benjamin's son) placed under house arrest. Not intimidated, he issued a proclamation calling for the defunct Assembly to reconvene, an action that only put him in a New Jersey jail. There he secretly worked for the loyalist cause. Discovered, he was sent off to solitary confinement in Connecticut jails, until eventually exchanged two years later.

Pennsylvania's neutral governor, John Penn, was allowed to remain in office, because he never opposed the legislature's actions. However, while the British army occupied Philadelphia (parts of 1777 and 1778) he was temporarily forced to live under guard in Connecticut. After the war, the Pennsylvania legislature gave generous payment to his family for the confiscation of his estate during this period of banishment.

Maryland's governor, Robert Eden, appeared to be neutral, until April, 1776, when a letter to him from the Administration in London was intercepted by patriots. It incriminated him by thanking him for confidential information, and directed him to assist Virginia's royal governor in his military campaign against the rebels. Eden was arrested, then allowed to remain in the colony on parole. Two months later, when the radicals were becoming impatient for his imprisonment, the Maryland Committee of Safety arranged for a British warship to come, under a flag of truce, and carry him away to England.

The governor of Georgia, Sir James Wright, might have been expected to retain control because of the small number of patriots there. But what they lacked in numbers they made up for in energy. When British warships arrived off the coast in June, 1775, a patriot named Joseph Habersham entered Wright's house and took him prisoner to prevent him from communicating with the ships. However, he soon escaped and fled to one of the ships. He failed in attempts to enlist the colony's Council in his plan to attack Savannah, and he soon sailed for England.

At Charleston, South Carolina, patriots on April 19, 1775, seized and opened official mail arriving from London. Included were docu-

184

ments disclosing British intentions to suppress all the colonies by force, not just Massachusetts. This discovery was promptly reported, via express riders, to the other colonies and to the Congress. The recently appointed royal governor, Lord William Campbell, finding the Assembly opposed to him, dissolved it, and began a fairly successful effort to recruit and organize loyalist regiments. However, by September, 1775, he also was forced to seek refuge on a British warship. Although control of the colony had by then passed into patriot hands, the loyalists were strong enough to make life in South Carolina truly a civil war for the next six years.

North Carolina's Governor Martin tried to bring some cannon to his house, but the Committee of Safety seized them. So he fled to Fort Johnson and declared himself ready to arm the colony's slaves. Before he could secure himself, though, Colonel Ashe collected militia to march against the fort. Martin quickly fled to a British warship, taking the fort's cannon and stores with him.

In Virginia, the House of Burgesses was replaced in March, 1775, by a Provincial Congress. On March 21st, they voted on the selection of delegates to the upcoming session of the Continental Congress. Then a proposal was made to shore up the colony's "much neglected" defenses. Sharing with Massachusetts a belief in a "well regulated militia" as the "only security of a free government," they debated two proposals: 1) adopting the New England custom of allowing the militia to elect their own officers, and 2) establishing local minuteman companies. These proposals were quickly opposed by conservatives as being premature. It was then that Patrick Henry rose from his chair and carried the day with his famous speech:

> Mr. President: It is natural for man to indulge in the illusions of hope. We are apt to shut our eyes against a painful truth, and listen to the song of that siren till she transforms us into beasts. Is this the part of wise men, engaged in a great and arduous struggle for liberty? ...
>
> Shall we acquire the means of effectual resistance by

lying supinely on our backs, and hugging the delusive phantom of hope, until our enemies shall have bound us hand and foot? Sir, we are not weak, if we make a proper use of those means which the God of nature hath placed in our power. Three millions of people, armed in the holy cause of Liberty, and in such a country as that which we possess are invincible by any force which our enemy can send against us. ...

If we were base enough to desire it, it is now too late to retire from the contest. There is no retreat but in submission and slavery! Our chains are forged. Their clanking may be heard on the plains of Boston! The war is inevitable - and let it come! I repeat it, sir, let it come!

It is vain, sir, to extenuate the matter. The gentlemen may cry, "Peace, peace!" but there is no peace. The war has actually begun! The next gale that sweeps from the north will bring to our ears the clash of resounding arms! Our brethren are already in the field! Why stand we here idle? What is it that the gentlemen wish? What would they have? Is life so dear or peace so sweet as to be purchased at the price of chains and slavery? Forbid it, Almighty God. I know not what course others may take, but as for me, give me liberty or give me death!

By April 20th, Virginia's royal governor, Lord Dunmore, felt it was time to act. He removed the locks from all the muskets in the arsenal, buried the powder, and set a spring gun in the locked arsenal building. When the illegal new legislature demanded the keys, he handed them over. A servant was instructed to open the door. The spring gun went off, shooting him. The shocked patriots discovered that the muskets had been tampered with and the powder taken. When they demanded its return, Dunmore agreed to pay for it, since wetness had damaged it. But he boldly declared that unless all rebel activities stopped, he would reduce Williamsburg to ashes, arm his own slaves, and "receive all others that will come to me, whom I shall declare free."

Governor Dunmore had seriously underestimated the extent of rebel support, and now his threat to arm the slaves had the effect of uniting white Virginians almost solidly against him. He was soon reporting to London, "My declaration that I would arm and set free such slaves as should assist me if I was attacked has stirred up fears in them which cannot easily subside." Led by Patrick Henry, 10,000 patriots marched to Williamsburg to seize the governor, but he fled to the safety of a British warship. From there, like the governors of Georgia, the Carolinas and New York, he would direct Tory military actions.

So, by the summer of 1775, all thirteen colonies were under patriot control, although most of the colonies south of New England would experience some degree of guerrilla warfare between patriots and loyalists off and on throughout the long war.

* * * * *

After over ten years of political conflict, the war had finally come, and many Americans were confident that Britain would not be able to win it. The country seemed too large to be conquered. And, if the war became a long affair, sheer numbers would be an advantage for the patriot side. For size of families, even "Irishmen are nothing to the Yankeys," although some said that the Yankee custom of bundling gave them an unfair advantage. Even the aristocratic wives of the Virginia planters were said to be "great breeders." An Englishman who visited the colonies in 1768 foretold the Americans' ability to multiply as being dangerous to the Empire:

> The good people are marrying each other as if they had not a day to live. I alledge it to be a plot against the State. And the ladies, who are all politicians in America, are determined to raise young Rebels to fight against old England.

By the fall of 1775, it would be pointed out as proof of the hopelessness of Britain's position that Britain, during the first six months of war, had already spent 3,000,000 pounds on the war, killing only 150 Yankees, while 60,000 new babies had been born in the colonies.

Young Alexander Hamilton of New York, in a rebuttal to a Tory essay, wrote: "There is a certain enthusiasm in liberty that makes human nature rise above itself in acts of bravery and heroism." The editor of the <u>Boston</u> <u>Gazette</u> wrote: "The glory of God is on our side and will fight for us, and this makes us as bold as lions." Charles Lee, a former British officer now living in Virginia, recalled that, during the late French and Indian War, the British Regulars were resplendent in uniform, "but fatal experience taught us that they knew not how to fight" in the American wilderness. Lee claimed that since then the quality of the British army had deteriorated still further - instead of hardening themselves for battle and "seeking for glory in the stained field," British officers sought only to "captivate the softer sex, and triumph over virtue."

With arguments like these, the conviction of American impregnability was firmly fixed in the minds of most patriots. This was the spirit of '75. According to one Tory, such was the Whigs' overconfidence, that you could tell them that British veterans would flee before "an undisciplined multitude of New England squirrel-hunters, and they would swallow it without a hiccough."

At the same time, Britons were confident that "one tolerable drubbing would quickly end the uprising. After all, had the army not put down numerous minor insurrections in England, Ireland and Scotland in recent years? They knew how to squelch the riotous ambitions of mobs; England alone averaged five major riots and countless minor ones each year. Being 3,000 miles away from the scenes of action, it was easy to believe that the American mobs were still being duped by a few agitators, and that there was no widespread commitment to resistance. Few believed that the middle and southern colonies would send their sons to die with New Englanders. Past wars against the

French and Indians had shown that the thirteen colonies would not co-operate to fight a common foe. The same behavior would be exhibited in this new war; the rebels would soon become disillusioned and realize it was futile to resist the mother country.

The English had belittled the courage and strength of Americans for so long that it was difficult to take colonial resistance seriously. Whatever courage the militia might possess was said to come from rum - without rum the New Englanders "could neither fight nor say their prayers." The "leveling" custom of New Englanders would surely be their curse during the coming war. According to one London newspaper, if an officer of this "motley rabble" gave a command, his men would likely answer, "I vow, Colonel, do it yourself."

British military policy would be based partly on two key assumptions: 1) the rebels would run at the sight of British Regulars, and 2) a large number of loyalists would rise up to assist the British army in putting down the rebellion. As early as June, 1775, at Bunker's Hill, the rebels would prove the first assumption false. And, likewise, the expectation that the "friends of government" in America would transform themselves into armed legions to assist the British army would not come true either. British army commanders, in their reports during the course of the war, would repeatedly point out the truth about these fallacies, but their superiors back home would persist in not believing it, right down to the end of the war.

CHAPTER ELEVEN
ARNOLD, ALLEN, AND THE
"GREEN MOUNTAIN BOYS"

"The captain came immediately to the door with his breeches in his hand, when I ordered him to deliver to me the fort instantly; who asked me by what authority I demanded it. I answered 'In the name of the great Jehovah and the Continental Congress.'"

- Ethan Allen

The vital strategic position in eighteenth century North American warfare was the water passage from New York City due north to Canada, via the Hudson River, Lakes George and Champlain, and then the Richelieu River, which flowed into the St. Lawrence River. Serving as the main artery of Canada, the wide St. Lawrence originated in the Great Lakes and flowed past Canada's principal towns of Montreal and Quebec, before finally emptying into the Atlantic Ocean. For decades, France and England had transported armies along this water route to attack each other. Many New England Yankees and French Canadian habitants had lost their lives fighting to either capture or hold some fort along this route. The most important of the forts were Ticonderoga, on Lake Champlain, and Quebec, on the St. Lawrence.

"Ticonderoga" was an Iroquois word meaning "place between the big waters," since it separated the northern end of Lake George and the southern tail of Lake Champlain. Located on a rise of land overlooking Champlain's narrow tail and a stream connecting the lakes, Fort Ticonderoga was described as the military "key to the continent."

In eighteenth century warfare, the ability to transport armies by water instead of land was paramount. Now that war had broken out between Britain and her colonies, continued British occupation of "Fort Ti" and the lesser fortifications north of it would provide an easy invasion route to New York and western New England. On February 13, 1775, the Massachusetts Provincial Congress stated that it was "the manifest design of Administration to engage and secure the Canadians and remote tribes of Indians, for the purpose of harassing and destroying these Colonies and reducing them to a state of slavery." On that same day, it requested the Boston Committee of Correspondence "to establish intimate correspondence and connection with the inhabitants of the Province of Quebec."

John Brown, a lawyer from Pittsfield, was appointed the committee's agent for this mission. He went north, and in March wrote to Sam Adams from Montreal: "One thing I must mention to be kept as a profound secret, the fort at Ticonderogo must be seized as soon as possible, should hostilities be committed by the King's troops." Patriot control of this key fort would inhibit, or at least put an obstacle in the way of, any British attempts to invade New York and New England by way of the lakes and the Hudson River. Control of the Hudson, along with the British navy's blockade of the coast, could isolate the rebellious New Englanders, making it easier for Britain to convince the other, less zealous colonies to give up their resistance to Parliament.

In April, 1775, there were only a few hundred Regulars in all of Canada, spread out at posts from the Great Lakes to the Atlantic. Canada's governor, General Guy Carleton, had since 1767 repeatedly requested the restoration and ample garrisoning of the Champlain forts, in case the colonists' conflict with Britain should reach the point of open rebellion. Finally, in the fall of 1774, General Gage at Boston received orders from London for the forts to be "put into a proper state of defence." But Gage felt that he could not spare any of his troops from Boston, so he did not send any to reinforce the garrisons at Ticonderoga and Crown Point.

Six months later, on the day of Lexington and Concord, Gage sent a letter to Carleton suggesting he send some of his troops stationed in Canada to reinforce the Champlain forts. This letter would not be received by Governor Carleton until the middle of May. By then, events would have altered the situation dramatically. However, as early as March, 1775, Gage sent a letter to the commander at Ticonderoga, warning him to prepare for trouble in the shape of "disorderly people in arms coming to the fort and makeing enquirys of its situation, and [the] strength of the garrison."

Down in New Haven, Connecticut, the Sons of Liberty for some time had been formed into a militia company (the Governor's Foot Guard, still active today) by their leader, Benedict Arnold, a prosperous 34-year-old trader. Arnold had bought them fancy uniforms and had been drilling them in preparation for the expected conflict with the British army. When word first arrived of the Lexington alarm, the selectmen met and resolved that New Haven would remain neutral. However, Benedict Arnold and the 50 men of his company, newly augmented by several Yale students, were determined to march for Cambridge to support the patriot cause. But first, they needed a supply of gunpowder, so Arnold demanded the keys to the powder magazine. "This is colony property," selectman Colonel David Wooster told Arnold. "We cannot give it up without regular orders from those in authority."

"Regular orders be damned," Arnold shouted back. "Our friends and neighbors are being mowed down by redcoats. Give us the powder or we will take it." After objecting once more, Wooster was told by Arnold that he would tear the doors off and take what his men needed. Arnold declared, "None but Almighty God shall prevent my marching!" Wooster handed over the keys, and the company set out to meet the British.

On the way, Arnold met Colonel Samuel Parsons, who was just returning from Cambridge to recruit more men. Parsons expressed his concern about the patriots' lack of cannon. Arnold told him that on his frequent trips to Canada, to trade in horses and other merchandise, he had become familiar with Fort Ti's situation. He informed Parsons that he'd heard the fort contained about 80 iron cannon, 20 made of brass, and 10 or 12 mortars, plus large quantities of muskets, powder, lead and flints. And the fort was reportedly "in a ruinous condition and has not more than fifty men at the most," many of them too ill to fight, having received crippling wounds during the late French war. Crown Point was said to be in a similar situation.

Arnold continued on to Cambridge, where he discussed the Champlain forts with Dr. Joseph Warren, who was overseeing the blockade of Boston. Warren was intrigued by Arnold's ideas for capturing the forts, and asked him to submit a written proposal to the Committee of Safety.

Benedict Arnold concluded his proposal by stating that Ticonderoga, in its present state, "could not hold out an hour against a vigorous onset." On May 3rd, in agreement with its military commander, General Artemas Ward, the Massachusetts Committee of Safety issued Arnold a provisional commission as a colonel on "a secret service," the provision being that he recruit the necessary forces, "not exceeding 400 men," in western Massachusetts. He was instructed to capture the forts, leave garrisons to hold them, and then return to Cambridge with the majority of its cannon and other ordnance.

When he reached Stockbridge, in western Massachusetts, Arnold learned to his astonishment that his was not the only expedition heading north. Samuel Parsons, after talking to Arnold, had secretly met with Silas Deane and Samuel Wyllys, of Connecticut's Committee of Safety. Without waiting to seek permission from the Assembly, they'd withdrawn 300 pounds from the colony's treasury, leaving a signed note that they had taken it. They gave the money to Noah Phelps and Bernard Romans on April 28th, to entice the so-called "Green Mountain Boys" to perform the raid. On their way north, Phelps and Romans halted at Salisbury, in northwestern Connecticut, where they located Heman Allen and sent him north to the Green Mountains to enlist the services of his brother, Ethan Allen, a leader of the Green Mountain Boys.

In 1775, the area composing what is now Vermont was a sparsely settled wilderness known as the New Hampshire Grants. Claimed also by the colony of New York, it had within the last ten or twelve years been settled by independent minded pioneers from New England, mainly Connecticut. They had purchased titles to their lands from the New Hampshire government, and named their frontier village of Bennington after Governor Benning Wentworth. During the 1770s, these pioneers became engaged in an increasingly heated dispute with authorities from New York, who were trying to evict them from what New York's government considered New York land.

These dirt farmers and husbandmen were led by the Allen brothers, a cousin named Seth Warner, and two other rough and ready frontiersmen, Remember Baker and Peleg Sunderland. It was Sunderland who had guided John Brown on his spy mission to Canada.

Ethan Allen was the most prominent of these leaders, and claimed to be the "colonel" of the local militia, known as the "Green Mountain Boys." Originally from Cornwall and Salisbury, Allen was attracted to the Grants by the opportunity for land speculation. Unlike the short, sophisticated Benedict Arnold, Ethan Allen was a man of backwoods manners and unusual height (six and a half feet). Like another tall backwoods hero of a later day named Lincoln, Allen was broad shouldered, lean and strong. His short temper and fondness for profanity ("the best goddamned cusser this side of hell!") had on occasion led to brushes with the law in puritan-minded Connecticut. There, and in the Grants, he was known widely for his boasting, his courage, and the ability to consume large numbers of "stonewalls" at one sitting. (A "stonewall was a powerful drink, made of the hardest possible cider, liberally laced with rum. It fortified a man so that he could then go out and build those walls of heavy stones so common in New England.)

When the dispute between New York and the Green Mountain people had its day in court at Albany, the settlers chose Ethan Allen to represent them and defend their property rights. Although lacking in formal schooling, he was a self-educated man and skilled at using words to persuade people to his way of thinking. However, he could not persuade the judge, Robert Livingston, who himself owned a New York title to 35,000 acres of the disputed land. Allen later recalled the outcome of the trial:

The plaintiffs appearing in great state and magnificence, which, together with their junto of land thieves, made a brilliant appearance; but the defendants appearing but in ordinary fashion [homespun], having been greatly fatigued by hard labor wrought on the disputed premises, and their cash much exhausted, made a very disproportionate figure at court. Interest, conviction, and grandeur being all on one side, easily turned the scale against the honest defendant.

Judge Livingston ordered the settlers to vacate. Allen, on his way out of the courtroom, gave notice to the judge: "The gods of the valleys are not the gods of the hills." With that warning, the "war" was on. The settlers refusing to leave, New York first tried sending tax collectors to the Grants, where they were abused by Allen and his followers and sent home empty-handed. One New York justice of the peace, Benjamin Hough, received 200 lashes across his naked back before he was sent home. According to Allen, the Boys had "seized their magistrates, and chastised them with the whips of the wilderness, the growth of the land they coveted."

Allen and his followers were not content to simply resist New York authorities. They also wanted New York settlers to go home, as well. Allen called on the home of a "Yorker" settler one day to inform him that his house would be offered up "as a burnt sacrifice to the gods of the woods;" soon only ashes would remain of the dwelling. Other New York settlers received the same treatment.

In 1774, the New York Assembly passed the Act of Outlawry, commanding Ethan Allen, Seth Warner, and six others to surrender to New York authorities, or else be captured and suffer death without trial or benefit of clergy. Allen responded in print, calling the act "replete with malicious turpitude!" and vowing that "immediate death" would be the fate of whoever tried to arrest them.

New York then sent sheriffs to arrest the leaders. The sheriffs caught Remember Baker, wounded and arrested him, then headed back toward Albany. But Baker's friends tracked the posse and rescued him by force en route. Fortunately, no one was killed. It was at this time that the settlers obtained their name, Green Mountain Boys, when New York's Governor Cadwallader Colden declared he would drive that "rag-tail mob back into the Green Mountains." Now, in the spring of 1775, the conflict would be temporarily put aside so both sides could concentrate on a larger conflict - actual war with Britain.

When John Brown, patriot agent in Canada, had suggested to Sam Adams the capture of Fort Ti, he added, "The people on N. Hampshire Grants are the most proper persons for this jobb." Connecticut's Parsons, Deane and Wyllys had come to the same conclusion on April 28th, when they sent Phelps and Romans to find Ethan Allen. The next day, they sent forth Captain Edward Mott, with five others, to follow and join up with the expedition.

Captain Mott kept a journal during the expedition. His writing illustrates the character of the men, intent on safeguarding their homes from the threat of British and Indian raids emanating from Fort Ti. We pick up Mott's journal on May 1st, in northwestern Connecticut, heading north:

> Having augmented our company to the number of sixteen in the whole, we concluded it was not best to add any more, as we meant to keep our business a secret till we came to the new settlements on the Grants.
>
> We arrived at Mr. Dewey's in Sheffield and there we sent off Mr. Jer. Halsey and Capt. John Stephens to go to Albany in order to discover the temper of the people in that place, and to return and inform us as soon as possible. That night we arrived at Col. Easton's in Pittsfield, where we fell in company with John Brown, Esq. who had been at Canada and Ticonderoga about a month before. He advised us that as there was a great scarcity of provisions in the Grants, and as the people were gener-

ally poor, it would be difficult to get a sufficient number of men there; therefore we had better raise a number of men sooner.

We then concluded for me to go with Col. Easton to Jericho and Williamstown, to raise men, and the rest of us to go forward to Bennington and see if they could purchase provisions there. We raised 24 men in Jericho and 15 in Williamstown, and got them equipped ready to march. Then Col. Easton and I set out for Bennington.

That evening we met with an express from our people [that had gone ahead] informing us that they had seen a man directly from Ticonderoga, and that he informed them that they were reinforced at Ticonderoga and were repairing the garrison and were every way on their guard; therefore it was best for us to dismiss the men we had raised and proceed no further, as we should not succeed. I asked who the man was, where he belonged and where he was going, but could get no account; on which I ordered that the men should not be dismissed but that we should proceed.

The next day I arrived at Bennington. There overtook our people. I inquired why they sent back to me to dismiss the expedition when neither our men from Albany nor the reconnoitering pary were returned. They said they did not think that we should succeed. I told them that fellow they saw knew nothing about the garrison; that I had seen him since and had examined him strictly, and that he was a lying fellow and had not been at the fort. I told them with the two hundred men that we proposed to raise I was not afraid to go; and that the accounts we had would not do to go back with and tell in Hartford.

While on this discourse, Mr. Halsey and Stephens came back from Albany and both agreed with me that it was best to go forward; after which Mr. Halsey and Mr. Bull both declared that they would not go back for no story, till they had seen the fort themselves. ...

Then we proceeded to raise the men as fast as possible, and sent forward men on whom we could depend, to waylay the roads ... and that all who were passing towards those garrisons from us should be stopped, so that no intelligence should go from us to the garrison. And on Sunday night, the seventh of May, we all arrived at Cassel Town [Castleton], the place where we had appointed for the men all to meet; and on Monday the 8th of May we resolved that a party of thirty men, under the command of Capt. Herrick, should the next day in the afternoon take into custody Major Skene [the Tory] and his party and boats; and that the rest of the men, which consisted of about 140, should go through Shoreham to the Lake, opposite to Ticonderoga; and that a part of the men that went to Skenesborough [present day Whitehall, New York] should, in the night following, go down the Lake to Ticonderoga.

We also sent Capt. Douglas to go to Crown Point and see if he could not agree with his brother-in-law, who lived there, to hire the King's boats on some stratagem, and send up the Lake from there to assist in carrying over our men. It was further agreed that Col. Ethan Allen should have the command of the party that should go against Ticonderoga.

When Benedict Arnold had learned, in Stockbridge, about the Connecticut expedition, he had left the recruiting to his subordinates and, with only a servant, headed north as fast as his horse could take him. Arnold and his servant arrived at Castleton, a hamlet of 20 houses, in the evening of May 8th, but Ethan Allen had gone ahead that morning to oversee preparations at Shoreham, on the Grants side of the lake, across from Ticonderoga. Mott, at Castleton with his Connecticut recruits and most of Allen's Boys, continues his account:

> In the evening Col. Arnold came to us with his orders
> and demanded the command of our people, as he said
> we had no proper orders. We told him we could not
> surrender the command to him, as our people were
> raised on the condition that they would be commanded
> by their own officers. The next morning he proceeded
> forward to overtake Col. Allen.

Arnold reached Shoreham and, in a meadow near the shore but sheltered from the fort's view, he found the Green Mountain Boys and the men that Mott and Phelps had recruited on their way north. Arnold's own recruits were still in Massachusetts, so he had to contend with Allen alone. One of the officers relates what happened when the smartly uniformed, somewhat aristocratic Benedict Arnold came face to face with the rough backwoodsman, Ethan Allen, seeking the same glory of conquest.

> We were shockingly surprised when Colonel Arnold
> presumed to contend for command of those forces that
> we had raised, who we had assured should go under the
> command of their own officers, and be paid and main-
> tained by the Colony of Connecticut. Mr. Arnold, after
> we had generously told him our whole plan, strenuously
> contended and insisted that he had a right to command
> them and all their officers, which bred such a mutiny
> among the soldiers [that] our men were for marching
> home, but were prevented by Colonel Allen and Colonel
> Easton, who told them that [Arnold] should not have the
> command of them.

After violent argument, including threats to Arnold's life, it was obvious that neither Allen nor Arnold would willingly allow the other to lead the expedition alone. So they agreed to march side by side, at the head of the force, but Arnold would not be allowed to issue any orders. Perhaps, lacking a written commission to perform the raid, Allen felt that the inclusion of Arnold (with his commission from Massachusetts) would legitimize the raid. As a gesture of good will, Allen gave Arnold a short blunderbuss, since he had arrived with only his sword and pistols.

Sufficient numbers of boats could not be found for the combined forces to cross the lake. The raiding party, that had been sent south earlier to seize the Tory Philip Skene's schooner at Skenesborough could not find the ship. They were further delayed by Skene's wine cellar, it being conveniently stocked with "choice liquors." By 3 a.m., the patriot forces at Shoreham had only two 33-foot scows. These would allow less than half the 200 or more men in the combined force to cross at once. Allen and Arnold huddled in the rain and considered postponing the attack until the next night, since daylight was fast approaching. But they decided not to take that chance - the British might be reinforced, or somehow learn of the attack before then.

So the first division crossed the lake, about a mile wide at this point, in ninety minutes. They disembarked about a quarter mile from the fort, and sent back the boat for the rest. Ethan Allen himself later recalled the details of the assault. Not surprisingly, he made no mention of Arnold.

> I landed eighty-three men near the garrison, and sent the boats back for the rear guard, commanded by Col. Seth Warner. But the day began to dawn, and I found myself under a necessity to attack the fort before the rear could cross the lake; and, as it was viewed hazardous, I harangued the officers and soldiers in the manner following:
>
> "Friends and fellow soldiers - You have, for a number of years past, been a scourge and terror to arbitrary

power. Your valour has been famed abroad, and acknowledged, as appears by the advice and orders to me
from the general assembly of Connecticut, to surprise
and take the garrison now before us. I now propose to
advance before you, and in person conduct you through
the wicket-gate; for we must this morning either quit our
pretensions to valour or possess ourselves of this fortress in a few minutes. And in as much as it is a
desperate attempt, which none but the bravest of men
dare undertake, I do not urge it on any contrary to his
will. You that will undertake voluntarily, poise your
firelocks."

The men being at this time drawn up in three ranks,
each poised his firelock. I ordered them to face to the
right; and, at the head of the centre file, marched them
immediately to the wicket-gate aforesaid, where I found
a centry posted, who instantly snapped his fusee at me.
[The gun did not discharge.] I ran immediately toward
him, and he retreated through the covered way into the
parade [ground] within the garrison, gave a haloo, and
ran under a bomb-proof.

Despite Gage's letter warning the fort's commandant to be on the
alert, there was only one sentry on duty, and he had been dozing when
Benedict Arnold and Ethan Allen had sprinted up to his post, each trying to outrace the other. The frost heaving action of many severe
winters had disrupted the stone and mortar walls, making it impossible
to close the gates completely. This meant there was just enough room
for one man to squeeze through at a time. So the attackers made their
way through the gates "Indian file." Ethan Allen continues his account:

My party, who followed me into the fort, I formed on
the parade in such a manner as to face the two barracks,

which faced each other. The garrison being asleep, except the centries, we gave three huzzas, which greatly surprised them. One of the centries made a pass at one of my officers with a charged bayonet, and slightly wounded him. My first thought was to kill him with my sword, but in an instant altered the design and fury of the blow to a slight cut on the side of the head; upon which he dropped his gun and asked quarter, which I readily granted him, and demanded of him the place where the commanding officer kept.

He shewed me a pair of stairs which led up to a second story, to which I immediately repaired, and ordered the commander, Capt. Delaplace, to come forth instantly or I would sacrifice the whole garrison; at which the captain came immediately to the door with his breeches in his hand, when I ordered him to deliver to me the fort instantly; who asked me by what authority I demanded it. I answered, "In the name of the great Jehovah and the Continental Congress."

When Allen's narrative was published, that one phrase secured his place among the legendary heroes of the Revolution. Actually, it was not Captain Delaplace who came to the door in his underwear, but rather his second in command, Lieutenant Feltham. Here is Lieutenant Feltham's account of what happened, which differs considerably from Ethan Allen's account:

I was awakened by numbers of shrieks and the words "No quarter, no quarter!" from a number of armed rabble. I jumped up, about which time I heard the noise continue in the area of the fort. I ran undressed to knock at Capt. Delaplace's door and to receive his orders or wake him. The door was fast. The room I lay in being close to Capt. Delaplace's, I stept back, put on my coat and waist coat and returned to his room, there being no possibility of getting to the men, as there were numbers of the rioters on the bastions of the wing of the fort on which the door of my room and back door of Capt. Delaplace's room led. With great difficulty, I got into his room, being pursued, from which there was a door down by stairs into the area of the fort. I asked Capt. Delaplace, who was now just up, what I should do, and offered to force my way if possible to our men.

On opening this door, the bottom of the stairs was filled with the rioters and many were forcing their way up, knowing the commanding officer lived there, as they had broke open the lower rooms where the officers live in winter and could not find them there. From the top of the stairs I endeavoured to make them hear me, but it was impossible. On making a signal not to come up the stairs, they stopped and proclaimed silence among themselves. I then addressed them, but in a stile not agreeable to them. I asked them a number of questions, expecting to amuse them till our people fired, which I must certainly own I thought would have been the case.

After asking them by what authority they entered His Majesty's fort, who were the leaders, what their intent, &c, &c, I was informed by one Ethan Allen and one Benedict Arnold that they had a joint command, Arnold informing me he came with instructions received from the congress at Cambridge, which he afterwards shewed. Mr. Allen told me his orders were from the province of Connecticut and that he must have immediate possession of the fort and all the effects of George the Third, insisting on this with a drawn sword over my head and numbers of his followers' firelocks presented at me, alledging I was commanding officer and to give up the fort, and if it was not complied with, or that there was a single gun fired in the fort, neither man, woman or child should be left alive in the fort. Mr. Arnold begged it in a genteel manner but without success. It was owing to him they were prevented getting into Capt. Delaplace's room, after they found I did not command. ...

The plunder[ing] was most rigidly performed as to liquors, provisions, etc., whether belonging to His Majesty or private property.

For "the refreshment of the fatigued soldiary," Allen let his men empty 90 gallons of rum from Captain Delaplace's stock. (Allen gave Delaplace a receipt, and he was later reimbursed by Connecticut.) Soon the reserve came across the lake and joined in the celebration. The victors, all except the highly disapproving Arnold, were blissfully "in liquor," having "tossed about the flowing bowl," as Allen expressed it. He sent a letter to the "Massachusetts Provential Congress":

To inform you with pleasure unfelt before, by the order of the Colony of Connecticut [we] took the Fortress of Ticonderoga by storm. Not only in council but in the assault the soldiary behaved with such resisless fury that they so terrified the Kings troops that they durst not fire.

The fabled fort, which an army of 11,000 Americans and British had tried and failed to capture in 1758, had now fallen without a shot being fired. The smaller fort at Crown Point also was taken by Ethan Allen's men, as he explains:

Col. Warner, with the rear guard, crossed the lake and joined me early in the morning, whom I sent off without the loss of time, with about one hundred men, to take possession of Crown Point, which was garrisoned with a serjeant and twelve men; which he took possession of, also upwards of one hundred pieces of cannon.

The next day, Arnold wrote a letter to Dr. Warren, suggesting his Massachusetts Committee of Safety send someone else to take over. Arnold tried in vain to bring order to the chaos at the forts, resisted by the Connecticut men almost as much as by the independent minded Green Mountain Boys. Benedict Arnold explains in his letter:

> There is here at present near one hundred men, who are in the greatest confusion and anarchy, destroying and plundering private property. There is not the least regularity among the troops, but every thing is governed by whim and caprice - the soldiers threatening to leave the garrison on the least affront. Most of them must return home soon, as their families are suffering. Under our present situation, I believe one hundred men would re-take the fortress, and there seems no prospect of things being in a better situation.
>
> I have therefore thought proper to send an express to you of the state of affairs, not doubting you will take the matter into your serious consideration and order a number of troops to join those I have coming on here; or that you will appoint some other person to take the command of them and this place, as you shall think most proper. Colonel Allen is a proper man to head his own wild people, but entirely unacquainted with military service; and as I am the only person who has been legally authorized to take possession of this place, I am determined to insist on my right, and I think it my duty to remain here against all opposition until I have farther orders.
>
> I cannot comply with your orders in regard to the cannon, etc., for want of men. I have wrote to the Governor and General Assembly of Connecticut, advising them of my appointment and giving them an exact detail

of matters as they stand at present.

Two days later, on May 13th, Arnold was able to send off a more cheerful letter, since his own recruits were starting to arrive. "I expect," he wrote, "more every minute. Mr. Allen's party is decreasing, and the dispute between us subsiding." The next day he reported "being joined by Captains [John] Brown and [Eleazar] Oswald, with fifty men enlisted on the road, they having taken possession of a small schooner at Skenesborough; we immediately proceeded on our way for St. Johns" to capture the British sloop there.

Arnold and Allen jointly set out for "St. Johns" (St. Jean), on the Richelieu River, just beyond the northern end of the lake. It did not bother either of them that St. Johns was in Canadian territory. Allen's Boys set out in bateaux (oversized rowboats, each equipped with a sail), while Arnold, being the only experienced sea captain available, took command of the schooner confiscated from the Tory Skene. Having more sail than the bateaux, Arnold quickly outdistanced Allen's division. But Arnold did not sail all the way to St. Johns, for the winds shifted direction. Determined to go on, Arnold had the schooner's two longboats lowered and, with just 35 men, rowed the remaining 30 miles. One of these men recorded their arrival at St. Johns:

> After rowing hard all night, we arrived within half a mile of the place at sunrise, sent a man to bring us information, and in a small creek infested with numberless swarms of gnats and musquetoes, waited with impatience for his return. The man returning, informed us they were unapprised of our coming.

In fact, according to one Canadian, they had not yet heard about "the taking of Tiyondarogo or other disturbances abt. Boston." Continuing with the same account:

We directly pushed for shore, and landed at about sixty rods distance from the barracks. The British had their arms, but upon our briskly marching up in their faces, they retired within the barracks, left their arms, and resigned themselves into our hands. We took fourteen prisoners, fourteen stands of arms, and small stores. We also took the King's sloop, two fine brass field-pieces, and four boats. We destroyed five boats more, lest they should be made use against us.

It was fortunate for the Americans that Arnold had pushed on to St. Johns, instead of waiting for the winds to shift back to a favorable direction. Just the day before, Governor Carleton received orders from General Gage to send troops to the Champlain forts. These reinforcements were now on their way to St. Johns, as Arnold relates:

The [sloop's] captain was gone to Montreal, and hourly expected with a large detachment for Ticonderoga [and] a number of guns and carriages for the sloop, which was just fixed for sailing. Add to this, there was a captain of forty men at Chambly, twelve miles distant from St. Johns, who was expected there every minute with his party; so that it seems to be a mere interposition of Providence that we arrived at so fortunate an hour.

Setting out to return to Ticonderoga, Arnold met Allen's bateaux party, still rowing northward. Ethan Allen wrote that Arnold

saluted me with a discharge of cannon, which I returned with a volley of small arms. This being repeated three times, I went on board the sloop with my party, where several loyal Congress healths were drank.

Not to be outdone by Arnold, nor call an end to the campaign so soon, Allen thirsted for more action. Benedict Arnold explains, in a letter to Dr. Joseph Warren:

> I supplied him with provisions, his men being in a starving condition. He informed me of his intention of proceeding on to St. Johns and keeping possession there. It appeared to me a wild, impracticable scheme, and of no consequence, so long as we are masters of the lake. ... [Allen] arrived with his party at St. Johns, and hearing of a detachment of men on the road from Montreal, laid in ambush for them.

According to Daniel Claus, Canadian Superintendent of Indians, a Regular from the fort had "made his escape to Montreal and carried the news" of Arnold taking the fort. The British officer in Montreal immediately

> sent off a party with a field piece to St. Johns, and would have surprized the Rebels and taken them prisoners had not one Benton a merchant of Montreal got to St. Johns before the party and apprized them of it.

In Benedict Arnold's report, he claimed that Ethan Allen's men were awakened before dawn the next morning by Regulars firing at them, and were forced to make "a precipitate retreat." Claus states that Allen's men were already in their boats and were able to make their escape, "being luckily favored with a fair wind to carry them over the Lake to Tiyondarogo."

When Ethan Allen and a remnant of his force finally made it back to Ticonderoga, they found Arnold firmly in charge. Learning that British Regulars were on their way south (at least as far as St. Johns), Arnold set his men to work strengthening Crown Point. The carpenters and shipwrights, whom Arnold had set aides to recruiting in Connecticut as soon as he received his commission three weeks before, had now arrived. Arnold put them to work building carriages, to transport the fort's big guns, and bateaux for transporting the troops. And he sent another messenger to Cambridge, once again requesting more men and supplies. "You may depend, gentlemen, these places will not be given up unless we are overpowered by numbers, or deserted by Providence, which has hitherto supported us."

By early June, Arnold was sailing north again, on the verge of attacking St. Johns, which by now had been reinforced and was under the personal command of Quebec's governor, General Guy Carleton. Arnold, without any authorization, was planning to capture the British forts of St. Johns and Chambly on the Richelieu River, then continue on and try to take Montreal and even Quebec before reinforcements could arrive from England. He knew that Carleton had only about 600 Regulars to defend all of Canada. But, on June 9th, he received a letter from the Massachusetts Provincial Congress instructing him to cease all offensive operations.

The Massachusetts Committee of Safety, temporarily headed by Dr. Benjamin Church (General Gage's spy) convinced the Provincial Congress to abandon all support for the Lake Champlain campaign. So they asked the legislature of Connecticut to assume responsibility for maintaining the lake forts. New troops soon arrived from Connecticut, including a Colonel Hinman to take over command. According to one of his men, Benedict Arnold "declared he would not be second in command to any person ... [but] after some time contemplating the matter, he resigned his post" and returned to Cambridge.

As for Ethan Allen and Seth Warner, they set out for Philadelphia to persuade Congress to adopt the Green Mountain Boys into the "Grand Army of the United Colonies." Within months, both Benedict Arnold and Ethan Allen would partake in a much more ambitious campaign - a full scale invasion of Canada, authorized by the Continental Congress. Through his own imprudence (an unauthorized attempt to capture Montreal), Ethan Allen would be captured and sent to a prison in England. After his exchange in 1777, he would publish an account of his adventures that would increase his fame and educate the people about the sad plight of American prisoners of war.

Benedict Arnold would go on to become America's most competent field general. Sadly, though, history would remember him for his decision in 1780 to desert the cause and sell his services to the British.

Though the war had just started in the spring of 1775, the patriots, acting virtually on their own, without any military organization supporting them, had boldly seized two enemy forts, and secured for the time being the most strategic military route on the continent. The northern frontier was now in patriot hands, and the way was open for an invasion of Canada.

British attempts to recapture those Lake Champlain forts and push south to Albany, to control the Hudson River and isolate New England from the other colonies, would be a major part of Britain's efforts to win the war in both the 1776 and 1777 campaigns. Their final attempt would end in the surrender of General Burgoyne's entire army at Saratoga, New York, in October, 1777. It would be a turning point in the war, because that signal victory would finally convince the French King Louis XVI that it was worth the risk to openly ally his country with the Americans and declare war on the British Empire. Four years later, a combined French-American army would force the surrender of another British army at Yorktown, Virginia, finally convincing Parliament to end its support of King George III's war with his American colonists.

CHAPTER TWELVE
CONGRESS SEEKS PEACE THROUGH WAR
MAY - AUGUST 1775

"This will be the commencement of the decline of my reputation."

> *- George Washington, writing to Patrick Henry, after being appointed by the Congress as Commander-in-Chief*

The second Continental Congress convened as scheduled on May 10, 1775. By coincidence, it was the very day that Ticonderoga and Crown Point fell into American hands. This new session of Congress had only a few new faces, as most delegates were repeaters from the first Congress the previous fall.

Virginia's Peyton Randolph was again chosen by the delegates to serve as President of the Congress. However, within two weeks, the speakership of Virginia's House of Burgesses became vacant and Randolph chose to go home to accept that more important post. To replace him, the Congress chose the wealthy, vain Bostonian, John Hancock. As President, Hancock would have no more influence than any other delegate; his main duties would be to preside over that body while it was in session, and to serve as Congress's chief correspondent with the generals, governors and others. But Hancock, more concerned with titles and prestige than political influence, gloried in his new role.

Virginia replaced Peyton Randolph's delegate position with a 32-year-old lawyer named Thomas Jefferson. Jefferson had impressed people on both sides of the Atlantic the previous year with his pamphlet, *Summary View of the Rights of British America*. Randolph kept

Jefferson in the House of Burgesses long enough for him to write Virginia's rejection of Lord North's Conciliatory Offer, before releasing him to ride north to Philadelphia. Like John and Sam Adams, and his fellow Virginian Richard Henry Lee, Jefferson considered himself to be one of "the forward men" in Congress. When the time came to push for independence, a year later, they would lead the way. Jefferson, a tall, thin redhead, abhorred public speaking. He almost never spoke his mind during the debates in Carpenter's Hall (which would later be renamed Independence Hall). He contented himself with exercising persuasion in committee and with his eloquent and forceful pen.

Another newcomer was the extremely popular scientist, philosopher, and author of <u>Poor Richard's Almanack</u>, Pennsylvania's Benjamin Franklin, who had just arrived home from London four days before, and been unanimously elected by the legislature the next day to serve as one of that colony's delegates. Franklin was 70 years old now, and the most famous and respected American of his time, both at home and abroad.

Franklin had spent most of the past fifteen years in London, serving as "agent" (lobbyist) for several different colonies. There he had consistently declared his belief that compromise would bring Britain and her colonies back together. Indeed, he had expected to be chief negotiator for all the colonies in that reconciliation process. But then came Lexington and Concord, passage of the Fisheries Act, the King's decision to hire mercenaries, and his proclamation declaring all the colonies in a state of rebellion. Franklin soon abandoned all hope of a peaceful settlement and joined the radical faction desiring a complete break with Britain.

Some of the previous session's conservatives, most notably Joseph Galloway, had not returned to this second Continental Congress, having either moved to England or been voted out by their legislatures.

Now that the war had commenced, Congress could no longer be just a forum for debating political theories and drafting petitions of grievances, as the first session had been in the fall of 1774. This new Congress would, somewhat reluctantly, become a legislative body, and remain in session almost continuously for the next eight years while the country was at war. Although the majority of delegates were not yet ready to even consider debating independence, on the whole they were a slightly more militant group than their counterparts of the first Congress had been. Their predecessors' petitions had been ignored in London, blood had been shed on American soil, and evidence showed that Britain was determined to exert as much military force as necessary to subdue the colonies. So this new set of delegates was in the frame of mind now to demand that the expected reconciliation be on their own terms.

However, there were serious political differences between the moderate or conservative delegates and the more radical delegates. They disagreed as to what course Congress should pursue, and how far its actions should distance the colonies from the mother country. John Adams, for one, advocated the radical position. He later recalled the plan he had at the beginning of this new session, for how the Congress should proceed:

> We ought to recommend [that the colonies] institute governments for themselves; declare the colonies free, sovereign and independent states; and then inform Great Britain we were willing to enter into negotiations with them for the redress of all grievances, and a restoration of harmony between the two countries, upon permanent principles.

> I was also for informing Great Britain very frankly that, if the war should be continued, we were determined to seek alliances with France, Spain and any other power of Europe that would contract with us. That we ought immediately to adopt the army in Cambridge as a continental army, to appoint a General and all other officers, [and to] take upon ourselves the pay, subsistence, clothing, armor and munitions of the troops.

The first few days of the new session were spent reading corre-spondence from a colonial agent in London, who described the gov-ernment's rejection of the first Congress's *Declaration of Rights*. Next, the depositions taken at Lexington and Concord by a committee from the Massachusetts Provincial Congress were read aloud and or-dered to be published. Then came an official request from that body to have the army taken over by the Continental Congress "by appointing a generalissimo."

The debate over this request was dropped, however, when John Brown arrived with news of the capture of Ticonderoga and Crown Point. The delegates were stunned. The aggressive actions of those New England hotheads - Joseph Warren and Silas Deane - in authoriz-ing the expedition did not sit well with either the moderates or the conservatives. Both factions wanted the colonies to do nothing that would antagonize Britain and put the reconciliation in jeopardy. Even most of the radicals at the time felt that the colonies would inevitably make peace and remain in the empire.

Therefore, after a bitter debate, the majority resolved that, although the cannon and other stores at the Lake Champlain forts could be re-moved for use by the New England army, a complete inventory must first be taken "in order that they may be safely returned when the res-toration of the former harmony between Great Britain and these colonies, so ardently wished for by the latter, shall render it prudent."

That seemed reasonable, but then another resolution was passed, calling for the forts to be abandoned! This enraged the New England delegates, who had been using express couriers to keep their commit-tees back home informed of the debates. "Ticonderoga Deane" now told the Congress that the Connecticut Committee of Safety was pre-pared to send 1,000 militia to Lake Champlain to keep control of the captured forts, in defiance of the Continental Congress. This threat quickly led Congress to rescind the resolution for abandoning the forts.

Congress next considered a request for advice from New York, on what course of action that colony should take if British reinforcements were sent to Manhattan. Congress advised New York to allow them a peaceable landing, and to provision them according to the Quartering Act. But, in the same resolution, the colony was advised to "repel force with force," should the British take any aggressive action, such as constructing new fortifications or cutting off communications between the city and the countryside, as Gage had done at Boston.

The unusually hot month of May dragged on, and the short, stocky and balding John Adams became increasingly frustrated by Congress's reluctance to take bold steps. So far, it had only resolved that Connecticut should garrison the captured Champlain forts, New York should erect batteries on the Hudson River, all Americans should collect lead for bullets and saltpetre for making gunpowder, and the New England colonies should provide the troops surrounding Boston "with as much powder and other public stocks as they can possibly spare."

John Adams blew up in anger when the moderate John Dickinson, of Pennsylvania, proposed that Congress draft a new petition of grievances. Adams gave a long speech opposing the idea, after which Dickinson followed him into the courtyard to speak with him. Adams later recalled Dickinson's warning to him:

> "What is the reason, Mr. Adams, that you New Englanders oppose our measures of reconciliation? ... Look ye, if you don't concur with us in our pacific system, I and a number of us will break off from you in New England, and we will carry on the opposition ourselves in our own way."

Although infuriated by this threat, Adams was too shrewd to continue his opposition if it meant risking the support he needed and expected to eventually win from the moderates. So, the next day, he supported Dickinson's proposal for a petition. Two committees were appointed, one to draft a petition of grievances, the other to draft a declaration explaining why the colonies were in arms. Adams grumbled in his journal:

This measure of imbecility, the second petition to the King, embarassed every exertion of Congress, occasioned motions and debates without end ... In the mean time the New England army were left without munitions of war, without arms, clothing, pay. Every post brought me letters from my friends, urging in pathetic terms the impossiblility of keeping their men together without the assistance of Congress.

... [There is] a strange oscillation betweeen preparations for war and negociations for peace. We must have a petition to the King and a delicate proposal of negociation. This negociation I dread like death. But it must be proposed. We cant avoid it. Discord and total disunion would be the effect of a total refusal to petition and negociate.

Unlike his impatient cousin John, the older and politically more experienced Sam Adams realized that each step of the revolution must take place only when the mood of the people was ready. The majority of delegates in the spring of 1775 were concerned with finding a way to live harmoniously within the British Empire. The more patient Sam Adams noted that "the spirit of patriotism prevails among the members of this Congress, but from the necessity of things, business must be slower than one could wish."

Failing to receive an answer to his request for the appointment of a generalissimo, Dr. Warren drafted a formal petition to the Continental Congress from the Massachusetts Provincial Congress. It asked for two things: 1) advice on setting up a new, permanent government in the colony; and 2) that the Continental Congress take charge of the New England army blockading Boston. As soon as Warren's petition was read aloud on June 2nd, John Adams urged Congress to "recommend to the people of every colony to call conventions immediately, and set up governments of their own." However, Congress voted not to go that far, but to consider only the case of Massachusetts.

These requests forced upon Congress a question: Would it begin to act as a true continental legislature? A committee of five (none from New England) was appointed to consider the Massachusetts petition. One week later, the committee reported to the whole Congress, and their arguments carried the day. Congress resolved that, due to concerted attempts by both the British Parliament and General Gage to subvert the charter of the Colony of Massachusetts Bay,

> The Governor and Lieutenant Governor of that colony are to be considered as absent, and in order to conform to the charter, it be recommended to the Provincial Convention to write letters to the inhabitants, requesting them to choose such representatives, and that the Assembly when chosen exercise the powers of government until a Governor of His Majesty's appointment will consent to govern the Colony according to its charter.

Although this resolution only recommended formation of a temporary government, to last until the expected reconciliation, with its passage Congress had established a precedent, setting itself up as the central authority for the colonies.

Congress then took up the thorny second part of the request, adoption of the New England army. In drafting this appeal, Dr. Warren had played upon the traditional fear that Englishmen have always had of a standing army which could threaten civilian control of government. "We tremble at having an army (although consisting of our own countrymen) established here, without a civil power to provide for and control them." He was also aware that many people in the colonies to the south feared that Yankee radicals might attempt to rule the continent. Warren pointed this out in a letter to John Adams, the day after the petition was sent to Philadelphia:

If the southern colonies have any appehension from the northern colonies, they surely must now be for an establishment of civil government here; for as an army is now taking the field, it is obvious to everyone, if they are without control, a military government must certainly take its place.

By June 14th, Congress decided to establish a "Continental Army." It appointed a committee to draft the army's rules and regulations. The committee included two delegates with military experience: Virginia's George Washington, and New York's Philip Schuyler. This new army would include the New England army investing Boston, and the New York forces guarding points along the Hudson River, as well as several new companies of riflemen Congress was asking Pennsylvania, Maryland and Virginia to raise in their mountainous western counties.

Known for their superior marksmanship, these riflemen would be sent north to bolster the army outside Boston. John Adams observed, "They can kill with great exactness at 200 yards distance. They have sworn certain death to the Ministerial officers. May they perform their oath."

The common musket used by the British army and most Americans had a short barrel with a smooth bore, and was inaccurate beyond 50 yards. "Rifling" was a process, brought to Pennsylvania by German and Swiss gunsmiths, of machining spiral grooves in a barrel. The raised "lands" between the grooves squeezed the soft lead ball as it moved along and gave it a spin, which meant it would not wobble and tumble in the air as it sped toward the target. Accuracy was further enhanced by the use of a patch of greased cloth or leather to "seat" the ball on the powder charge, the patch creating a seal which prevented explosive gases from escaping and being wasted around the ball instead of behind it.

In August, as they marched north, the new rifle companies passed through towns where their appearance made a sensation. They were persuaded to perform exhibitions to amuse their audiences and instill in the people a confidence in their "grand American army." A correspondent for the <u>Pennsylvania Journal</u> witnessed such an exhibition:

These men have been bred in the woods to hardships and dangers from their infancy. They appear as if they were entirely unacquainted with, and had never felt, the passion of fear. With their rifles in their hands, they assume a kind of omnipotence over their enemies. One cannot much wonder at this, when we mention a fact which can be fully attested by several of the reputable persons who were eye-witnesses to it.

Two brothers in the company took a piece of board five inches broad and seven inches long, with a bit of white paper, about the size of a dollar, in the center; and while one of them supported this board perpendicularly between his knees, the other, at the distance of upwards of sixty yards, and without any kind of rest, shot eight bullets through it successively, and spared a brother's thigh! The spectators, appearing to be amazed at these feats, were told that upwards of fifty persons in the company could do the same thing; that there was not one who could not plug nineteen bullets out of twenty within an inch of the head of a tenpenny nail. Some of them proposed to stand with apples on their heads while others at the same distance undertook to shoot them off; but the people who saw the other experiments declined to be witnesses of this.

At night a great fire was kindled around a pole planted in the court house square. The company, with the captain at their head, all naked to the waist and painted like savages, indulged a vast concourse of people with a perfect exhibition of a war-dance, and all the maneuvers of Indians - holding council, going to war, circumventing their enemies by defiles, ambuscades, attacking, scalping, &c.

Now that Congress had established an army, it logically followed that it must appoint a general to lead that army. John Adams determined to nominate someone who was not a New Englander. In his autobiography, he claimed that at the time there was in Congress "a southern party against a northern and a jealousy against a New England army under command of a New England general." Connecticut delegate Eliphalet Dyer agreed it was "absolutely necessary in point of prudence" to select someone from outside New England to head this new "continental" army, since "it removes all jealousies, more firmly cements the southern to the northern, and takes away the fear of the former, lest an enterprising New England general, proving successful, might with his victorious army give law to the southern or western gentry."

John Adams was impressed with the economy of words, quiet patriotism, and imposing presence of the only delegate who wore a uniform while Congress was in session: George Washington. Eliphalet Dyer described the Virginian as "clever, and if anything to modest. He seems discreet and virtuous, no harum starum ranting swearing fellow, but sober, steady and calm." Washington had earlier stated that it was his "full intention to devote my life and fortune in the cause we are engaged in, if need be." An improbable story, but one believed at the time, held that "on hearing of the Boston Port Bill, Washington had offered to raise an army and lead one thousand men himself at his own expense."

Through the preceding years of crisis, Washington had established a reputation for patriotism that was noted for its moderation, contrasting with some of his fellow Virginian Burgesses, radical thinkers such as Patrick Henry and the brothers Richard Henry Lee and Francis Lightfoot Lee. Although Washington realized that the time had come for all "virtuous" men to take up the sword, he favored reconciliation, so the colonies could remain within the British Empire. Because of his status as a wealthy "gentleman planter" and his moderate politics, Washington's appointment to head the army was expected to influence the middle and southern colonies to support the formation of a truly continental army. His appointment would give the army a more conservative flavor, in contrast to its prior leadership by "Boston radicalism." The less egalitarian middle and southern colonies would rest easier, knowing that the New Englanders would be less likely to spread their philosophy of social leveling to the other troops.

On June 14th, John Adams suggested that a Commander-in-Chief be appointed, someone "among us and very well known to all of us, a gentleman whose skill and experience as an officer, whose independent fortune, great talents, and excellent character would command the approbation of all America; and unite the cordial exertions of all the colonies better than any other person." At that moment, Congress's vain president, John Hancock, smiled and readied himself to make a speech reluctantly declining the office. But then Adams finished his speech and named the man he was proposing for Commander-in-Chief: George Washington. As Washington left the room, so that his nomination could be debated, Hancock's broad smile quickly disappeared. John Adams later recalled observing Hancock at that moment:

> I never remarked a more sudden and striking change of countenance. Mortification and resentment were expressed as forcibly as his face could exhibit them. Mr. Samuel Adams seconded the motion, and that did not soften the President's physiognomy at all.

John Adams was both surprised and gratified that the nomination was seconded by his cousin Samuel, who "very rarely spoke in Congress." But they were not joined by the other delegates from Massachusetts - Robert Treat Paine and Thomas Cushing. Adams continues his account:

The subject came under debate, and several gentlemen declared themselves against the appointment of Mr. Washington, not on account of any personal objection against him, but because the army were all from New England, had a general of their own, appeared to be satisfied with him, and had proved themselves able to imprison the British army in Boston, which was all they expected or desired at that time. Mr. Pendleton of Virginia, and Mr. Sherman of Connecticut, were very explicit in declaring this opinion; Mr. Cushing and several others more faintly expressed their opposition, and their fears of discontents in the army and in New England. Mr. Paine expressed a great opinion of General Ward and a strong friendship for him, having been classmates at college.

The day's session ended without a vote being taken. John Adams spent the evening visiting those who had spoken against Washington, finally persuading them to withdraw their opposition. The next day, June 15th, the tall, 43-year-old Virginian was unanimously elected as "Commander-in-Chief of all the continental forces raised or to be raised for the defense of American liberties." On the 16th, Washington gave his acceptance speech:

Mr. President: Tho' I am truly sensible of the high honour done me in this appointment, yet I feel great distress from a consciousness that my ability and military experience may not be equal to the extensive and important trust. However, as the Congress desires, I will enter upon the momentous duty, and exert every power I possess in their service for the support of the glorious cause. I beg they will accept my most cordial thanks for this distinguished testimony of their approbation.

But lest some unlucky event should happen unfavourable to my reputation, I beg it may be remembered by every gentleman in the room, that I this day declare with the utmost sincerity, I do not think myself equal to the command I am honoured with.

As to pay, Sir, I beg leave to assure the Congress that as no pecuniary consideration could have tempted me to have accepted this arduous employment (at the expense of my domestic ease and happiness), I do not wish to make any profit from it: I will keep an exact account of my expenses; those I doubt not they will discharge, and that is all I desire.

Two days later, Washington wrote to his wife, Martha, to break the news as gently as he could:

You may believe me, my dear Patsy, when I assure you, in the most solemn manner that, so far from seeking this appointment, I have used every endeavor in my power to avoid it, not only from my unwillingness to part with you and the family, but from a consciousness of its being a trust too great for my capacity, and that I should enjoy more real happiness in one month with you at home than I have the most distant prospect of finding abroad, if my stay were to be seven times seven years. But as it has been a kind of destiny that has thrown me upon this service, I shall hope that my undertaking it is designed to answer some good purpose.

You might, and I suppose did perceive from the tenor of my letters, that I was apprehensive I could not avoid this appointment, as I did not pretend to intimate when I should return. That was the case. It was utterly out of my power to refuse this appointment, without exposing [my] character to such censures as would have reflected dishonor upon myself, and given pain to my friends.

This, I am sure, could not, and ought not, be pleasing to you, and must have lessened me considerably in my own esteem. I shall rely, therefore, confidently on that Providence which has heretofore preserved and been bountiful to me, not doubting but that I shall return safe to you in the fall. I shall feel no pain from the toil or the danger of the campaign; my unhappiness will flow from the uneasiness I know you will feel from being left alone. I therefore beg that you will summon your whole fortitude, and pass your time as agreeably as possible. Nothing will give me so much sincere satisfaction as to hear this, and to hear it from your pen.

Unfortunately, George Washington would not return to his dear Patsy "in the fall." Instead, he would be away from his home for eight long years. During some of the winters, though, his wife came to stay with him at headquarters. For much of the war, he transported with him a portable folding four poster bed. He needed a fairly comfortable bed because of his rheumatism, attacks of the "bloody flux" (dysentery), recurring toothaches, and other problems. Or perhaps he brought his own bed with him because of the unlikelihood of finding one long enough in the many houses in which he lived during the war. At a time when the average American man was five feet, eight inches tall, George Washington stood six feet, two and a half inches. The typical British soldier, because of poorer diet, stood only five feet, five inches.

Congress expected Washington to bring a semblance of order to the chaotic mob that was the New England army, and somehow turn it into an effective fighting force with the unenviable task of opposing the mightiest military power in the world. Perhaps this was too much to ask of any man. But Washington's character was widely known long before his appointment. As a teenager, he had spent parts of three years surveying the wilderness of the Ohio Valley. At 22, just before the start of the French and Indian War, he had been sent back into that wilderness by Virginia's governor to find the French commander near Lake Erie and tell him to depart from British soil. This was an assignment requiring not only courage, but the hardiness of a backwoodsman and the shrewdness of a diplomat.

During the French and Indian War, Washington rose to the rank of colonel in the Virginia militia, and distinguished himself at General Braddock's disastrous defeat by taking charge after Braddock was shot and leading a successful retreat away from the ravine where the French and Indians had sprung their ambush. Over the course of those war years, while in charge of Virginia's 350-mile frontier, he learned a lot about the militia's fickleness, as well as the deep rooted provincialism that made men from one region balk at aiding those from another. He also had to cope with shortages of food, powder and men. So, in June, 1775, he must have had some idea of the formidable task he was being asked to perform. He confided to Patrick Henry after his appointment, "This will be the commencement of the decline of my reputation."

As an experienced politician, George Washington also understood the legislative mind, an essential attribute for a commander who, countless times, would have to find ways to keep his ill-fed, inadequately clothed army in existence. During the Revolutionary War, he would correspond tirelessly with the Congress and the state governors. He would also have to cope with the incompetence, arrogance, and selfishness of subordinate officers. His capture might have meant the collapse of the struggle. Most historians agree that his leadership was the only thing that kept the Revolution going during the many desperate times.

During the war, Washington would lose most of his battles against his more skilled and better equipped British adversaries, but he would manage, through careful planning and British sloth, to retreat to safety numerous times, preventing the total destruction of his army. Eventually, his ability to keep his ragged forces from giving up or being annihilated in battle, together with a comparatively few victories, would lead to the wearing down of Britain's will to continue this costly war.

George Washington had the kind of temperament to withstand the temptation to take rash offensive actions that might, if unsuccessful, result in the capture of his own army. He knew that defensive war was the more appropriate strategy for his weaker, less trained army. He also realized that vigorous American operations would be foolhardy until such time as supplies could be organized and readily available. He would often be criticized for refusing to take offensive action, and at times would become exasperated by such criticism. In February, 1776, he would write:

> To have the eyes of the whole continent fixed, with anxious expectation of hearing of some great event, and to be restrained in every military operation for want of the necessary means of carrying it on, is not very pleasing.

Now that a Commander-in-Chief had been appointed, Congress set about commissioning subordinate officers. Since most of the present army blockading the British in Boston was from Massachusetts, that colony's Artemas Ward was chosen to be "first major general," ranking just below George Washington. Ward, 58, was described by General Charles Lee as "a fat old man" better suited for "church warden" than general. Within a year, Ward would resign due to poor health.

Many delegates wanted Virginia's Charles Lee as second in command. He was selected as "second major general," ranking just below Ward. A recent emigrant from England, the 43-year-old Lee was an intellectual and a student of military tactics. As an outspoken member of the British army, he had declared that it was not effective during the French and Indian War until the troops forgot everything they were taught by their officers. Lee brought badly needed organizational, tactical, and engineering skills to the infant army. During his first year in the American army, he would be praised by Dr. Benjamin Rush for "inspiring our citizens with military ideas and lessening in our soldiers their superstitious fears of the valor and discipline of the British army."

Lee had a reputation for being eccentric, impetuous, obnoxious and lacking manners. He was considered an "odd fish," a "strange animal," etc. Wherever he went, he offended the civilian leaders whose support the army desperately needed. Washington described Charles Lee as "the first officer in military knowledge and experience we have in the whole army. He is zealously attached to the cause, honest and well meaning, but rather fickle and violent, I fear, in his temper." John Adams admitted that "we must put up with ten thousand oddities in him on account of his abilities and his attachment to the rights of humanity." John and Sam Adams strongly urged his selection as a major general, perhaps because of his radical political views. In the fall of 1775, nearly six months before it would become an acceptable view, Lee would openly advocate a declaration of independence. An ugly man, Charles Lee was remembered by Alexander Milliner, a drummer boy attached to Washington's staff, as being

> a large man. He had a most enormous nose. One day a man met him and turned his nose away. "What do you do that for, you d----d rascal?" exclaimed Lee. "I was afraid our noses would meet," was his reply. Lee laughed and gave him a dollar.

The same drummer boy also recalled the unemotional Washington, who would often pat him on the head after playing "Reveille," and call him "my boy." "He was a good man, a beautiful man. He was always pleasant; never changed countenance, but wore the same in defeat and retreat as in victory." At times though, Washington had an explosive temper, which he worked hard to keep under control.

After Ward and Lee were appointed as major generals, Congress chose five brigadier generals, only to discover that, for political reasons, more must be appointed. As one Congressman put it, the colonies all "insist, with great justice and sound policy, on having a share of the general officers in some proportion to the quotas of troops they are to raise." So two additional major generals had to be appointed, and three more brigadier generals.

One of the two major generals was Philip Schuyler, a member of Congress who was a large landholder from Albany. Eliphalet Dyer viewed Schuyler's appointment as an attempt "to sweeten and keep up the spirit in that province." Showing the typical distrust that Connecticut men had for "Yorkers," Dyer resented the New York delegates' reluctance to commit their colony to the kind of war preparations Congress was now taking.

> Their cautious men are for saving for themselves and the province a safe retreat, if possible. We readily see they most carefully avoid taking any hand in these matters; therefore the more they are brought to move and apply, the more they will give us a stronger security for their future firmness in the general cause. About 12 hundred [Conn. troops] are ordered to York [Ticonderoga and Crown Point] for more reasons than one.

Because of Connecticut's hefty commitment in troops, and prompt and bountiful supplies of food to the army around Boston, the final major general would have to come from that colony. Israel Putnam was chosen over his two superior militia officers, David Wooster and Joseph Spencer. Although Wooster and Spencer were appointed brigadiers, they were mortified by this insult. Spencer left the army to go home, and only after much persuasion by Governor Trumbull did he agree to return and serve. Wooster flatly refused his commission, preferring to head up the home militia, rather than serve under Putnam.

For Putnam, the timing was perfect. He had just captured the country's attention by aggressively skirmishing with a British detachment on a foraging expedition to an island in Boston's harbor. Congressman Roger Sherman explained in a letter to Wooster that, "Gen. Putnam's fame was spread abroad, and especially his successful enterprise at Noddle's Island, the account of which had just arrived; it gave him the preference. His appointment was unanimous among the colonies." Silas Deane wrote that Putnam's "health has been the second or third [toast] at almost all our tables in this city." On the very day of his appointment, June 17th, "Old Put" was again in action, this time at a place called Bunker's Hill, outside Boston.

An authentic backwoods hero, this 57-year-old tavernkeeper from northeastern Connecticut had survived, among other exploits: capture and torture by Iroquois Indians, a shipwreck off the coast of Cuba, and a venture into a dark cave to kill a wolf that had been terrorizing his village. During the French and Indian War, he demonstrated his Yankee shrewdness when a British officer challenged him to a duel. As the recipient of the challenge, Israel Putnam was, of course, given his choice of weapons. He chose kegs of gunpowder. Though this was an unorthodox choice, honor would not allow the challenger to refuse. So Putnam selected two kegs, which were then rolled to an open spot of ground and attached with long fuses.

The two duelists each sat on his respective keg, and the fuses were lit by each man's second, as the crowd of British and American soldiers quickly scurried away to watch from a safe distance. The two barrels being close together, each man stared into the other's eyes and tried not to look at the burning fuses coming closer and closer. Finally, after a quick glance down at his fuse, the Briton, deciding he would rather be a live coward than one of two dead fools, jumped and ran. Putnam remained seated on his barrel until the fuses reached the inside of the kegs and, surprisingly, extinguished themselves. After waiting a sufficiently safe amount of time, each man's second ran over and opened his respective keg. Then, together they announced, to the delight of the bipartisan crowd, that both kegs were filled with onions!

Congress took other actions to prepare the colonies for war, such as establishing a hospital department for the army, to be headed by Boston's Dr. Benjamin Church (Congress had not yet found out that the good doctor was spying for General Gage). Congress also authorized creation of a new postal system, "for the speedy and secure conveyance of intelligence from one end of the continent to the other." It would be directed by Benjamin Franklin, and have stations from

Georgia to Maine (part of Massachusetts).

Reluctantly, due to a distressing lack of munitions, Congress was forced to relax the trade boycott a bit, so that the colonies would be allowed to export produce to the British West Indies in exchange for munitions. Efforts were made to keep word of this compromise out of the newspapers. In other Congressional actions, the various colonial legislatures were advised to strengthen their militia organizations, fortify their harbors, and establish Committees of Safety.

Congress not only endeavored to maintain civilian control over the army, but wanted this new army to be known for its humanitarian and moral code. The army's regulations would include punishments for such infractions as uttering "any profane oath," or behaving "indecently or irreverently at any place of divine worship." Except for a few serious crimes requiring the death penalty, the most severe punishment was limited to 39 lashes. A soldier found guilty by court-martial could appeal to the commander of his regiment or any general, in hopes of obtaining a pardon or a lessened sentence.

Washington felt that three things prompted men to perform their duty and not run away, while under fire from the enemy: bravery, hope of reward, and fear of punishment. Congress hoped that the third could adequately be replaced by the "spirit and confidence that so universally prevails throughout America, the best substitute for discipline." But experience would soon show that more than spirit was needed to build and maintain a disciplined army. Congress would be advised in 1776 that "thirty-nine lashes is so contemptible a punishment that it is very frequent" for a soldier being thus chastised "to offer to take as many more for a pint of rum." So the penalty for desertion would be increased that year to 100 lashes, and later to 200. Late in the war, Washington would feel it necessary to recommend it be set at 500 lashes, but his proposal would be defeated in Congress.

Looking to the frontier, Congress appointed commissioners "for the purpose of securing the neutrality of the Indians: one for the Six Nations and other tribes toward the north; a second for the Creeks or Cherokees towards the south; and a third for the intervening tribes towards the west." Because it considered alliances with "heathens" to be repugnant, Congress sought only their neutrality. A speech prepared for the chiefs ended with this summation:

> This is a family quarrel between us and old England. You Indians are not concerned in it. We don't wish you to take up the hatchet against the King's troops. We desire you to remain at home, and not join on either side, but keep the hatchet buried deep. What is it we have asked of you? Nothing but peace.

The tribes initially agreed to this, but the artifices and bountiful gifts of British agents, and the desire of young warriors to fight, would prove too strong for their neutrality to last long.

A proposal by Virginia's Richard Henry Lee, to open American ports to trade with all non-British nations, was defeated. John Adams angrily wrote: "We have had in contemplation a resolution to invite all nations to bring their commodities to market here, and like fools have lost it, for the present." The majority of the delegates felt such an action would ruin any chance for reconciliation, since it could be interpreted as a tacit declaration of independence.

Now that Congress had created an army, it must find some way of paying and provisioning it. The easiest way - simply printing money - was chosen, in the hopes that the people would honor its printed value, despite the lack of a hard currency to back it. On June 22nd, it was "Resolved, That a sum not exceeding two millions of Spanish milled dollars be emitted by the Congress in bills of credit for the defence of America." Each colony was to redeem its quota of these "continentals." Paul Revere was contracted to print them. During the course of the war, Congress would find it necessary to print more and more money to keep the war going. The new paper money depreciated slowly during the first three years of the war, the number of continentals needed to purchase one Spanish dollar's worth of gold rising from one in 1775 to eight in October, 1778. By January of 1781, however, inflation had jumped the figure to 100.

Revere found it difficult to obtain the quantities of copper necessary to make the plates from which to print the paper continentals, but even more difficult was procurement of the paper itself. He was forced to use other materials. The bills were sometimes so thick that the British scornfully called them "pasteboard currency." Often the printing press would run out of ink, resulting in blank bills. With the tremendous inflation, a common joke of the day was that, since everything seems to be going up in price, the blank bills would soon be worth more than the printed ones.

The depreciation of the continental currency partly explains why much of the army was shoeless, almost naked, and without food for long stretches of time. For example, while the American army was starving and freezing to death at Valley Forge, nearby farmers sold their crops and firewood to the British, who were offering hard money. A popular new derogatory phrase was "not worth a continental." By 1781, difficulties caused by the depreciation of the currency were so profound that they could be candidly reported by Congressman James Lovell:

> Foreign [French] troops are to garrison West Point because foreign troops <u>can</u> feed themselves and <u>are</u> paid. Our Quartermaster General has been obliged to sell some of his provision to enable himself to <u>transport</u> the rest to a skeliton of an army in want of the very pounds of meat or flour which he has been forced to part with.
>
> If you know of a compliance with one requisition of Congress, <u>in time and quantity</u>, do let me have it, that I may show it to the delegates, who cannot produce a single instance. We are in an uproar here about the money. Sailors with clubs parade in the streets instead of working for paper. The beer houses demand hard for a pot of drink.

The committee for drafting a petition to the King, of which John Dickinson was the principle member, presented its draft. Dickinson, whose famous *Letters from a Pennsylvania Farmer* seven years earlier had won him the admiration of all the Whigs, had by June, 1775, come under pressure from his wife and mother, both Tory sympathizers. Philadelphian Charles Thomson confided to John Adams that he had heard Dickinson's strong-minded mother tell her son, "Johnny, you will be hanged, your estate will be forfeited and confiscated, you will leave your excellent wife a widow and your charming children orphans, beggars and infamous." So Dickinson insisted on producing this one last petition of grievances to the King. According to Eliphalet Dyer, "the Farmer" had now become "not very highly esteemed in Congress." Indeed, John Adams referred to him as a "piddling genious" whose petition "has given a silly cast to our whole doings."

But Dickinson firmly believed that the King's ministers were responsible for the present armed conflict, and that the Congress should convince the King to rid himself of them. In Dickinson's words, "Why should nations meet with hostile eyes because villains and ideots have acted like villains and ideots." In debating the petition draft, he declared that prior petitions had met with rejection because they'd offended the dignity of either the King or Parliament. So, on July 5th, Congress approved, by a clear majority, Dickinson's new petition to King George III. The *Olive Branch Petition* was signed by the delegates as individuals, rather than as representatives of their respective colonies. It was carried to London by the loyalist, Richard Penn. The petition reaffirmed the colonists' loyalty to their sovereign King, and asked him to remove the army and to protect the colonies from Parliament until a reconciliation could be worked out. Thomas Jefferson noted:

> The disgust against this humility was general; and Mr. Dickinson's delight at its passage was the only circumstance which reconciled them to it. The vote being passed, although further observation on it was out of or-

der, he could not refrain from rising and expressing his satisfaction, and concluded by saying, "there is but one word, Mr. President, in the paper which I disapprove, and that is the word "Congress;" on which Ben Harrison rose and said, "There is but one word in the paper, Mr. President, of which I approve, and that is the word "Congress."

The petition was not well received in London, where it was denounced in the press as "an insult and mockery." As Englishmen conceived it, England could not possibly yield to the demands of an illegal congress without humiliating itself in the eyes of all Europeans and without sacrificing its sovereignty over the colonies. Richard Penn was frustrated in his attempts to have the petition presented to King George III. His ministers told Penn, "His Majesty will receive no petitions from a rebel body." In fact, by the time Congress's *Olive Branch Petition* reached London, King George III had already issued his *Proclamation of Rebellion*, declaring that a general rebellion existed in the colonies, and "utmost endeavours" should be made "to suppress such rebellion, and to bring the traitors to justice."

Congress drafted other documents, too, that summer, including one prepared by Thomas Jefferson and revised by Dickinson. It was intended to "be published by General Washington, at the camp before Boston." Titled a *Declaration of Reasons for Taking up Arms*, it presented a by now familiar history of grievances, then concluded:

> We are reduced to chusing between an unconditional submission to the tyranny of irritated ministers, or resistance by force. The latter is our choice. We have counted the cost of this contest, and find nothing so dreadful as voluntary slavery. Our cause is just. Our union is perfect. Our internal resources are great, and, if necessary, foreign assistance is undoubtedly attainable.
>
> With hearts fortified with these animating reflections,

we most solemnly, before God and the World, declare that the arms we have been compelled by our enemies to assume, we will, in defiance of every hazard, with unabating firmness and perseverence, employ for the preservation of our liberties; being with one mind resolved to dye free-men rather than live slaves.

Lest this declaration should disquiet the minds of our friends and fellow subjects in any part of the empire, we assure them that we mean not to dissolve that union which has so long and so happily subsisted between us, and which we sincerely wish to see restored. We have not raised armies with ambitious designs of separating from Great Britain, and establishing independent states.

Congress did not stop there, but went on during that summer to produce separate *Addresses* to the peoples of Great Britain, British West Indies, Ireland, Canada, and the Six Nations of the Iroquois Confederation, as well as a response to Lord North's Conciliatory Offer. Thomas Jefferson, having already written one for Virginia, was unanimously selected to do the same for "The Twelve United Colonies" (Georgia had not yet sent delegates). Jefferson's new document for the Congress would be similar to the one he had written for Virginia - a scathing rebuke of Lord North's offer, in which he declared that "the proposition is altogether unsatisfactory, because it imports only a suspension of mode, not a renunciation of the pretended right to tax us."

One document, or rather a rough draft, was not adopted: *Articles of Confederation and Perpetual Union*, authored by Benjamin Franklin. It was his own idea to prepare such an instrument. Although he probably knew the delegates and colonies were not ready for such a step, Franklin could not resist presenting it to Congress as food for thought. Copies were sent to the colonial legislatures, with the suggestion that it be viewed "as a subject which will be proposed to the Continental Congress at their next session," and with the expressed wish that the ideas put forth in the *Articles* "be dispassionately debated and approved or condemned" by the legislatures so their delegates will know how to act when and if it comes up for a vote in Congress.

Those few who were shown the draft agreed with Franklin that the delegates should be given a chance to "turn the subject in their minds" on the idea. So, on July 21st, he presented it to Congress, advising that it was being offered as a rough basis for preparation of a more perfect instrument, if and when one should become necessary. Franklin was not putting it up for debate, though, because some "were revolted at it" and, in Jefferson's words, would "suspect we had lost sight of reconciliation with Great Britain." Those who Jefferson characterized as "timid members" insisted that no mention of Franklin's *Articles* be made in the official journal of Congress, lest the British government find out and be alarmed. However, with so many loyalists in Congress, it was impossible to keep such information from the British; a copy soon found its way to London.

The delegates had a respite from their work when a humorous incident occurred. A loyalist from the Ticonderoga region, Major Philip Skene, had been in London, conferring with authorities, when the fort was taken by Ethan Allen and Benedict Arnold on May 10th. Skene's family had been seized and carried off to Connecticut to ensure his proper conduct when he returned. However, when he returned to America from England, he sailed directly to Philadelphia. He brought with him funds from the royal treasury, to bribe as many Congressmen as necessary into voting for acceptance of Lord North's conciliatory plan. Upon entering the Congressional chambers, Skene was promptly arrested, since Congress had been warned that he was "a dangerous partizan of Administration, charged with a power to influence the members of Congress by arguments drawn on the treasury." This was confirmed by an examination of his papers, which also included his appointment as "Governor of Ticonderoga, Crown Point, and the Lakes," and other commissions to serve as "Surveyor of his Majesty's Woods" and commander of a Canadian regiment of militia.

The members of Congress burst out laughing when these papers were read aloud. Pennsylvania's John Morton stated, "It has happened so that the said governor has no government to go to, the New England men having some time since taken possession of those important places. Now, John Adams added, "He must dispute for his government with Arnold and Allen." Skene was sent to Connecticut to join his family as "a prisoner under parole." Eliphalet Dyer wrote him a letter of introduction to the governor, explaining his arrest, and commenting:

> How amazingly was he chagrined. The dunce imagined he should have easy work to settle the whole controversy. I dare say he told the Ministry so and they fully believed him. It is amazing how they can be so reduced as to employ such a genius as this Major Skene, open, exposed, unguarded, and his abilitys but moderate.

On August 5th, after twelve hot, humid weeks, Congress recessed for four weeks. Since the beginning of its first session in September 1774, Congress had evolved from being a forum for debating political theories and writing petitions, to become a body that now effectively acted as a central government for a collection of estranged colonies forced into a war against the mightiest military power in the world. Despite the temporary frustration of having to spend valuable time creating more petitions, declarations and addresses, even John Adams would later admit that these documents "were necessary to give popularity to our cause, both at home and abroad." By this two-pronged strategy of waging war while seeking peace, Congress hoped to convince the King to oust Lord North and other hard-liners of his administration, and replace them with men such as Lord Chatham (William Pitt), who, when he heard the news of Lexington and Concord, exclaimed "I rejoice that America has resisted!"

Unfortunately, the Congressmen, like most Americans, did not realize that Lord North and the other members of King George III's inner circle were simply carrying out his wishes. Contrary to the popular American misconception that he was being duped, or at least strongly influenced by these men, the progressively harsher and more militaristic answers to "the American question" were the brainchild of the King himself. Only after his complete correspondence was made available to historians, several decades after the war, would the King's true role in Britain's loss of her colonies become known.

CHAPTER THIRTEEN
TIME TO BREAK OUT OF BOSTON
JUNE 1775

"What! Ten thousand peasants keep five thousand King's troops shut up? Well, let us get in, and we'll soon find elbow room!"

> *- John Burgoyne, one of three generals from England arriving in Boston Harbor with reinforcements*

In Boston, General Gage and his army had been penned up inside the peninsular town ever since the night of April 19th, when his soldiers had stumbled home from their disastrous expedition to Concord. Within a few days, approximately 17,000 Yankees from all parts of New England arrived and took up positions in a semi-circle of earthworks surrounding Boston. In their haste to "meet the British," the Yankee farmers, shopkeepers, and artisans that made up the militia had, in many cases, rushed from home without stopping to pack food, clothing or bedding. Much to their surprise, they soon realized that Gage was unwilling to venture out of Boston again, and the Yankee commander, General Artemas Ward, was equally unwilling to launch an attack.

Therefore, with the emergency apparently over, and responsibilities calling at home, the Yankees began leaving. James Warren wrote to John Adams that "the army is in a shifting, fluctuating state, continually coming and going." It appeared that Thomas Hutchinson would be right in his prediction that they "must soon disperse, as it is the season for sowing their Indian corn." These farmers were willing to die in defense of their liberties, but they saw no reason to stay and do nothing but dig trenches.

To feed and shelter those who stayed, to keep as many of them as possible in camp, to repel the expected attack from Gage, and to somehow make an army out of this confused mass of volunteers were formidable tasks. Fortunately, General Ward was ably assisted by the Massachusetts Committee of Safety's energetic and resourceful Doctor Joseph Warren. Warren rode back and forth from his Cambridge headquarters to Watertown, five miles to the west, where he also served as President of the Massachusetts Provincial Congress. But, despite the best efforts of Ward and Warren, their "army" was accurately described by one of its own as "no better than a mob."

Dr. Warren attempted to strike a balance between the overly cautious Ward and his subordinate, Connecticut's impatient General Israel Putnam. After one of Putnam's characteristically rash actions - a foraging expedition that resulted in a skirmish of little significance but tremendous waste of precious powder and ball - Warren called Putnam aside and told him, "I admire your spirit, and respect General Ward's prudence. We shall need them both, and one must temper the other."

Inside Boston, the Regulars and townspeople fully expected the rebels to attack the city. Two hundred Tories had offered their services to Gage on April 19th. Gage provided them with arms, and under the direction of Tory Timothy Ruggles, formed the Loyal Associated Volunteers. Although they trained and drilled vigorously, they were never utilized by the British commanders. They were not the first loyalist troops in Massachusetts. The previous November, Colonel Thomas Gilbert had organized Tories in Freetown with the help of 300 muskets received on request from Gage. However, on April 9th, they were taken prisoner by Whigs from nearby Taunton while Gilbert was out of town. Gage, preoccupied with his own plans, did not come to their rescue.

Boston's population had changed much in recent months. Thousands of Whigs had moved to the countryside. Remaining were only those financially unable to risk leaving their homes and businesses, and those too stubborn to depart. One who decided to stay reported that "the soldiers plunder everyones house and store who leaves town." Across the river, Charlestown was now completely deserted, as its former inhabitants expected it to be destroyed in the coming battle. Just as Whigs fled from Boston, so also did Tories flock into town from the countryside, leaving their homes and shops to be plundered by local Sons of Liberty, or confiscated by their Committees of Safety.

Massachusetts was not the only colony where Tories led "a devil of a life." In parts of every colony, especially New England and Virginia, life was hot for them. Some escaped persecution by signing oaths of allegiance to the principles of American liberties, and keeping their opinions to themselves. Others chose or were forced to flee - some to England, where, to their surprise, the depression caused by the cessation of trade with the colonies made refugees unwelcome. Others moved to Canada, the British West Indies, or the frontier.

The blockade was making food scarce for both the soldiers and citizens of Boston. Gage's troops were forced onto emergency short rations. There was no longer hay for their horses, which were now being fed Indian corn. Canada was the closest province that would send provisions, and these were subject to the risk of capture by American "privateers." Privateers were privately owned vessels (usually former merchant ships, refitted for war) whose captain carried a "letter of marque" from Congress or some other body authorizing him to seize enemy provision ships. Throughout the war, privateers would be a thorn in the side of Britain's efforts to supply its armies. From Boston, Henry Pelham wrote to his brother:

> We have been obliged to live intirely upon salt provisions and what stores we have in the house, and I think we are very fortunate. It is inconceivable the distress and ruin this unnatural dispute has caused to this town and its inhabitants. Almost every shop and store is closed. No business of any kind going on.

James Bowdoin, an elderly Whig on the town council, courageously remained in Boston and presided over the Town Meetings which sent numerous petitions and delegations to Gage, demanding that any Bostonians who wished to leave the city be allowed to. At first, the general agreed to do this, provided Dr. Warren would also give safe conduct to any Tories trying to get into Boston. Neither side allowed the migrants to bring any weapons, food, livestock, or useful supplies with them. Before allowing any Whigs to leave Boston, Gage insisted that all the inhabitants, whether leaving or staying, surrender their weapons to the town selectmen, supposedly to be returned at a future, more peaceful time. Altogether, 1,778 muskets, 973 bayonets, 634 pistols, and 38 blunderbusses were turned in. A correspondent provided the Pennsylvania Journal with a desciption of the situation in Boston. It was published in the Philadelphia newspaper on May 21st.

> The anxiety indeed is so great to get out of town, that even were we obliged to go naked, it would not hinder us. But there are so many obstructions thrown in the way, that I do not think those who are most anxious will be all out in less than two or three months. Vastly different from what was expected; for the general at first proposed, unasked, to procure the admiral's boats to assist the inhabitants in the transportation of their effects, which is not done [the admiral refused], and there are but two ferry boats allowed to cross.

William Cunningham, who would later become notoriously famous as the cruel provost-marshall in charge of captive American soldiers, is mentioned by John Greenwood, a patriot soldier, in his recollection of a typical scene one day at the Charlestown ferry:

> "Granny Gage" gave permission to the inhabitants, before the battle of Bunker's Hill, to leave the town, but placed a fellow by the name of Cunningham at the ferry stairs, to search their trunks and little bundles and take

from the women and children their pins, needles, and scissors, in short anything he pleased, which, with his noted cruelty, he would throw in the river while the poor helpless children were weeping.

Soon the Tories in Boston convinced Gage that, if he continued to let the Whigs leave, the rebels would set fire to the town. Therefore, he broke his agreement with the town council and stopped issuing passes. Abigail Adams related this in a letter to her husband John, writing, "Pharoah's heart is hardened, and he refuseth to hearken to them, and will not let the people go. May their deliverance be wrought out for them, as it was for the children of Israel."

Whigs were not the only people leaving Boston, as Frederick Mackenzie, a British lieutenant, noted in his journal: "We here, by some persons who came in within a day or two, that there are a good many British deserters in arms with the Rebels." One of these was Private John Howe, who in March had been sent out by General Gage to spy the countryside in preparation for the march to Concord. According to Howe, on May 10th:

> I put on my Yankee dress again, I called on Col. Smith and I told him I had a notion to make a trip to Rhode Island and Connecticut and see what preparations the Rebels were making. Smith answered, "John, the devil's in you, you'll get hanged before youre done, but if you have a mind to try again you shall have some money."

The colonel gave him fifteen pounds and a pass. That night, Private Howe walked over Boston Neck to Roxbury, and kept moving until he reached Albany, New York, where he enlisted in the New York patriot forces. After the war he settled on the Ohio River.

The Massachusetts Provincial Congress sent a flowery letter to the Stockbridge Indians, a small, Christianized tribe from western Massachusetts. The letter stated the hope that they would smoke their pipes, speak with their Indian brothers toward the setting sun (the powerful Iroquois Confederation), and if some of their young men "should have a mind to see what we are doing here, let them come down and tarry among our warriors." The Continental Congress may have recoiled at the thought of allying itself with "savages," but the British army was not in Philadelphia.

Many Stockbridge Indians arrived, as well as a handful of Mohawks. Their principal contribution was to frighten the British sentries, and they killed a few. They enjoyed moving dangerously close to the British lines, where they would "flourish their scalping knives, and yell by way of insult," according to one British officer. But they were even less suited to the camp life than the Yankees. As one militia officer put it, "They were too fond of liquor; they grew troublesome; there was no bush fighting to employ them in; and they were dismissed."

General Gage was reluctant to initiate any action until the scheduled reinforcements, including three major generals, arrived from England. The Tories and soldiers inside Boston, as usual, were frustrated with the inaction of "Granny Gage." Lieutenant Barker wrote in May:

> We are anxiously awaiting the arrival of the genl. officers and troops that are expected; we want to get out of this coop'd up situation. We cou'd now do that I suppose but the G does not seem to want it; there's no guessing what he is at; time will shew.

Finally, on May 25, the transport *Cerberus* arrived with nearly 2,000 troops and three more generals, William Howe, Henry Clinton, and John Burgoyne. A London newspaper had noted their departure:

> Behold the *Cerberus*, the Atlantic plow,
> Her precious cargo - Burgoyne, Clinton, Howe.
> Bow, wow, wow!

As the ship neared Boston Harbor, it passed one bound for England. Burgoyne hailed it, yelling, "What news is there?" After being informed that there had been a battle at a village called Concord, and the present status of Gage's forces, Burgoyne turned to the soldiers on deck and exclaimed: "What! Ten thousand peasants keep five thousand King's troops shut up? Well, let us get in, and we'll soon find elbow room!" This little joke became popular with the troops, and soon also with the Bostonians, but it would come back to haunt "General Elbow Room." Years later, when Burgoyne returned to Boston, this time as a prisoner of war after his defeat at Saratoga, an old woman in the crowd would cry out, "Make way! Make way! The General's coming! Give him elbow room!"

Since General Jeffrey Amherst, hero of the late French war, had declined the King's request to replace Gage, these three were the best that Britain could offer. They each brought with them excellent records of accomplishment, Burgoyne himself referring to them as a "triumvirate of reputation."

William Howe had the senior ranking of the three and, in a few more months, would supplant Gage as Commander-in-Chief. He and his brothers had been shining stars during the late war against the French. One brother, "Black Dick" Howe, was now the most popular admiral in the navy. The eldest brother, George Augustus Howe, had accompanied Robert Rogers and his famous Rangers during that war to learn their methods of fighting "Indian style," a method disdained by other British officers. He had discarded his ornate uniform in favor of buckskins. A colonial carpenter in the army wrote of him:

> It was not extravagant to suppose that every soldier in the army had a personal attachment to him, he frequently cam among the carpenters and his manner was so easy and fermilier, that we loost all the constraint we feale when addressed by our superiors whose manners are forbiding.

While attacking the French-held Fort Carillon (Ticonderoga) with the Rangers, George Augustus Howe's friend and subordinate, Israel Putnam, had pleaded with him to not expose himself so recklessly. A few minutes later, Howe was shot in the heart and died in Putnam's arms. The citizens of Boston paid to have a statue of George Augustus Howe erected in London. Now his brother, William, would be opposing Israel Putnam and these other colonists rebelling against the mother country.

William Howe, 46, had gained fame in his own right during the war. Learning from Braddock's disastrous defeat in the wilderness of western Pennsylvania, Howe established a new type of fighting unit, the "Light Infantry," by extracting the fastest men from the regular line infantry. During the climactic assault on Quebec, Howe personally led his Light Infantry battalion up the cliffs and onto the Plains of Abraham outside the city, then held off an enemy force four times his size, while the main American and British army under General Wolfe followed up the cliff. The French General Montcalm then led his army out of their fortress and onto the Plains, where he not only lost his life and the battle, but with it all of Canada.

In 1774, as a Whig in Parliament running for re-election, William Howe assured the voters of Nottingham that he would never fight against "our American brethren." Later, when requested by his distant cousin, King George III, to do just that, Howe's reply was: "Is that a request, or an order, Your Majesty?" When the King informed him it was an order, Howe reluctantly agreed. He later explained to his critics that he "could not refuse without incurring the odious name of backwardness to serve my country in distress."

The next in rank among the new arrivals was Henry Clinton, 37. He had made his mark on the battlefields of Europe in that same war, while serving in a British regiment assisting Frederick the Great's Prussian army. Officers who had served under Frederick, a military genious, considered themselves the elite of the British army, claiming that "men were made in the late war, but only in Germany." Graduates of "the German school" looked down their noses at those who had gained their experience in "the American school," and vice versa. Clinton would also eventually progress to Commander-in-Chief and, like his predecessors, Gage and Howe, fail to bring the war to a successful conclusion; and, in turn, he would also be replaced.

The lowest ranking new general to arrive, although the oldest at 53, was "Gentleman Johnny" Burgoyne. He had earned this nickname from his fondness for the high life of women, drinking, and cards. He was also known for his good treatment of his troops. Burgoyne, unlike other officers of the time, was reluctant to administer excessively brutal whippings for the least infraction. Officers were almost always from the upper class, and scorned the common soldiers as, in the words of the Duke of Wellington, "the scum of the earth." Burgoyne was also a man of letters, having earlier that spring seen one of his plays performed in a London theater.

Like the other new arrivals, General Burgoyne had gained his military reputation in the recent French war. His came from leading a cavalry charge in a decisive battle in Portugal. Not content to serve under three superior generals, Burgoyne left England for Boston only after obtaining Lord North's assurance that the King would see to it that he was given an important independent command somewhere outside of Boston by the next fall, or else he would be allowed to return home. John Burgoyne would ultimately be given that command; it would not result in the glory he anticipated, but rather his ignominious surrender at Saratoga.

General Gage had only requested more Regulars, not generals, too, but he listened to the advice these newcomers offered. Clinton suggested deserting Boston in favor of an invasion of Rhode Island from the sea, as punishment for the *Gaspee* affair three years before, and to provide the navy with an excellent base. From there, British warships could patrol Long Island Sound and blockade the port of New York, and those of the Connecticut coast as well. Like Clinton, Howe also wanted to desert Boston, but he favored locating the army at New York, to maintain control the lower Hudson River. Deferring to the more senior generals, Burgoyne offered no advice. Gage politely listened to Howe and Clinton, but took no action for almost three weeks. He would formulate his own plan to break out of Boston, there being no doubt in his mind that the army that had beaten the French and Austrians could easily rout an untrained mob of colonial farmers and shopkeepers.

Just after the reinforcements arrived, they were able to witness an action precipitated by attempts on both sides to secure for its own use all livestock and crops within reach. Not surprisingly, Israel Putnam was in the thick of the fighting. In fact, it was he who arranged for the skirmish by laying an ambuscade for the British foragers. Taking place on two islands in Boston Harbor, it was the most significant of the many skirmishes that occurred between April 19th (Lexington and Concord) and June 17th (Bunker Hill). The following account, from a Yankee correspondent, was published in both the Pennsylvania Journal and the Virginia Gazette:

> May 28. Yesterday a party of the American army at Cambridge, to the number of between two and three hundred men, had orders to drive off the livestock from Hog and Noddle's Islands. In attempting to carry out these orders, they were attacked by the King's troops. The combat began on Hog Island about five o'clock in the afternoon, and continued almost incessantly till midnight. The attack was made with cannon, swivels, and small arms, from an armed schooner, sloop, and eight or ten barges, upon our people who had small arms only, but were very advantageously posted by Putnam, who got to them just in season to station and command them properly. He placed them in a ditch up to their wastes in water, and covered by the bank to their necks. The schooner, sloop and boats full of men came within twelve or fifteen rods of them, and gave our people a fine opportunity to place their shot well.

About midnight the fire ceased a little, and our people retreated to the main land, where they were soon after joined by Captain Foster with two field-pieces ...

At daylight this morning the combat was renewed, and as the schooner passed the ferry way she was briskly attacked by our people, with the field-pieces and small arms, which soon clearing her deck, she drifted on shore, where our people set fire to her, and she blew up, notwithstanding the utmost endeavors of the people in the boats to tow her off, and save her from destruction. In this they exposed themselves much to our fire, and suffered greatly. When they found the schooner was lost, they with difficulty towed off the sloop, much disabled, and retired to their den; and thus ended the combat.

This afternoon our people got out of the wreck twelve four-pounders, six swivels, and every thing else that was valuable, without molestation; they afterwards destroyed or removed from both the islands all the stock, a large quantity of hay, and burned all the barns and houses.

All this was done in sight, and as we may say, under the noses of the whole fleet and army at Boston without molestation. General Gage's crew of enemies to the English constitution have suffered as much as in their precipitate flight from Lexington on the memorable 19th of April. Our killed none! wounded three! Heaven apparently, and most evidently, fights for us, covers our heads in the day of battle, and shields our people from the assaults of our common enemies.

The correspondent went on to estimate British casualties at Noddle Island as around three hundred, an exaggeration for propaganda purposes. Actually, they suffered only a dozen combined killed and

251

wounded, although they did lose the schooner, and the sloop that tried to come to its rescue was put out of action almost immediately by Putnam's two small cannon, and - most humiliatingly - had to be towed out of range by sailors in longboats. The estimate of American casualties appears to be confirmed by other sources, including the diary of one of the participants, Amos Farnsworth: "There was not a man of us kild. Surely God has a favor towards us. Thanks be unto God that so little hurt was done us when the bauls sung like bees round our heds."

The so-called "Battle of Noddle's Island" had expended much of the army's supply of ball and powder, with little gained but "spirit." Old Put, however, was not one to reflect on the critical supply problem he had just worsened. Ebullient with the joy of victory and the sheer excitement of his first real action of yet another war, the old veteran returned to camp covered with mud, and declared, "I wish we could have something of this kind every day. It would teach our men how little danger there is from cannon balls."

Although a very minor skirmish, reports were so positive that it resulted in Putnam's appointment by Congress as a major general. It also provided great material for the patriot propagandists. Typical was the following, published in the Pennsylvania Journal:

> May 30. A captain who was lately seized by Admiral Graves and taken into Boston has just come out; he says he was at the wharf at Noddle's Island when the battle began. The master of the *Diana* schooner told him, that guns were never better served than the Americans'; that not a shot missed him. One man was carried on board for dead, but the next morning he came to, and had not the least wound about him; others were frightened almost to death.
>
> There is an amazing difference in the looks and behavior of the enemy since the battle. Now all is still and quiet. From the general down to the common soldier,

they seem to be in a great panic, and are afraid to go to bed for fear the Yankees will kill them before morning.

A few days after his arrival, Burgoyne served as ghostwriter for Gage, producing a long-winded proclamation intended to frighten the "rabble in arms" into giving up. The following are excerpts from the June 12th proclamation offering amnesty.

> The infatuated multitude, conducted by certain well known incendiaries and traitors, have at length proceeded to avowed rebellion. ... With a preposterous parade of military arrangement they affected to hold the army beseiged; while part of their body made daily and indiscriminate invasions upon private property and with a wantonness of cruelty ever incident to lawless tumult carry depredation and distress wherever they turn their steps. ...
>
> In this exigency of complicated calamities, I avail myself of the last effort within the bounds of my duty to spare the effusion of blood; to offer in His Majesty's name his most gracious pardon to all persons who shall forthwith lay down their arms and return to their duties of peaceable subjects, excepting only Samuel Adams and John Hancock, whose offences are of too flagitious a nature to admit of any other consideration than that of condign punishment.

Fresh from the successes of Concord and Noddle's Island, the "infatuated multitude" was not in the frame of mind to give up the fight so soon. One of them wrote home:

> After the windy proclamation of the 12th, our troops became enraged [that] they were not led on to action. This learned proclamation was burned by the hands of

the common hangman. Many went off in disgust that nothing was done; the different parishes sent them back.

The proclamation inspired the Reverend Roger Cleveland, Congregational minister of Ipswich, Mass., to preach against General Gage, and to write an open letter to him:

> Thou profane wicked monster of falsehood and perfidy, your late infamous proclamation is full of notorious lies, as a toad or rattlesnake of deadly poison. Without speedy repentence, you will have an aggravated damnation in Hell. You are not only a robber, a murderer, and usurper, but a wicked rebel: a rebel against the authority of truth, law, equity, the English constitution of government, these colony states, and humanity itself.

Gage's proclamation achieved a similar notoriety in London's Whig newspapers. One anonymous essayist, like the Reverend Cleveland, also alluded to the English Revolution of 1688 and portrayed the King's administration and generals as the real rebels:

> According to our constitution, the very head that wears the crown may be an incendiary. By encouraging a faction devoted to a vile administration against the constitution, they are traitors to the people.
>
> General, you should always reason sword in hand. The pen is not your forte. You are lost upon paper, and must at last submit to be vanquished in the field. Putnam is in earnest.
>
> Blood was unnaturally and unjustifiably drawn by our hireling cut-throats at Concord; and then the General, in commiseration of the calamities which his murderous army has occasioned, most humanely offers his Majesty's most gracious pardon to these unhappy sufferers. Your

treacherous offer is disdained - away with it! - and massacre (if you can), but without an insult, the bravest men
in the British empire.

The die is cast, and those who would RISE AGAIN
to the STATE and LIBERTIES of ENGLISHMEN
must RISE through BLOOD.   The parricides of this
constitution, General, are to be found in England, NOT
IN AMERICA, nor can HAPPINESS, PEACE, LIB-
ERTY, and LAW be now restored (unless Providence
miraculously intervenes) but by ANOTHER REVOLU-
TION.

On June 12th, the same day that he issued his offer of pardon, Gage
decided on an attack. After all, he did need some "elbow room," as
Burgoyne later explained in a letter home:

Boston is a peninsula, joined to the mainland only by
a narrow neck; arms of the sea and the harbor surround
the rest. On one of these arms, to the north, is Charlestown. and over it is a larg hill. To the south is a still
larger scope of ground containing three hills, joining also
to the main by a tongue of land called Dorchester Neck.
The heights, both north and south, command the town;
that is, give an opportunity of erecting batteries above
any that you can make against them, and consequently
are much more advantageous.   It was absolutely
necessary we should make ourselves master of these
heights and we proposed to begin with Dorchester.

In a letter to his brother, the admiral, General Howe explained that
the rebels would soon be driven from Dorchester Heights, then the rebel lines in nearby Roxbury (near Boston Neck) would be attacked.
After Boston had thus been made safe from an attack in that direction,
Gage planned to have Howe take a large force across the water to

Charlestown Heights (Breed's Hill and Bunker's Hill), and cross Charlestown Neck to attack the rebel headquarters at Cambridge. He confidently added, "I suppose the Rebels will move from Cambridge, and that we shall take and keep possession of it." Gage set Sunday, June 18th, as the date for the expedition.

CHAPTER FOURTEEN
BUNKER HILL
JUNE 17, 1775

"It is probable that I will be taken in arms. But I will never be taken alive. The Tories will never have the satisfaction of seeing me hanged."

- Colonel William Prescott

The British plans soon leaked out to the patriot spy network. Numerous fishermen and ferryboatmen, all with legitimate errands to perform for the British in Boston, could be relied on to carry a message to Dr. Joseph Warren. General John Burgoyne, himself, as well as some "inferior officers," had been overheard discussing the plans. By June 15th, three days before the scheduled attack, Warren knew of Gage's plans, and suggested to General Ward that he call a council of war.

The proposal being discussed was to forestall the British attack on the Dorchester and Roxbury end of the lines by forcing Gage to attack in a place more advantageous to the Americans. Artemas Ward and Joseph Warren had both been opposed to earlier suggestions that Charlestown Heights be fortified. Now that the proposal was being suggested again, more forcefully this time, they reiterated their opposition. They reminded Israel Putnam and the others in favor of the idea that there was barely a thousand barrels of gunpowder left in the whole camp. Without adequate supplies, it seemed unlikely that any fortification could be held for long against the expected British attack.

Putnam, however, was strongly in favor of seizing and fortifying Charlestown Heights before the British could. General Ward objected, predicting it "would lead to a general engagement" with the enemy, something he wanted to avoid, for the inexperienced militia might run away. To this, Putnam declared, "The Americans are not at all afraid of their heads, though very much afraid of their legs; if you cover these, they will fight forever." He wanted a battle, as long as the Americans were in the advantageous position and not out in the open, where the well trained Regulars would have the upper hand. Putnam said he would only risk 2,000 men.

> We will defend ourselves as long as possible and, if driven to retreat, every stone wall shall be lined with their dead. And, at the worst, suppose us surrounded and no retreat; we will set our country an example of which it shall not be ashamed.

Warren paced up and down the floor, then leaned on his chair and said, "Almost thou persuadest me, General Putnam, but I still think the project rash." General Seth Pomeroy, of Massachusetts, vouched that his men "would fight the enemy with but five cartridges apiece." Putnam recalled aloud how he knew Pomeroy to many times go out with only three charges of powder and bring home "two and sometimes three deer." Colonel William Prescott, of Massachusetts, then voiced his approval of the plan. It was he who had suggested the idea in early May, before Putnam had wasted so much of the powder supply on Noddle's Island.

Faced with a majority in favor of the plan, General Ward acquiesced, although he repeated his objections. He then appointed Colonel Prescott - not Putnam - to lead the expedition, and authorized him to take 900 Massachusetts men along. Although Putnam outranked Prescott, he would not be in charge, because most of the men were from outside his colony and, therefore, not likely to obey any of his orders. Putnam would make his presence felt, encouraging the troops and bringing on reinforcements.

Another 175 from Connecticut would be led by Captain Thomas

Knowlton. Shortly after the council, upon hearing of the expedition, Knowlton would tell Putnam to his face that it was suicidal, and that he objected to it. But, out of loyalty to Putnam, Knowlton agreed to do his part.

William Prescott, 49, had a commanding presence about him; he led men with his quiet but forceful personality; he did not act rashly like Israel Putnam. As a lieutenant in the provincial forces under Howe back in 1759, during the attack on Novia Scotia's Louisbourg fortress, Prescott's courage, coolness under fire, and leadership abilities had caught the attention of the British officers. He was offered a commission in the British army, a rare compliment for a colonist. Prescott refused it, and returned to his farm in Pepperell, Massachusetts.

Later, when war against Britain appeared imminent, he accepted a position as colonel in the local militia, and began drilling the farmers. His sister, married to a Tory, was very concerned about her brother being taken in arms by the British, and because of it losing his estate and perhaps his life, hung for treason. Prescott's brother-in-law, Abijah Willard, visited him shortly before the war started at Lexington to tell him of his sister's anxiety. Prescott answered by stating his position firmly: "It is probable that I will be taken in arms. But I will never be taken alive. The Tories will never have the satisfaction of seeing me hanged."

Among those going with Colonel Prescott was Amos Farnsworth, who noted in his journal:

> Friday, June 16. Nothing done in the forenoon. In the afternoon we had orders to be ready to march. At six, agreable to orders, our regiment preadid [paraded] and about sunset we was drawn up and herd prayers; and about dusk marched for Bunker's Hill under command of our own Col. Prescott.

The militia, including the officers, were dressed in their typical myriad of colors and styles of clothing and arms. One witness recorded their appearance as they left Cambridge Common at nine o'clock, after listening to a prayer for success spoken by the president of Harvard College:

> To a man they wore small-clothes, coming down and fastening just below the knee, and long stockings with cowhide shoes ornamented by large buckles, while not a pair of boots graced the company. The coats and waist-coats were loose and of huge dimensions, with colors as various as the barks of oak, sumach and other trees of our hills and swamps could make them, and their shirts were all made of flax, and like every other part of the dress were homespun. On their heads was worn a large round and broad-brimmed hat. Their arms were as various as their costume.

At Charlestown Neck, they were met by Putnam with wagons loaded with tools, as well as *gabions* (wicker baskets to be filled with dirt) and *fascines* (tightly bundled brushwood and sticks). These would give structure to the fort's earthen walls. Colonel Prescott sent a captain and ten men to the village of Charlestown to listen for evidence that the British sentries had noticed them. But all they would hear until 5 a.m. would be the sentries' periodical "All's well!" Prescott continued the march up Bunker's Hill with "dark lanterns open only at the rear."

Charlestown peninsula was about three and a half miles long, a half mile wide, and connected to the mainland by a narrow "neck" of land, which was "not a stonethrow across." Three hills composed its backbone. Near the Neck rose the gently sloped Bunker's Hill, rising 110 feet above sea level. Further down the middle of the peninsula was the steeper Breed's Hill, 75 feet high. Beyond that, near the tip farthest from the Neck, was the 35 foot high Moulton's Hill. Along the south slope of Breed's Hill, facing Boston, the village of Charlestown rose from the Charles River. Along the north shore flowed the Mystic

River. Except for the village, most of the peninsula was composed of hayfields marked off by low stone walls topped by split rails (a combination popular with farmers because it was "pig tight and cow high").

The silent column of slowly moving militia halted, as planned, on the grassy summit of Bunker's Hill. There, General Putnam urged Colonels Prescott and Richard Gridley, the chief engineer, to change the site of the proposed "redoubt" (earthen fort) to Breed's Hill, which was 500 yards closer to Boston. Putnam wanted to make sure the British would be alarmed enough to fight. He won the long argument that ensued, and they proceeded to Breed's Hill, where the "Battle of Bunker Hill" would actually take place. The coming battle would be misnamed, for two reasons: first, the original plans called for it to be on Bunker's Hill, so the official dispatches from headquarters mentioned that site; and second, even the British accounts of the battle referred to Bunker's Hill, since it was the higher of the two hills.

Prescott later recalled the scene atop Breed's Hill: "We arrived at the spot, the lines were drawn by the engineer, and we began the intrenchment about twelve o'clock." Private Israel Potter later recalled that the men "laboured all night without cessation and with very little refreshment." Against the wishes of chief engineer Gridley, Prescott insisted that half the men maintain an armed watch, while the other half work at constructing the fort. Five short hours would bring daylight and discovery by the British artillerymen aboard the ships in the harbor and atop Copp's Hill in Boston's north end.

Henry Clinton, walking along Boston's north shore late that night, as the restless British general often did, heard the sounds of picks and spades striking stones up on Breed's Hill. So Clinton quickly walked back to headquarters and pulled General Howe away from the gambling tables to whisper the news. Irritated at the interruption, and always disrespectful of Clinton's opinions, Howe disagreed with his assessment that immediate preparations should be made to launch an assault at dawn. Frustrated but not surprised, Clinton then went to the Commander-in-Chief, Thomas Gage, who also declined his advice. Disgusted with his superiors, Clinton returned to his quarters and completed that day's entry in his journal:

> I have given a proposal in writing. If we were of active disposition, we should be landed tomorrow at daybreak. As it is now, I fear it must be postponed until two.

Two o'clock in the afternoon would be the next high tide after daybreak. So the British generals went to bed totally ignoring the rebel fortifications being constructed on a hilltop only half a mile away. Not knowing whether the work on Charlestown Heights was a serious effort, or whether the Americans would still be there in the morning, Gage had thought it unwise to wake his army in the middle of the night. Daylight would soon show him what course of action to take.

At 4:45 a.m., as soon as it was light enough to see, a sailor aboard the sloop *Lively* observed what appeared to be a miracle: a fort on the top of a hill which had been covered only by grass at sunset eight hours before. He called the ship's captain, who immediately swung the vessel broadside to the target and commenced firing with everything he had. The guns woke up Admiral Graves, who angrily sent a messenger to order the *Lively* to cease firing without orders. But soon, after the admiral had taken his own observations and consulted with General Gage, he ordered all the ships within range to open fire, and the batteries on Copp's Hill in Boston joined in the bombardment.

The Americans had brought four light field pieces with them to Breed's Hill, but were saving their gunpowder to oppose the expected British landing. So the Americans did not fire back at the warships. Elihu Phelps noted the diggers' anxiety:

> The soldiers kept enquiring if there war no more cannon comeing. ... [The British] kept continually playing with large cannon and bombs which would seem as though it would tare the whole hill to peices. Some of our soldiers talked of deserting the breast works.

The digging site on Breed's Hill was slightly out of range of the British guns. One of the many Bostonians watching the action from rooftops and cupolas across the river observed that each time Prescott's men saw a flash from a British cannon, "we could plainly see them fall down, and mount again as soon as the shot was passed." Even the British must have been impressed, for a London magazine months later noted that, "The Americans bore this severe fire with wonderful firmness and seemed to go on with their business as if no enemy had been near."

However, about 8:00 a.m., Asa Pollard, a militiaman from Billerica, Massachusetts, suddenly dropped, headless, to the ground. In the words of Colonel Prescott:

> [Pollard] was killed by a cannon ball which struck his head. He was so near me that my clothes were be-smeared with his blood and brains, which I wiped off, in some degree, with a handful of fresh earth. The sight was so shocking to many of the men that they left their posts and ran to view him. I ordered them back, but in vain. I then ordered him to be buried instantly.

As best he could, Prescott urged the men to hurry the burial so they could return to the digging, but they stubbornly insisted on a proper prayer service and burial. The British generals, observing the scene in their looking glasses, must have thought it an odd time for a formal burial service, what with cannon balls falling all around.

After the burial service, Colonel Prescott could not persuade the men to return to work; they seemed preoccupied with the cannon balls still coming over. So Prescott climbed atop the redoubt's six foot high "parapet" (outer wall) and walked up and down its length. Prescott was tall and blue-eyed, with a sword buckled to his side. He wore homespun clothes, a light loose-fitting coat, and a broad-brimmed round farmer's hat. The men watched how coolly he walked atop the parapet, defying the danger of the British cannon balls; they took heart and went back to work.

The Yankees, many of them green troops who had never seen action before, could not help but be shaken by "the melancholy fate of their companion," and some began stealthily slipping away. Some of them halted on Bunker's Hill and "tarried" (lingered) there throughout the day's battle. Others did not stop until safely across the Neck. One who stayed on Breed's Hill recalled that Pollard's shocking death

> caused some of our young country pple to desert, apprehending the danger in a clearer manner than the rest, who were more diligent in digging and fortifying ourselves. We began to be almost beat out, being tired by our labor and having no sleep the night before, but little victuals, no drink but rum.

Colonel Prescott did nothing to try to stop these men from deserting, other than staring in silent contempt. He knew it was better to let cowards go now. For, if they were forced to stay and then ran off when the battle was underway, their panic could spread through the ranks and start a mass exodus. Even two of his fellow regimental commanders, Colonels Bricket and Bridge, deserted at this time. They came to Prescott and announced that they were exhausted and would retire to a house on Bunker's Hill. The effect of the desertion of these two colonels was compounded, since "most of the men under them deserted the party."

Colonel Prescott was everywhere, urging on his men, "Dig, men! Dig for your lives!" and joining them in the digging at times. Years later, one of these men, recalling the battle, declared: "I tell ye, that if it had not been for Colonel Prescott, there would have been no fight." They continued working "till they had thrown up a small breastwork extending from the north side of the redoubt" downhill toward the Mystic River, "under a very warm fire from the enemy's artillery."

It was 9:00 a.m. now, and the men began to grumble - why had the relief force not shown up yet, so they could go back to Cambridge and finally get some sleep. "The danger we were in," Peter Brown wrote, "made us think there was treachery, and that we were brot there to be all slain." Prescott's officers approached him, urging him to demand that General Ward send replacements for his exhausted, sleepless men, so they could return to camp. Prescott refused, suspecting that any replacements Ward might send would desert. He answered his officers:

> The men who have raised these works are the best able to defend them. They have learned to despise the fire of the enemy; they have the merit of the labor, and shall have the honor of the victory.

However, he did agree that he would need reinforcements, so he ordered Major John Brooks to borrow one of the artillery horses and ride to Ward's headquarters. But the artillerymen, saving their horses for what would turn out to be their own desertion, would not lend Brooks a horse. So he had to walk the three and a half miles on foot. When he arrived, Ward refused Prescott's request, claiming he needed all his forces to protect against a possible British move elsewhere. Gage had been bombarding the rebel lines near Boston Neck all morning, deceiving Ward into believing that the attack against Charlestown Heights would be a diversion, that the main British thrust would be against the lines in Roxbury near Boston Neck.

Shortly after 11:00 a.m., General Putnam returned from Cambridge, where he had tried in vain to persuade General Ward to send reinforcements. Crossing the Neck, Putnam rode as if he didn't even notice the shelling from British flatboats that had been rowed closer than the warships could go. A Yankee walking across the Neck at the same time saw Putnam pass him, "on a horse. I expected to see him knocked off." But Putnam made it safely across and rode up to the digging site atop Breed's Hill. He reined in his white horse and leaned over to urge Prescott to send some of the intrenching tools to Bunker's Hill, so that under Putnam's direction the men milling around there could build a fall-back fortification, in case those on Breed's Hill should be forced to retreat. According to William Heath:

> The Colonel replied that, if he sent any of the men away with the tools, not one of them would return; to this the General answered, they shall every man return. A large party was then sent off with the tools, and not one of them returned; in this instance the Colonel was the best judge of human nature.

When Colonel Prescott gave the order to carry the tools to Bunker's Hill, he observed that "An order was never obeyed with more readiness. From every part of the line within hearing volunteers ran; some picked up one, some two shovels, and hurried over the hill."

Putnam was again at headquarters when Major Brooks arrived with Prescott's request for reinforcements. After watching Artemas Ward refuse the request, Putnam decided to take the request higher up - to the Committee of Safety, which was meeting in another room of the same house. One of its members, Richard Devens, a Charlestown resident, was so "impassioned and vehement" in urging the request be honored that General Ward finally relented and sent two New Hampshire regiments, those of Colonels James Reed and John Stark.

Stark, 46, had been a captain in the famous Rogers Rangers during the late French war. Stark's fame and ability were so well known that he easily attracted 800 backwoodsmen to join him when the news of Lexington and Concord reached the New Hampshire frontier. He and his recruits took only a day and a half to march the 55 miles to Cambridge. Two years later, he would rally his men again and march from New Hampshire to the Vermont-New York border for a decisive victory - the Battle of Bennington, a key step on the way to the complete surrender of Gentleman Johnny Burgoyne's army at Saratoga.

As the New Hampshire men crossed Charlestown Neck, young Captain Henry Dearborn, marching beside Stark at the head of the long column, became anxious. The shelling from the floating batteries in the Charles River hit some of the men, knocking them, screaming, out of the column. He asked the colonel if he should think about "quickening the march of the regiment, that it might sooner be relieved of the galling crossfire of the enemy." Many years later, Dearborn could still vividly recall how Stark answered him:

> With a look peculiar to himself, he fixed his eyes upon me and observed with great composure, "Dearborn, one fresh man in action is worth ten fatigued ones," and continued to advance in the same cool and collected manner.

Stark and Reed continued to march their regiments at that deliberate pace until they reached the summit of Bunker's Hill about 1:00 p.m. There they halted to observe the defenses and the enemy, by now landing at Moulton's Point. The two New Hampshire colonels quickly realized where the weak point in the defenses was - the left flank, along the lower slope leading to the Mystic River. Here, below and behind the redoubt's breastwork extension, was a split rail fence, 250 yards long. Captain Thomas Knowlton had just led his 175 Connecticut men down there from the redoubt, at the suggestion of Colonel Prescott, who was concerned about his left flank.

Colonel Stark "harangued his regiment in a short but animated address," to which they responded with three cheers, "Huzzah! Huzzah! Huzzah!" Stark and Reed then led their two New Hampshire regiments "at the double" down the slope to join Knowlton.

They tore down a nearby fence and, together with Knowlton's men, used these rails to build a new one about a foot in back of the one already there. They filled the gap between the rail fences "with bushes, hay and grass which they found on the spot ready cut." Although it may have made a deceivingly formidable appearance to the advancing redcoats, one of the men knew it would be only "a slight defence against musquet-ball." It would certainly not stop anything shot from the light cannon the British would bring over with them from Boston.

No one doubted that the British army would surely come, to force them off the peninsula.

At the bottom of the slope, along the shore of the Mystic River, Stark noticed the narrow beach protected by a bluff eight feet high. He fully expected the enemy to take advantage of it in an attempt to flank the Americans. In Stark's own words, "It was a way so clear that the enemy could not miss it." He therefore had his men carry and roll large stones from nearby walls to make a stone barrier on the beach, just below the bottom of the rail fence. Then he personally led its defense, with a triple row of his best marksmen. He instructed the men how to fire when the enemy column approached along the beach: each row must "reserve their fire" until ten seconds after the row in their front had fired. This would produce frequent volleys and not allow enough time for the British to reform their lines and make their fearsome bayonet charge. John Stark walked 35 feet in front of the stone barrier, hammered a stake in the sand, and gave the order, "Not a man is to fire until the first Regular passes that stake."

Going back to the morning, General Thomas Gage, Commander-in-Chief of the British forces, had called a council of war. It appeared obvious to the senior officers attending that their "venture out of town" planned for the next day would have to be changed. After observing the Americans on Charlestown Heights, it "became necessary to alter our plan, and attack on that side," instead of starting with Dorchester. While they were discussing what to do, the Americans tested their light cannon on Breed's Hill by firing a few times, without success, at the batteries on Copp's Hill in Boston's north end. Burgoyne noticed that "two cannon ball went a hundred yards over our heads."

Burgoyne, the most junior of the generals, did not offer a plan of attack. But, of course, Clinton had one. He suggested that "he might be landed with 500 men near Charlestown Neck," Howe land a larger force at the other end of the peninsula, and Admiral Graves's ships shell the mainland side of the Neck to prevent reinforcements from coming to rescue the trapped rebels. The rebels could then either be attacked by Howe, or simply starved into submission. Gage rejected this plan, reminding Clinton that, "A commander should never place his army between two enemy armies," a fundamental rule of warfare.

Burgoyne and Howe agreed, pointing out also that Clinton's plan was a slightly unmanly approach. "The hill was open and of easy ascent, and ... [will] be easily carried," they predicted. It was simply inconceivable that untrained rebels could stand in the face of over one thousand highly trained, bayonet-wielding Regulars. Later, General Clinton would vent his frustration in his journal once again:

> Mr. Gage thought himself so well informed that he would not take any opinion of others, particularly of a man bred in the German school, which that of America affects to despise.

Howe's proposed plan was the one selected. It called for a single landing of a large force at Moulton's Point. The rebel defenses would be attacked by a frontal assault, in conjunction with a flank attack along the lower slope near the Mystic River, as follows: While most of the troops would slowly march up the hill and pour diversionary fire at the rebels, eleven companies of Light Infantry would move quickly along the Mystic beach, past the Americans above them, then turn and move uphill along a dirt road to attack the rebels from behind. At the same time, the main force would charge with the bayonet from the front. The rebels would be forced to either surrender or be torn to pieces.

It is important to remember that, at the time Howe formulated this plan, the only Americans on Breed's Hill were those within the redoubt. Its left flank was still open at that time; Prescott had not yet ordered construction of the redoubt's breastwork extension, and he had not yet sent Knowlton to take post at the rail fence to the rear, lower on the slope.

The sight of fleeing Yankees would give renewed confidence to the Regulars, while instilling the proper fear in "the infatuated multitude," who might then reconsider their participation in this silly rebellion.

The whole spectacle would be viewed by thousands of Boston's inhabitants, both Whig and Tory, on the city's hills, rooftops, and cupolas. The whole "battle" - rout would be a better word - was expected to be over so quickly that Gage planned to make it the first stage in his original, though slightly altered, plan to take the countryside surrounding Boston and scatter the rebel "army." The British generals expected the rebels to flee at the first bayonet charge. Howe would then signal Clinton, atop Boston's Copps Hill, to launch 600 waiting troops to row up the Charles River. They would land near Charlestown Neck and join in a combined attack on the rebel headquarters at Cambridge.

Because this was to be the first step in breaking out of Boston, each Regular carried three days' provisions, a full *cartouche* of 60 rounds, toiletries, a change of clothes, a blanket, and a share of his mess's tent and equipment - canvas or poles, eating or cooking utensils, cast-iron cooking pot, etc. Altogether, including his 15-pound Brown Bess musket, the average private's burden, according to one British officer, "may be estimated at one hundred and twenty five pounds."

Although Howe's plan seemed sensible at the time it was formulated, it could only succeed if executed with utmost speed, before the rebels improved their defenses. However, Gage and Howe, true to their nature, took their time, opting to wait for a favorable tide. Howe wrote to his brother, the admiral: "As the shore where it was judged most proper to land was very flat, the landing could not be made with facility after the tide of ebb was much run off." It was thus necessary to wait for "high water at two o'clock in the afteroon."

These extra hours allowed the British cooks to boil beef and bake biscuits, enough to last several days. However, the extra hours also allowed the Americans time to build their earthen breastwork extending downhill from the redoubt toward the Mystic River, as well as three *fleches* (small V-shaped earthen breastworks) beyond the lower end of the breastwork extension. It was also during this time that Prescott assigned Knowlton to take post along the split rail fence in the rear and lower on the north slope (to be precise, at the base of

Bunker's Hill), and Reed and Stark arrived with their large New Hampshire forces to bolster the left flank. By the time Howe's troops arrived within shooting range, the American left flank was no longer a weak point.

By two o'clock, Howe was transporting his 1,550 soldiers across the Charles River to Moulton's Point in longboats rowed by sailors from the men-of-war. On Boston's north shore were 700 more red-coats - the reserve, ready if needed. Time was finally running out for the men and boys atop Breed's Hill, as they frantically worked on extending their defenses down the slope toward the Mystic River. To cover his right flank, Prescott detached a party of two hundred from the redoubt, and ordered them to take positions in houses on the upper streets of Charlestown.

With the exception of the capable Prescott, Stark and a few subordinate officers, the Americans were without adequate leadership. There were no staff officers to carry messages between the spread-out forces, or to and from General Ward's headquarters on the mainland. There was no single officer in charge to coordinate the overall defense efforts. Prescott was busy directing the defenses in and near the redoubt. Stark was on the Mystic beach; Knowlton and Reed were behind the rail fence; Putnam was the highest ranking officer, but was there only as a volunteer with no real command. Putnam would spend part of his time behind the rail fence, the rest of it atop Bunker's Hill directing construction of fallback breastworks.

Upwards of 2,000 militia lingered either on nearby Bunker's Hill or on the mainland side of Charlestown Neck. Many had come without orders, compelled by their own curiosity. Lacking specific orders and assertive officers, these fresh troops did not join the battle, much to the exasperation of the tired men and boys manning the defense lines. A few hundred did move up, though, coming singly or a few at a time. In a few cases, a whole company of thirty or forty decided they should be wherever they felt they were needed most, and thus moved up to fill gaps along the line.

Colonel Samuel Gerrish was later court-martialled and cashiered

271

out of the army for his cowardice that afternoon. A soldier from New-bury, Massachusetts, wrote after the battle:

> Gerrish was ordered to Charlestown with a reinforce-ment, but he no sooner came in sight of the enemy than a tremor seiz'd him & he began to bellow, "Retreat! re-treat! or you'll all be cut off!" which so confus'd & scar'd our men that they retreated most precipitately, & our soldiery now sware vengeance against him & determine not to be under his command.

Major Scarborough Gridley, son of Colonel Gridley, and also an artillery officer, was proving that nepotism is a terrible vice to have in an army. He was ordered to advance from Cambridge to the battlefield. But, when he saw solid shot from British artillery landing on Charlestown Neck, he decided he could do just as much good setting up his four-pounders on one of the hills on the safe, mainland side of the Neck. From there, he had his men waste their ammunition shooting at British ships a mile away.

One of his officers was so disgusted by this show of cowardice that he defied Gridley's orders and led some of the men and two cannon across the Neck to the battlefield. Colonel Mansfield soon came along with his regiment, bound for the redoubt. Gridley hailed him and or-dered him to take a position alongside him to "protect" his guns. Although Gridley had no authority to issue such an order, Mansfield acquiesced, assuming that the son of the chief engineer and artillery of-ficer in the army must know what he is talking about. Soon Colonel Scammons also arrived with a regiment and was taken in. Gridley spent the afternoon safely surrounded by 700 fresh troops with full ammunition pouches desperately needed on Breed's Hill.

Colonel Jonathan Ward's regiment was about to cross the Neck to reinforce Prescott when a horseman rode up, shouting, "Who gave you orders to advance?" "General Ward," was the reply. "The Committee of Safety countermands it," the rider retorted, then galloped away.

Although no one could identify him then, several later claimed it was Dr. Benjamin Church, the British spy. The colonel was perplexed: the Committee of Safety had absolute authority, even over Artemas Ward, the Commander-in-Chief. Did he dare refuse this countermand? Captain Seth Washburn decided for him. "I don't care who gave that order," he said. "I say it's a Tory order, and we should ignore it." Without waiting for his colonel, Washburn led his company across the Neck on the run. Two other companies followed him, then the colonel raced after them, leaving most of his regiment behind to make up their own minds whether to stay or follow.

The British navy stepped up the shelling to cover Howe's landing. Despite this, Prescott sought to make it uncomfortable for them at Moulton's Point. Private Peter Brown described it in a letter to his mother:

> When our officers saw that the Regulars would land, they ordered the artillery to go out of the fort and prevent their landing, if possible. The artillery captain took his pieces and went right off home to Cambridge fast as he could, for which he is now confined and we expect will be shot for it.

While the artillerymen were deserting, the rest of the Americans on Breed's Hill prepared themselves for the assault, while keeping an eye on the approaching British. Private Israel Potter recalled the wait:

> We were now harangued by Gen. Putnam, who reminded us that, exhausted as we were by our incessant labour through the preceding night, the most important part of our duty was yet to be performed, and that much would be expected from so great a number of excellent marksmen. He charged us to be cool, and to reserve our fire until the enemy approached so near as to enable us to see the whites of their eyes.

After landing, Howe stood upon little Moulton's Hill and observed the extended defenses as well as the numerous militia in the distance, on Bunker's Hill, thinking they were reinforcements coming to help. He decided he just might need those 700 troops held in reserve, after all.

> Their works were crowded with men, about 500 yards from us. From the appearance of their situation and numbers, and seeing that they were pouring in all the strength they could collect, I sent to General Gage to desire a reinforcement.

Howe then instructed the troops to take off their packs and eat lunch. If all went well, they would have to march all the way to Cambridge and fight another battle there later that day, so he wanted the troops to have enough energy to do it. Some of the veterans didn't eat, though, knowing that a man receiving a ball in his middle suffers less damage if his belly is empty. Before they finished their lunch, several officers and soldiers came up, cursing and shouting. Howe asked what the disturbance was about, and was told that five Regulars had been caught trying to desert to the American lines. Howe promptly had two of the five deserters, which he seemingly picked at random, hung from the nearest tree, to serve as examples. He sent the other three back to their ranks, saying he would need every soldier he had for the assault. Howe had no more trouble about desertions after that.

Major General William Howe then divided his forces. He and his second, Brigadier General Robert Pigot, would each take about 750 to 800 men. Pigot, on the left, would advance straight uphill against the redoubt and its breastwork extension. Howe would lead his own division along the slope on the right, advancing against the "grass fence." Before setting out, he spoke to his army:

> Gentlemen, I am very happy in having the honor of

commanding so fine a body of men. I do not in the least doubt that you will behave like Englishmen and as becomes good soldiers. If the enemy will not come from their entrenchments, we must drive them out. At all events, the town of Boston will be set on fire by them. I shall not desire any of you to go a step further than where I go myself at your head. Remember, gentlemen, we have no recourse to any resources if we lose Boston but to go on board our ships, which will be very disagreeable to us all.

Peter Oliver, the Bostonian Tory, explained in his history of the war what Howe meant by "behave like Englishmen and as becomes good soldiers." According to Oliver, the definition of such "English courage" was "standing, undaunted, in an open field to be shot at." They would have to show a great deal of that English courage this day.

"Our troops advanced with great confidence, expecting an easy victory," one British officer wrote. "Many of our great men were heard to say, 'Let us take the bull by the horns' as they marched." The uphill march through waist-high hayfields and over stone walls and rail fences was exhausting for the heavily-laden soldiers. They sweated profusely in their heavy boots, tight-fitting trousers, vests (called waist-coats and pronounced "weskits"), woolen regimental coats, and heavy packs. Their high, stiff collars forced their faces to look up, into the sun. The British uniform was designed for the parade ground, not the battlefield.

It was a humid day, with thermometers reaching the mid-nineties, and no wind to provide relief. The officers looked particularly ridiculous as white streaks streamed down their faces, for the flour they used to powder their wigs was now mixing with perspiration and rolling down their foreheads. But they had to endure this indignity, for it would not do to allow the men to see their officers wiping their faces as they marched.

The advance was slow; the drummers, walking three steps behind the troops, beat out the standard 80 steps per minute. The advance was "frequently halted to give time for the artillery to fire." The heavier field pieces were not able to be pushed forward to where they could be effective, because they sank in the swampy areas and were left behind. The lighter field pieces were able to move up with the troops. But they were soon useless, for when their ammunition was used up the discovery was made that the reserve supply brought along was the wrong size - twelve pound balls, for six-pounder guns. One officer later bitterly criticized the man he thought responsible:

> The wretched blunder of the over-sized balls sprung from the dotage of an officer in that corps who spends his whole time dallying with the schoolmaster's daughters. God knows he is old enough. He is no Sampson, yet he must have his Dalilah.

About 3:00 p.m., Howe's division moved forward into a swale, where they were temporarily hidden from the Americans' sight. The Light Infantry, as planned, filed off to the right and dropped down the steep bank. Forming on the narrow beach, they quickly moved forward. The remaining troops, along the hillside, marched in wide lines, ready to make their bayonet charge against the spread-out American defenses. Each rank was close behind the one in its front, and each man marched about twelve feet from the one on his left or right.

General Burgoyne, watching from Boston, later described the scene of pageantry, and the beginning of the battle:

> Howe's disposition was exceedingly soldier-like, in my opinion it was perfect. As his first arm advanced up the hill, they met with a thousand impediments from strong fences, and were much exposed. They were also exceedingly hurt by musquetry from Charles Town, though Clinton and I did not perceive it till Howe sent us word by a boat, and desired us to set fire to the town,

which was immediately done. We threw a parcel of shells, and the whole was instantly in flames. Our battery afterwards kept up an incessant fire on the heights; it was seconded by a number of frigates, floating batteries, and one ship of the line.

And now ensued one of the greatest scenes of war that can be conceived. If we look to the height, Howe's corps ascending the hill in the face of entrenchments, and in a very disadvantageous ground, was much engaged; to the left the enemy pouring in fresh troops by thousand, over the land, and in the arm of the sea our ships and floating batteries cannonading them. Straight before us, a large and noble town in one great blaze; the church steeples being of timber, were great pyramids of fire above the rest. The hills round the country covered with spectators, the enemy all in anxious suspense, the roar of cannon, mortars and musquetry, the crash of churches, and whole streets falling together in ruin to fill the ear. The storm of the redoubt with the objects above described to fill the eye; and the reflection that perhaps a defeat was a final loss to the British Empire in America to fill the mind.

Pigot's advancing left flank, as Burgoyne described, was tormented by American snipers in Charlestown's upper houses. Again and again, a Regular dropped to the ground with a groan or cry. Without orders, several of Pigot's men began firing wildly at the houses. This being their first action of the day - and for many of the Regulars, their first action ever - the panic spread, and the entire line under Pigot began to falter. They stopped their forward progress and began shooting back at their unseen enemy, snipers in Charlestown's upper houses.

Pigot was forced to temporarily forget his own plans for a flanking operation on the redoubt's south side, and shift Major Pitcairn and his Marines to the left, to flush out the snipers. The Marine major sent his men charging into the town and a bloody house-to-house struggle commenced. Here the British met with success, shooting and bayoneting many of the outnumbered pockets of militia, while others retreated to the safety of the redoubt. But throughout the afternoon, many of these Massachusetts men, led by Captain Benjamin Walker, stealthily returned to the houses closest to Pigot's line, to "hang on the flank."

After several minutes of this activity, Pigot sent a messenger to Howe, telling him that he could not advance unless something was done about the snipers in Charlestown. Conveniently, at that moment, Admiral Graves stepped ashore "to be near General Howe for the sake of seeing whether any further aid could be given." He was asked by Howe "to set fire to that town over there." The admiral, who had suggested it be burned the day after the unsuccessful expedition to Concord, gladly obliged and "immediately sent to the ships to fire red hot balls, which had been prepared with that view, and also to Copp's Hill battery to desire they would throw carcasses into the town." Carcasses were hollow balls filled with greased rags, and lit before being shot from the guns. Like the "hot shot" from the ships, these carcasses would set ablaze houses wherever they landed.

Many Bostonians, Whig and Tory alike, shed a tear as they watched Charlestown burn. Some of them had, months before, moved their valuable furniture, silver, portraits, and other possessions to the cellars of Charlestown homes for safe keeping. Among the losses was the 200- year-old library of the Mather family.

Admiral Graves also ordered two floating batteries, which had been bombarding Charlestown Neck, to leave the Charles and row around to the Mystic, where they could be in a position to fire upon the rail fence. However, "the tide being against them," the rowers never reached their destination, over a mile and a half away. If, instead, Graves had ordered one of his wind-powered vessels up the Mystic, as Howe had requested in the morning, the battle might have been the rout that Howe had envisioned. The planned flanking operation would have been unopposed, since the New Hampshire and Connecticut troops would've been forced from their posts by the ship's fire.

But, remembering how his nephew's sloop *Diana* had run aground at Noddle's Island, the admiral refused to risk sending any of his ships into uncharted waters. Despite having been in Boston Harbor for several weeks, the admiral had never ordered soundings taken in the Mystic River's channel. This was an example of the kind of halfhearted cooperation that was typical between the British army and navy; it would play its part in their losing the war.

Between the efforts of Pitcairn's Marines and the rapidly spreading flames, Pigot soon was able to report that the snipers had been flushed out, so Howe ordered the advance to continue. He felt he didn't have enough time to wait for the floating batteries to reach the Mystic - it was now after 3:30, and he still hoped to reach the rebel headquarters at Cambridge before dark.

On the Mystic beach, where the action began sooner than on the slope above, three times the crack Light Infantry companies charged past Stark's stake, only to be cut to pieces by his three rotating ranks of sharpshooters behind their makeshift stone wall. Finally, the Light Infantry turned and ran back down the beach to Moulton's Point. Ninety-six of Britain's finest soldiers lay dead on the narrow beach. Stark had never seen "sheep lie as thick in the fold" as these dead redcoats now lay.

A messenger rushed the outcome to General Howe just as he and Pigot were in place and waiting to see the Light Infantry climb up the bluff and form up behind the Americans. Howe was shocked to hear the result of his critical flanking movement, and sternly told the messenger to keep his voice down. Howe was now faced with a difficult choice: either retreat and wait for artillery support to reach the Mystic River, or continue the attack despite the lack of a flanking column. Howe chose the latter. He knew that, if he waited, his men would learn of the Light Infantry's demise, and lose heart. He was encouraged by hearing his impatient soldiers shouting, "Push on! Push on!" "Let's get at the dogs!" So Howe issued the order to his officers, and sent a runner to inform Pigot: "Attack all along the line."

Despite the American officers' orders to their men to hold their fire until ordered to fire, or until they could see "their buttons," "their gaiters," "the whites of their eyes," etc., fingers were tense on their "trickers" and a few men, unable to restrain themselves, fired prematurely. One Yankee recalled the man next to him firing early: "He did it singly and with a view to draw the enemy's fire, and he obtained his end fully, without any damage to our party."

One of Prescott's officers became so incensed at these men who could not wait that he jumped onto the parapet and walked along it, kicking up their muskets with his feet. Prescott reprimanded them, reminding them that "powder was scarce, and must not be wasted. Keep your heads down." Behind the rail fence, Putnam rode up to a spot where someone had also just fired, drew his sword and threatened to "take off the head of the next man that fired without orders."

After the Regulars' unauthorized fire was halted by their officers, they reformed their lines and continued the advance. They marched in perfect formations, with bayoneted muskets held waist-high and leveled at their enemy, ready for the order to charge. Some of them were now within fifty paces of the rebel redoubt, but they could hardly see any Yankees. Perhaps most of the cowards had snuck away after all, rather than face those terrible 14-inch bayonets. Polished, they shimmered in the sunlight as the redcoats marched up the hill.

A few more steps, and then from behind the American lines came shouts of "Make ready!" Hundreds of heads, some bare, others with dirty, broad-brimmed hats, ominously rose up and leveled muskets atop the walls. "Take aim!" The Yankees pointed those muskets at the slowly marching redcoats, now just fifteen yards away. In their red regimental coats - some new, others faded by long exposure to the sun to a brick color - and with those broad white belts running across their chests, they were easy targets. The officers were conspicuous in their silver and gilt braided, scarlet coats. Officers' coats contained an expensive dye, made from dried skeletons of female cochineal insects, that produced a more lasting and brighter color, as suited an officer. The militia heard their own shabbily clad officers remind them, "Fire at none but the reddest coats." Corporal Francis Merrifield recalled that the officers "looked too handsome to be fired at, but we had to do it."

After a pause, the harsh command, "Fire!" was snarled all up and down the long American lines. The discharge of muskets sounded "like the roll of a hundred drums" to observers on Boston's Beacon Hill, who saw the front rank of redcoats "fall like grass" before the farmer's scythe. The perspective of those redcoats facing that stream of lead balls coming at them was much different than that of the spectators in Boston. Sergeant Richard Pope was in the front rank, one of its few survivors. He thought the rebel fire "resembled a continuous sheet of lightning and an uninterrupted peal of thunder."

Those who had just fired now quickly ducked down to reload while others took their turn at the hated lobsterbacks. One militiaman recalled, "While they were filling up their ranks to advance again, the Yankees gave them the second fire with the same effect."

The British survivors, who had been in the third and fourth ranks, now found themselves to be the front rank facing these Yankee muskets. They stopped their advance to fire back at the Yankees, contrary to orders. They stood there, surrounded by the bloody bodies of their comrades at their feet, some lying still and silent, others writhing and screaming in pain. Finally, they turned and ran back down the hill, Pigot's men and Howe's, too. All along the lines, Yankees cheered, huzza-ing their victory. Some, seeing the enemy retreating, jumped over their walls to pursue them, but by "the prudence of the officers they were prevented leaving so advantageous a post."

Behind their barriers, the Americans that afternoon were making the best possible use of their resources. They did not all fire at once, but rotated in groups, just as Stark had instructed his men to do down on the beach. A British soldier later explained that he'd seen an American sharpshooter "attended by two men, one on each side of him to load pieces for him so that he had nothing to do but fire as fast as a piece was put into his hand." These tactics explain why British accounts of the battle consistently refer to the "incessant fire" of the Yankees. The following is an excerpt from one of the many bitter letters that British officers sent home in the days after the battle:

That the officers suffered so much must be imputed
to their being aimed at. The dexterity which the Americans by long habit had acquired in hitting beasts, birds,
and marks was fatally applied to the destruction of our
officers. From their fall much confusion was expected;
they were, therefore, particularly singled out.

For deadly effect, the militia used their traditional "buck and ball" -
four pieces of buckshot with each musket ball. After they ran out of
these, they used stones they gathered on the site. For accuracy, in
most cases, they waited until the enemy was within twenty yards before firing. They were instructed to "take good sight," "fire low," and
"aim at the waistbands" so the recoil of the musket upon firing, which
invariably threw it up slightly, would result in the ball hitting the target
in the trunk of his body.

In contrast, the British Regulars fired their muskets as they were
taught to do it - simply holding them up in front of their chests and
pulling the "tricker" without aiming ("Present! ... Fire!"). This tech-
nique, when used by a large number of men at the same time, was
known as a "mass volley" and was thought to be more efficient than
having the men take the time to aim, since it took less time (three volleys per minute, instead of two) and could be quickly followed by the
more important part of the attack - the bayonet charge. The result, according to one American soldier, was "forty-nine out of fifty balls
flying six feet over our heads." An apple tree behind the breastwork
extension had its branches cut to pieces, while not a mark was found
on its trunk.

Much has been said about the "untrained" militia's lack of discipline,
but on Breed's Hill those men who stayed and fought showed remarkable restraint and ingenuity in the use of their weapons, unlike the
"highly trained" professional soldiers they were opposing, many of
whom stopped their advance to fire back, contrary to orders.

One veteran Yankee behind the rail fence recognized a wounded

British officer who had been notorious in the preceding weeks for claiming that Yankees were all cowards. As the British officer was carried from the battlefield, the Yankee called out to him, "Colonel Abercrombie! Are the Yankees cowards now?"

Except for the men in Charlestown run down by Pitcairn's Marines, the Americans had suffered very few casualties during the first assault. True to their frontier heritage of fighting against French Canadians and Indians, they kept their bodies hidden except when firing. However, their officers, standing to survey the battlefield and shout orders, suffered for their courage. Colonels Brewer and Nixon, of Massachusetts, were carried from the field, as was Captain Isaac Baldwin, of New Hampshire. Hit in the chest, he managed to fire three more rounds before collapsing. As he was carried away, he was heard to say, "You'll beat them, boys. I'll be back as soon as the doctor tends this." He died that night.

Fifteen-year-old Private John Greenwood was on his way to the battle about this time, trying to find his company (he had been on furlough).

> As I passed through Cambridge common I saw a number of wounded who had been brought from the field of conflict. Everywhere the greatest terror and confusion seemed to prevail, and as I ran along the road it was filled with chairs and wagons, bearing the wounded and dead, while groups of men were employed in assisting others, not badly injured, to walk. Never having beheld such a sight before, I felt very much frightened, and would have given the world if I had not enlisted as a soldier; I could positively feel my hair stand on end.
>
> Just as I came near the place, a negro man, wounded in the back of his neck, passed me and, his collar being open and he not having anything on except his shirt and trousers, I saw the wound quite plainly and the blood

running down his back. I asked him if it hurt him much, as he did not seem to mind it. He said no, that he was only going to get a plaster put on it, and meant to return. You cannot conceive what encouragement this immediately gave me. I began to feel brave and like a soldier from that moment, and fear never troubled me afterward during the whole war.

At Moulton's Point, Howe and Pigot rallied their men for a second try. Some had to be pulled out of the longboats. This time, speeches and songs of bravado would not suffice. The officers had to "push forward the men with their swords." As Pigot again led his division toward the redoubt and its breastwork extension, Howe concentrated his own forces against the hundred yard long gap between the lower end of the breastwork and the upper end of the rail fence. This was the area of the three *fleches*. The British Ensign Henry DeBerniere commented on his map of the peninsula and battle, that this was a "Place from where the Grenadiers received a very heavy fire" during the second assault.

While Howe regrouped, the Americans were confidently bracing themselves for the second attack, only five minutes since the end of the first one. Israel Potter later recalled this lull in the action:

We were now again harangued by "old General Put," as he was termed, and requested by him to aim at the officers. Their approach was with a slow step, which gave us an excellent opportunity to obey the commands of our General in bringing down their officers.

This time, the better marksmen did not wait until the advancing Regulars were within close range before they aimed and fired at their officers. The following, from a British soldier's letter home, appeared in a London newspaper:

General Howe on the march to attack the breastwork found that the strength was such that the troops could do nothing against it without cannon, which quite deranged his design to make the attack by a bold and sudden effort without a halt. The lines had to halt several times, exposed all the time to a dreadful though irregular fire from their infernal rifles, which cut down our officers at a distance never fired by regular troops. Our men dropped incessantly, while at such a distance that their fire arms against men behind a breast-work had no effect. Had the cannon been properly provided they might have moved with sufficient expedition. It was this horrid fire that threw the troops into such confusion.

In the first assault, the actual fighting had taken between 10 and 15 minutes. For the second, it lasted twice that. But the British did not quite reach the American lines this time either. Pigot and Howe, seeing the ranks so depleted, at last had the drummers sound the retreat. One of Howe's soldiers describes the attack against the rail fence:

As we approached, an incessant stream of fire poured from the rebel lines. It seemed a continued sheet of fire for nearly thirty minutes. Our Light Infantry were served up in companies against the grass fence, without being able to penetrate - indeed how could we penetrate? Most of our Grenadier and Light Infantry, the moment of presenting themselves lost three-fourths, and many times nine-tenths, of their men.

For the second assault, Howe had ordered the troops not to use their muskets, but to charge as fast as they could and rely on their bayonets. However, a fence had to be climbed over before the rebel defenses could be reached. It was when the Grenadiers stopped their charge, to climb over this obstacle, that the militia behind the rail fence opened up, not waiting this time until the British were within fifteen yards. Instinctively, the British ranks stopped, and began firing instead of continuing their charge. Howe explains that his Grenadiers

> set forward to attack with bayonets ... [but] were checked by a difficulty in getting over some very high fences of strong railing, under a heavy fire, well kept up by the Rebels. They began firing, and by crowding fell into disorder and in this state the second line mixt with them. The Light Infantry at the same time being repulsed, there was <u>a moment that I never felt before</u>.

At one point, Howe found himself the only man in his immediate area still standing. Although the general's white trousers were spattered with the blood of his staff officers, all of whom had been hit, Howe was so far unscathed. Major John Small, too, stood alone momentarily in front of the rail fence, deserted by his retreating Grenadiers. According to his own account of the battle, he saw three Yankees raise their muskets and aim at him when, suddenly, Putnam, recognizing his old friend Small, rode up and knocked their guns up with his sword.

Howe later blamed the fences, which his heavily loaded men had to climb over, for his disastrous casualties. One of the officers wrote of them: "These posts and rails were too strong for the columns to push down, and the march was so retarded by getting over them, that the next morning they were found studded with bullets, not a hand's breadth from each other.

Up at the redoubt, the action was equally hot. The following is taken from the memoirs of Judge William Prescott, based on conversations with his father, Colonel William Prescott:

> The discharge was simultaneous the whole length of the line, and though more destructive, as Col. Prescott thought, than on the former assault, the enemy stood the

first shock, and continued to advance and fire with great spirit; but before reaching the redoubt, the continuous, well directed fire of the Americans compelled them to give way, and they retreated a second time, in greater disorder than before. Colonel Prescott spoke of it as a continuous stream of fire from his whole line, from the first discharge until the retreat. The ground in front of the works was covered with the dead and wounded - some lying within a few yards.

By the time Pigot and Howe reached Moulton's Point again on their second retreat, the reserve of 700 fresh Regulars was beginning to arrive from Boston. John Greenwood described the riverfront scene in his memoirs:

As my father lived near the ferry, my brothers were at this point, and the river being only half a mile wide, saw the whole battle. The wounded were brought over in the boats belonging to the men-of-war, and they were obliged to bail the blood out of them like water. These boats carried back the fresh troops who stood ready to reinforce those engaged. My brother told me that the wives or women of the British soldiers were at the ferry encouraging them, saying: "D--- the Yankee rebels, my brave British boys, give it to them!"

He observed likewise that the soldiers looked as pale as death when they got into the boats, for they could plainly see their brother redcoats mowed down like grass by the Yankees, the whole scene being directly before their eyes.

After the second assault failed, General Pigot and some of the other officers tried, in vain, to persuade Howe to give up, telling him that it would be "criminal" and "butchery" to send the troops against such deadly fire again. Howe, however, had not only the army's reputation at stake, but his own, too. He knew he surely would be summoned home for a court-martial if he gave up and took his forces back to Boston, ignominiously defeated by irregulars. Therefore, he refused to give up, and ordered a third assault. The hot, exhausted men who had survived the first two attempts were quite naturally reluctant to try again.

> It was with very great difficulty their officers could persuade them to rally, telling them they must, as British valor and courage were at stake. Officers were seen to drive their soldiers on to the charge with swords and bayonets.

For the third assault, Howe ordered the men to remove from their backs their heavy knapsacks, containing iron kettles, portions of canvas tents, etc., and leave them at Moulton's Point. Many of the men also, without orders, deposited their heavy coats. Howe could not help but see this, but made no objection. The hot sun continued to beat down on the soldiers from the clear, windless sky. The men were instructed to march in columns this time, instead of wide lines. Again, the emphasis was to not stop and fire their muskets, but continue charging, and rely on the effectiveness of their bayonets.

The heavy field pieces were hauled out of the muck and ordered forward to a spot just downhill from the lower end of the rebel breastwork, so as to fire *enfilade* (along its length). The artillery officers objected, pointing out that this would place their men in danger from the Yankees at the rail fence, only 100 yards away from the artillery's proposed location. Howe glared at them a moment, then told them firmly that they would be hung on the spot for cowardice if they disobeyed this order. The two deserters still hanging from the nearby tree served as a reminder that Howe was deadly serious; the artillery officers shut their mouths and obeyed orders. Their crews would do their duty well, but almost every gunner would be killed or wounded in the upcoming third attack.

Howe's division would again advance against the uppper end of the rail fence. But, just before coming within musket range, most of them would wheel to the left and move uphill against the breastwork and redoubt. The Light Infantry would stay, though, to keep the rail fence's defenders occupied with a diversionary fire. And, once the rebels were forced from their breastwork extension, the British field pieces aimed at the breastwork could easily be turned ninety degrees to the right to keep the militia at the rail fence from moving uphill to assist Prescott's outnumbered defenders in the redoubt.

On Howe's left, Pigot was bolstered by both his half of the reinforcements and the arrival of General Henry Clinton. During the second assault, Clinton had seen about 200 wounded troops without officers milling about at the bottom of Breed's Hill. So, without orders, he had jumped in a boat and headed across the Charles River to organize them and lead them back up the hill in the next attack. On the way across the river, two of Clinton's rowers were hit by sharpshooters lingering in burning Charlestown. When he landed, Clinton "collected all the guards and such wounded men as would follow, which to their honor were many, and advanced with as much parade as possible, to impress the enemy."

At 5:00, the Regulars once more advanced up the hill, their eyes stinging from the drifting smoke of the Charlestown fire. This time, they shouted, "Conquer or die!" as they came on. Howe had taken so much time planning this third attack that some of the Americans thought he'd given up. To their dismay, they now saw the redcoats approaching again, with the addition of the 700 fresh men that had composed the reserve. By now, many of the Yankees were out of balls or powder. Some wondered aloud where the promised relief force was. Robert Steele, arriving with rum at the redoubt, noted, "It went very quick.. We found our people in confusion and talking about retreating." Prescott grimly confined the retreating to just talk.

From his vantage point inside the redoubt, Prescott could see that Howe's new strategy was working perfectly, as the men behind the breastwork fled either to Bunker's Hill or to the redoubt, and the rail fence's defenders were kept at bay by the Light Infantry and the British field pieces. It was at this point that Prescott realized his poorly armed and now vastly outnumbered garrison inside the redoubt would be overwhelmed. He had two choices: retreat; or stand firm and fight to the end, hoping Putnam would arrive with reinforcements. There was no doubt in his mind what he would choose.

Putnam, on Bunker's Hill trying to coax the hundreds of militia there to build a fallback breastwork on that hilltop, was unaware of Prescott's desperate situation, since there were no staff officers to carry messages. Colonel Jonathan Ward's regiment, with full ammunition pouches, arrived at Bunker's Hill on their way to the redoubt. Putnam promptly convinced Ward to stay and build breastworks instead of proceeding to Breed's Hill. Eventually, but too late, Ward saw this was an error in judgement, and took a couple of companies forward. On the way, he was struck down by a bullet and killed.

So Prescott and his men - about 300 now, counting those who had moved up from the breastwork being raked by the British artillery - prepared once again for the onslaught as the enemy neared the redoubt. The colonel ordered some men to break open three unused artillery cartridges and carefully distribute the powder. He charged the recipients "to not waste a kernel of it, but to make it certain that every shot should tell." Once again, he ordered his men to hold their fire until the enemy was close. This time, no one disobeyed the order.

The Committee of Safety's Reverend Peter Thacher, after watching the battle, was assigned to write the official American account of it, to be sent to England and the other colonies. He described the final advance of the British:

> Having formed once more, they brought some cannon
> to bear in such a manner as to rake the inside of the
> breastwork, and having drove the provincials thence into
> the redoubt, they determined to make a decisive effort.
> The fire from the ships and batteries, as well as from the

cannon in front of their army, was redoubled. Innumerable bombs were sent into the fort. The officers behind the army of Regulars were observed to goad forward their men with renewed exertion.

The dispersal of the militia previously manning the breastwork allowed Howe to turn his division left and move uphill to converge his forces with those of Pigot and Clinton. Together, they stormed the redoubt's walls. It was a costly charge, though. One of the British casualties in these final moments was Major John Pitcairn, who had commanded the Regulars that started it all on Lexington Common, eight weeks before.

At the far left of Pigot's line, Pitcairn's Marines ran around to the Charlestown side of the redoubt, to attack the fort from that flank. But Pitcairn's men were met with a blast of accurate fire that cut down many of them. They stopped and began to fire back at the hated Yankees. Major Pitcairn tried to rally them to the charge again, shouting that the enemy had abandoned the fort. Hearing him, a boy within the fort called out, "We are not all gone!" Just then, a Negro named Salem Prince shot Pitcairn through the head. He fell into the arms of his son, who with help carried him down to the boats, kissed his dying father, and returned to the battle, to be wounded himself within minutes. Adjutant Waller, observing near him a captain also shot down, realized that,

> had we stopped there much longer, the enemy would have picked us all off. I saw this, and begged Colonel Nesbitt of the 47th to form on our left, in order that we might advance with our bayonets to the parapet. I ran from right to left, and stopped our men from firing. When we had got in tolerable order, we rushed on, leaped the ditch, and climbed the parapet, under a most sore and heavy fire.

Before the British scaled the walls, Prescott ordered every man who had a bayonet to man the walls, and those who still had ammunition to join Dr. Warren at the rear of the redoubt so they could shoot over their comrades' heads at the redcoats as they emerged on top of the parapet. When the bayonet-wielding Regulars climbing over the walls became too numerous, Prescott finally ordered a retreat. The redoubt, that had preserved his men through so much, now became a nightmarish deathtrap. The smoke and dust made the air "as dark as pitch, obliging them to feel about for the outlet." They desperately sought the narrow opening at the back, while fending off the bayonet thrusts of a frustrated and enraged enemy by now mad with a blood lust for revenge. Many of the retreating men used their muskets as clubs, as they slowly fell back, overwhelmed by numbers. Thirty of them never made it out and were killed inside the fort.

Fortunately for the Yankees, the dust and smoke prevented the British, pouring in on three sides, from firing their muskets, for fear of hitting their comrades. But once out of the redoubt, the Yankees found themselves being squeezed by charging Regulars on both flanks. Israel Potter recalled the scene:

> A close and bloody engagement now ensued to fight our way through a very considerable body of the enemy, with clubbed muskets (for there were not one in twenty of us provided with bayonets). Fortunately for me, at this critical time, I was armed with a cutlass, which although without an edge, and much rust-eaten, I found of infinite more service to me than my musket.
>
> In one instance, I am certain it was the means of saving my life - a blow with a cutlass was aimed at my head by a British officer, which I parried and received only a slight cut with the point on my right arm near the elbow, which I was then unconscious of, but this slight wound cost my antagonist at the moment a much more serious one, which effectually dis-armed him, for with one well

directed stroke I deprived him of the power of very soon again measuring swords with a "yankee rebel!"

We should have been mostly cut off, and compelled to yield to a superiour and better equipped force, had not a body of Connecticut men held the enemy at bay until our main body had time to ascend the heights, and retreat across the Neck.

Covering the retreat was Captain John Chester's company, from Wethersfield, Connecticut, which had just arrived from Cambridge. Putnam, without seeking permission from General Ward, had sent his son to order them to Breed's Hill. It had taken a couple hours to reach it, the company having to weave their way through hundreds of sightseeing and deserting militia. Chester recalls his company's brief action:

> While we were going over the Neck, we were in imminent danger from the cannon-shot, which buzzed around us like hail. At last I met with a considerable company who were going off rank and file. I called to the officer that led them, and asked why he retreated. He made me no answer. I halted my men, and told him if he went on, it should be at his peril. He still seemed regardless of me. I then ordered my men to make ready. They immediately cocked, and declared, if I ordered, they would fire. Upon that, he stopped short, tried excuses, but I could not tarry to hear him. I ordered him forward, and he complied.
>
> We joined our army on the right of the centre, just by a poor stone fence, two or three feet high, and very thin, so that the bullets came through. Here we lost our regularity, as every company had done before us, and fought as they did, every man loading and firing as fast as he could. As near as I guess, we fought standing about six

minutes ... [and] covered their retreat till they [the British] came up.

When the British did reach the Wethersfield company, hand-to-hand combat ensued at their "stone fence." Lieutenant Samuel Webb later wrote to Silas Deane, relating the bravery of one of his comrades:

Edward Brown stood side by side with Gershom Smith in the intrenchments. Brown saw his danger, discharged his own and Smith's guns when they came so close as to push over our small breastwork. Brown sprang, seized a regular's gun, took it from him, and killed him on the spot.

The retreat was surprisingly slow and orderly. Despite the need for haste, many of the Americans struggled to carry off their wounded. A British officer wrote that the Yankees fought "from one fence or wall to another until we entirely drove them off the peninsula." Colonel Prescott "stepped along with his sword up," parrying bayonet thrusts that missed his body but pierced his coat in several places. As Burgoyne wrote, "The retreat was no flight: it was even covered with bravery and military skill."

Expecting the Yankees to flee, the British were surprised to find them "a set of infuriated beings, whom nothing could daunt or intimidate and who, after their ammunition failed, disputed the ground, inch by inch ... [with] clubbed muskets, rusty swords, pitchforks and billets of wood." It appeared that many preferred, like old Jonas Parker had on Lexington Common, to stand their ground and fight to the death, rather than retreat from the hated lobsterbacks. Lord Rawdon, who himself showed much bravery that day, thought the Yankees fought "more like devils than men" inside the redoubt. Howe, in his official report, mentioned that "thirty of the Rebels were killed with bayonets in it."

The Connecticut and New Hampshire troops behind the rail fence used what little ammunition they had left, trying to stop the pursuing British and cover Prescott's retreat. It was during this retreat that the Americans suffered most of their casualties. Peter Brown recalled that he "ran for about half a mile where balls flew like hailstones and cannons roared like thunder."

On Bunker's Hill, Prescott passed Putnam sitting atop his horse, surrounded by the hundreds of men who had lingered there during the battle. The irate Prescott demanded to know from Putnam, "Why did you not support me with your men according to our agreement?" "I could not drive the dogs up," Putnam replied, wearily. To which Prescott answered, "If you could not drive them up, you might have led them up!" Israel Putnam had been quite ineffectual all day. His location during most of the battle - either on Bunker's Hill or en route to and from Cambridge - was deemed by many unworthy of a general. Colonel Stark's son, who had been in action along the rail fence, later wrote that "when Gerrish's conduct was arraigned it was a subject of conversation why Gen. Putnam was not called to trial as well. I am inclined to think that his reputation for bravery and his great popularity in Connecticut and [such a trial's] effect on recruiting" were the reasons why he was not also court-martialled.

One of the Yankees lagging behind to cover the others' retreat was Dr. Joseph Warren. The night before, Warren had had dinner with the Hunt family in Watertown, where the Provincial Congress was in session. Years later, Betsy Hunt recalled that the young doctor "at dinner said, 'Come, my little girl, drink a glass of wine with me for the last time, for I am going on the hill tomorrow and I shall never come off.'" The morning of the battle, he was at work in Cambridge, at the Committee of Safety headquarters. He talked there with Elbridge Gerry, and they both agreed that occupying Charlestown Heights was folly. Folly or not, Warren announced he had to go there. Gerry tried to stop him, saying, "It would be madness for you to expose yourself. As surely as you go there, you will be slain." Warren had not slept at all the night before, and was still "sick, feverish, and suffering from a splitting headache." After talking with Gerry, he went upstairs and slept a few hours until noon. When Warren awoke, he hurried off to the battlefield.

He was still wearing his good white suit with its silk-fringed waistcoat, and came carrying a book of poetry, but no weapon. As the battle was beginning, he obtained a musket and ammunition from a deserting sergeant. Since, three days earlier, the Provincial Congress had commissioned him a major general, with rank just below Artemas Ward, Israel Putnam offered him the command of the rail fence. Dr. Warren declined, but asked, "Where will the attack be the hottest?" Putnam, pointing to the redoubt, answered, "That is the enemy's object. If that can be maintained, the day is ours."

At the redoubt, Colonel Prescott offered Dr. Warren the command, as he had done to Brigadier General Seth Pomeroy when he had walked up a few minutes before. Pomeroy had declined, preferring to fill an empty spot behind the rail fence. Now Doctor Warren likewise declined, saying, "I did not come to take command but to act as a volunteer. I shall be happy to learn from a soldier of your experience."

Nothing had angered Joseph Warren more than assertions by the British and Tories that, once the fighting began, the Whigs would run. He'd once told a student, Dr. William Eustis, "They say we will not fight. By God, I hope to die up to my knees in British blood." After Howe's Grenadiers filled the redoubt, Warren's wish came true, as he was shot in the head near the fort's exit. An American reported his death in a letter to a relation in England:

> Almost the last shot they fired they killed good Dr. Warren, who had dressed himself like Lord Falkland, in his wedding suit, and distinguished himself by unparalled acts of bravery during the whole action, but particularly in covering the retreat; he was a man of great courage, universal learning, and much humanity. It may well be said he is the greatest loss we have sustained.

The man Lord Rawdon had called "the greatest incendiary in all

America" was now dead. General Howe, sleeping the night after the battle on a pile of hay, was awakened and told that Joseph Warren had been identified among the dead. Howe went to the burial site to investigate. Captain Sloane Laurie was in charge of the burial detail, the same man who had been in command at the North Bridge in Concord two months before. So it was with no love lost for dead rebels that Laurie acknowledged to the commander that, yes, he had indeed found Warren's body. And he'd instructed his men to "stuff the scoundrel with another Rebel into one hole, and there he and his seditious principles may remain." Since the death of an enemy leader must be verified, Howe ordered Warren's remains dug up, for proper identification. Hearing of this, General Burgoyne immediately came over from Boston to view the body. Howe declared Warren's death "worth five hundred men to me."

The patriots were not sure what had happened to Warren, since it was so dark in the redoubt, and all but a few of the defenders had left by the time he was shot. Two days later, the Provincial Congress elected James Warren (no relation) as President, to replace "the good doctor" who was "supposed to be killed in the late battle."

Captain John Chester, of the Wethersfield company, wrote down his thoughts about the Massachusetts troops who had remained in the redoubt when the British broke into it:

> 'Tis said many of them, the flower of the province, have sacrificed their lives in the cause. Some say they have lost more officers than men. Good Dr. Warren, God rest his soul, I hope is safe in Heaven! Had many of their officers the spirit and courage in their whole constitution that he had in his little finger, we had never retreated.

By the third day after the battle, stories were circulating about Warren's supposed last words spoken while expiring: "I am a dead man; fight on, my brave fellows, for the salvation of your country." (A difficult statement for a man shot through the head to make.) His death was not confirmed until nearly a year later, after the British left, when his brothers and friends dug the gravesite. It had been learned from the British that his one companion in the grave had been "a person wearing a frock coat." This was one of the identifying clues. The other was two artificial teeth held in place by silver wire, which Paul Revere identified as his own dental work.

* * * * *

One by one, several of the Boston radicals who had helped bring on this war were dying off. Will Molineaux - the extremist thought to be the speaker who, at the corner of King Street the night of March 5, 1770, had incited the mob to attack the British sentry and precipitate the Boston Massacre - had died of tuberculosis.

Illness had also taken the life of Josiah Quincy, Jr., the brilliant young lawyer who, with John Adams, had defended the British at the massacre trial. Quincy had gone on to help lead the constitutional arguments phase of the crisis, but died in March, 1775, of consumption. He was on his way home from London with news so urgent and secret he had felt he must personally carry it to Sam Adams and Joseph Warren, despite his failing health which should have kept him from making the trip. No one ever found out what his news was.

Then there was the tragic case of James Otis, Jr., who had started the embryo of resistance with his stirring anti-government speech in 1761 in a court case testing the Writs of Assistance. As Advocate General for the colony, Otis was supposed to present the government's case, so he resigned his post and delivered a four hour oration so powerful that, although he lost the case, it made a lasting impression on all who heard it or read of it in the press. During that speech, he coined the phrases, "A man's house is his castle," and "Taxation without representation is tyranny." John Adams, years later, recalled, "Otis was a flame of fire! American independence was then and there born; the seeds of patriots and heroes were then and there sown."

In the next few years, Otis had gone on to raise the consciousness of the citizenry concerning their "rights as Englishmen." However, he gradually went insane and had to be cared for at his relatives' country home. Occasionally, during the 1770s, he would be lucid when speaking out again in the legislature and the courts, but would soon lapse into irrational behavior, and have to be bound and carried away. When he heard that the British were landing at Charlestown, he rushed to the scene and participated in the battle, exposing himself recklessly, but escaping injury. He often had spoken aloud his desire to be killed by a bolt of lightning. One stormy day not long after the battle, while he was out walking on his cousin's farm, his wish came true.

* * * * *

Returning to the American retreat across Charlestown Neck, Burgoyne wrote that it "proceeded no farther than to the next hill, where a new post was taken, new intrenchments instantly begun." This was Winter Hill, on the mainland side of the Neck. Putnam's Connecticut regiment, under Lt. Colonel Ebeneezer Storrs, arrived and were put to work by Putnam. Storrs wrote in his journal, "we immediately went to entrenching; flung up by morning an entrenchment 100 feet square." These men "were expecting to come to an ingagement," as it was thought the British "intend to take Cambridge." Private Elihu Phelps wrote home to his mother in Wethersfield, "we was ordered to sleep with our fire locks in our arms." But to their surprise, the British did not pursue them across the Neck. Clinton was for it, and began forming the troops on Bunker's Hill, but Howe did not want to risk running into American reinforcements and more fortifications. In his memoirs, Clinton recalled, "I desired I might go forward with the light troops, but he called me back."

Colonel Prescott asked General Ward for three fresh regiments, well equipped with ammunition and bayonets, so he could retake the heights. Fortunately, Ward refused to permit Prescott to lead any more men into the trap from which he had been lucky to escape.

The last casualty of the battle occurred on Charlestown Neck a few hours after the retreat. Major Andrew McClary was a six-foot-six giant of a man who had led his New Hampshire militia into Fort William Mary in Portsmouth the previous December to seize the cannon and powder there. Like Putnam, he had been one of Rogers' Rangers and, on April 20, 1775, had been plowing his fields when the news of Lexington reached him. McClary ran to his horse, flung his saddlebags on it, and promised his sons he would "kill a redcoat" before he returned, then rode off to Cambridge. During the Battle of Bunker Hill, he had stood his tall, broad frame behind the rail fence and barked out orders in the deepest voice heard anywhere along the entire line, oblivious to the danger he was exposing himself to.

The evening after the battle, McClary convinced Captain Henry Dearborn that they should take Dearborn's company and cross the Neck to reconnoiter British activity on Bunker's Hill, so as to discover whether Howe was planning a sudden move against Cambridge the next day. When they reached the Neck, it was still being bombarded by British artillery. This dissuaded all but the major from proceeding across it. Dearborn begged his friend to give up the idea. McClary laughed enormously and boasted, "The cannon shot hasn't been made that will kill me yet." He casually walked across the narrow Neck, and for ten minutes observed the British, working hard with picks and shovels, throwing up defensive works atop Bunker's Hill. Satisfied, he headed back. Dearborn describes McClary's return:

> He was returning towards me and was within twelve or fifteen rods of where I stood with my company when a random cannon shot from one of the frigates passed directly through his body. He leaped two or three feet from the ground, pitched forward and fell dead upon his face.
>
> He was my bosom friend; we had grown up together on terms of the greatest intimacy. I loved him as a brother.

CHAPTER FIFTEEN
NOW WE ARE ENEMIES

"[If Parliament means to master America], some other mode must be adopted than gaining every little hill at the expense of a thousand Englishmen. They must lay aside the notion that hurting America is ruining Great Britain, and permit us to restore the dominion of the country by laying it waste, and almost extirpating the present rebellious race. Upon no other terms will they ever possess it in peace."

> *- A British officer, writing to Lord George Germain, newly appointed Secretary of War*

At British headquarters in Boston, General Gage was now more convinced than ever that Boston was not a desirable place for his army. Reporting the battle results to Lord Barrington, the Secretary of War, Gage wrote:

> The loss we have sustained is greater than we can bear. Small armys cant afford such losses. I wish this cursed place was burned. It is the worst place either to act offensively from, or defensively.
>
> I have before wrote your Lordship my opinion that a large army must at length be employed to reduce these people, and mentioned the hiring of foreign troops. I fear it has come to that, or else to avoid a land war and make use only of your fleet.
>
> I dont find one province in appearance better disposed than another, tho' I think if this army was in New

York we should find many friends, and be able to raise
forces in that province on the side of Government.

Howe agreed that no further "ventures into the countryside" around
Boston should be attempted. His superior, Thomas Gage, called off
the planned attack on rebel headquarters. General Howe expressed his
own conclusions in a letter home:

> It is my opinion, with the strength we have, we must
> not risk endangering the loss of Boston. The intentions
> of these wretches are to fortify every post in our way;
> wait to be attacked at every one, having their rear se-
> cure, destroying as many of us as they can before they
> set out to their next strong situation and, in this defen-
> sive mode they must in the end get the better of our
> small numbers.

Of the 2,250 Regulars engaged, 226 were killed that day and 828
wounded, for a total loss of 1,054 - by far the highest proportion of
any British battle since Braddock's infamous ambuscade by the French
and Indians twenty years before. Especially appalling were the figures
for officers: 19 killed and 73 wounded, more than in any other battle
of the entire "American War," as the British would come to call our
Revolutionary War.

In comparison to the 1,054 British casualties, the American losses
(115 killed, 305 wounded, 30 captured) seemed quite favorable. The
populous colonies could more easily sustain losses than the small,
peacetime-sized British army. Rhode Island's General Nathanael
Greene would write, "Upon the whole, I think we have little reason to
complain. Wish we could sell them another hill at the same price."
One member of Parliament said to Prime Minister Lord North, "Eight
more such victories, and we will have no one left to report them."

Unlike General Greene, many Americans did feel there was indeed
reason to complain. The clamor was such that the Provincial Congress

on June 20th appointed a committee of five "to enquire into the grounds of a report which has prevailed in the army that there has been treachery in some of the officers." Apparently, Peter Brown was not the only one who had thought "we were brot there to be all slain." The committee found no evidence which would support the claim, and emphatically stated as much, declaring that the rumors had been started by some of those cowards who had deserted before Howe's first attack began.

Despite the favorable casualty figures, the Yankees had been forced from the field of battle. Therefore, the American people, in general, saw the battle as a defeat. The immediate reaction was to lay the blame on the man in charge of American forces - Artemas Ward. James Warren, the new President of the Massachusetts Provincial Congress, wrote to John Adams, then at Philadelphia:

> Had our brave men had a Lee or a Washington, instead of a general destitute of all military ability and spirit, to command them, it is my opinion the day would have terminated with as much glory to America as the 19th of April. This is our great misfortune, and it is remediless from any other quarter than yours. We dare not supersede him here.

The British troops, after the battle, were equally bitter about their "victory." As one put it, "We have got a little elbowroom, but I think we have paid too dearly for it." One officer wrote, "A universal murmur now runs through the army, which ever most disagreeably invades the General's ears." Another wrote that, "there is an air of dejection through all our superiors which forbodes no good, and does not look as things ought to do after a victory. If we have not 10,000 reinforcements soon, I hope ------ ------- will be hanged." The name, perhaps, Lord North's, was deleted before the letter was printed in a London newspaper. Another published letter came from an officer who wrote bitterly of the ill-planned expedition:

Too great a confidence in ourselves, which is always dangerous, occasioned this dreadful loss. "Let us take the bull by the horns" was the phrase of some great men among us, as we marched on. We went to battle without even reconnoitering the position of the enemy. Had we only wanted to drive them from their ground, without the loss of a man, the *Cymetry* transport which drew little water and mounted 18 nine-pounders could have been towed up the Mystic Channel and brought to within musket-shot of their left flank, which was quite naked. Had we intended to have taken the whole rebel army prisoners, we needed only have landed in their rear and occupied the high ground above Bunker Hill.

Even our manner of attacking in front was ruinous. In advancing, not a shot should have been fired, as it retarded the troops, whose movement should have been as rapid as possible. They should not have been brought up in line, but in columns with Light Infantry in the intervals, to keep up a smart fire against the top of the breastwork. If this had been done, their works would have been carried in three minutes, with not a tenth of our present loss.

Another circumstance equally true and astonishing is that Gen. Gage had undoubted intelligence early in May that the rebels intended to possess Bunker Hill; yet no step was taken to secure that important post, though it commanded all the north part of town.

We are all wrong in the head. My mind cannot help dwelling upon our cursed mistakes ... brave men's lives were wantonly thrown away. Our conductor as much murdered them as if he had cut their throats himself on Boston Common. Had he fallen, ought we to have regretted him?

When news of the battle reached London, it caused a sensation in the newspapers. Gage's official report, mentioning the casualty figures, impressed the readers, as did a quote taken from Colonel Abercrombie moments before he died: "My friends, we have fought in a bad cause, and therefore I have my reward." The bad news did not help the lagging recruiting effort. The war was unpopular, especially in Ireland, a traditionally good area for recruiting. Compounding the problem was the fact that the American boycott of trade with Britain had sent domestic farm prices soaring, because of the shortage of wheat and rice normally bought from the colonies. This unusual prosperity helped keep down on the farm peasants who otherwise might consider enlistment as a means of escaping poverty. John Pownall, General Clinton's friend in Parliament, wrote to him that, "unless it rains men in red coats, I know not where we are to get all we shall want."

In England, popular opinion had for many decades held that wars were to be fought by small professional armies, and the masses did not owe their country any military service, except in a case where England itself was invaded. Appeals to the Canadians also fell on deaf ears. The only recruiting success was achieved in the highlands of Scotland, where the poverty-stricken peasants kept down by a feudalistic clan system were lured into the army by promises of free farms in America, to be confiscated from the rebels.

So King George III arranged with money-hungry German princes to rent him soldiers, drafted from among the peasant and working classes. During the course of the war, 30,000 Germans would serve in the British army, at a cost of nearly five million pounds. More than half of them came from the two prinicpalities of Hesse-Cassel and Hesse-Hanau, explaining why the British and Americans would collectively refer to all the German soldiers as "Hessians." There was much criticism in Parliament and the English press about the hiring of foreign mercenaries to kill English subjects. But, as usual, King George III and his ministers ignored the protests. He wrote, "I am clear as to one point: that we must persist and not be dismayed by any difficulties that may arise on either side of the Atlantick; I know I am doing my duty, and therefore can never wish to retract."

Also that summer, the King issued a *Proclamation for Suppressing Rebellion and Sedition*, binding all officers and subjects to aid him in putting down the revolt in America. He managed, over much Whig opposition, to push the moderate Secretary of War, Lord Barrington, out of office, replacing him with the hard-liner, Lord George Germain. The King was not bothered by Germain's lack of experience; rather, he was determined to carry on the war as he saw fit, and have it managed by men who saw things as he did. Colonel William Phillips, a member of Parliament, wrote to General Henry Clinton, who shared a common contempt for Germain: "They attempt to carry on a war of such magnitude without a serious consultation of any military men."

The man now chosen to direct the war, George Germain, was thoroughly despised by virtually the entire British military. While an officer during the last French war, Germain had been court-martialled for cowardice and dismissed from the army in disgrace. King George II, who had hated Germain because of his friendship with his rebellious teenage grandson, Prince George, had ordered the verdict to be read to every unit in the army. But now the rebellious grandson was King; and, despite opposition from Parliament and the military, he wanted his old friend to direct the war with the strong hand he felt was needed to bring the Americans to a proper obedience.

Ironically, the man pronounced "unfit to serve his majesty in any military capacity whatsoever" was now directing that same army from which he had been cast out. Almost from his first day in office, Secretary of War Germain worsened the long-standing feud between the navy and army by lashing out at the corruption and inefficiencies in the navy. Throughout the war, Germain would not be able to get along with the Secretary of the Navy, the Earl of Sandwich. Their unwillingness to cooperate would, of course, be passed down to lower levels and be a factor in the failure of several "combined" operations during the war.

The battle on June 17th for Charlestown Heights proved to any remaining cynics the seriousness of the revolt. These rebels - a "rabble in arms" - would not be such easy pushovers as many had believed. One officer concluded that "the Americans, if they were equally well commanded, are full as good soldiers as ours; and as it is, are very little inferior to us." Bunker Hill proved that Britain would have a rough road to travel if it was determined to keep its colonies. Captain William Glanville Evelyn wrote home, expressing a view he shared with the King and his new minister, Germain. It was his opinion that, if Parliament meant to continue mastering America,

> some other mode must be adopted than gaining every little hill at the expense of a thousand Englishmen. They must lay aside the notion that hurting America is ruining Great Britain, and permit us to restore the dominion of the country by laying it waste, and almost extirpating the present rebellious race. Upon no other terms will they ever possess it in peace.

The Battle of Bunker Hill convinced King George III and his ministers who controlled Parliament that only a full scale war would keep their American colonies in the British Empire. Parliament, in its weakness, had repealed the Stamp Act and most of the Townshend Duties. This had only encouraged more boldness by those colonists who were infatuated with republican ideas. Now blows must decide.

The battle had a profound effect on William Howe, who would soon replace Thomas Gage as Commander-in-Chief. Howe would serve in that capacity for most of the first half of the war, when Britain had its best chances for victory. But, time and again, Howe would have Washington's army on the verge of annihilation, but then he would call back his troops, rather than send them against American marksmen fixed behind earthworks. Howe's behavior would appear inexplicable to his critics, but the American General Henry Lee would attribute it Howe's memories of Bunker Hill: "The sad and impressive experience of this murderous day sunk into the mind of Sir William

Howe; and it seems to have its influence on subsequent operations."

The battle also convinced the southern and middle colonies - who were somewhat wary of joining the New England hotheads - that they, too, should risk their lives and fortunes in "the common cause." The Yankees' marksmanship and courage, and the tremendous casualties they inflicted on the Regulars were dramatically spelled out in newspapers for all to see, and then believe, that indeed a united America did stand a chance to win this war. The Yankees had forced Gage into a battle, and they had stood their ground against the best army in the world.

This was the reason that John Coffin, a Massachusetts loyalist who later became a general in the British army, regarded Bunker Hill as the key battle of the war that brought about American independence. When some Americans visited Coffin in London, after the war, he declared to them:

> You could not have succeeded without it. Something
> in the then state of parties was indispensable to fix men
> somewhere, to show that the Northern people were in
> earnest. That, that did the business for you.

SELECTED BIBLIOGRAPHY

Author's Note: Many of the sources, both primary and secondary, listed below were first published in the late eighteenth or nineteenth century, and later reprinted in the twentieth century. I have listed here not necessarily the original edition, nor the most recent reprint, but rather the edition that I consulted.

<u>Primary Sources</u>

Allen, Ethan, *The Narrative of Colonel Ethan Allen.* New York: Corinth Books, 1961.

Chapin, Noah, *Journal* kept by Corporal Noah Chapin of Somers, CT, during the blockade of Boston, April 18, 1775 - July 19, 1775. Unpublished manuscript in the Connecticut State Library.

Church, Benjamin, *Letter*, dated July 22, 1775, to Mijah Cain in England, describing war preparations and a drift toward independence. Unpublished manuscript in the Connecticut State Library.

Clinton, Henry, *The American Rebellion, Sir Henry Clinton's Narrative of his Campaigns, 1775-1782, with an Appendix of Original Documents.* Edited by William B. Wilcox. New Haven, CT: Yale University Press, 1954.

Commager, Henry Steele, and Richard B. Morris, ed., *The Spirit of 'Seventy-Six, The Story of the American Revolution as told by the Participants.* New York: Harper & Row, 1975.

Commager, Henry Steele, and Allan Nevins, ed., *The Heritage of America.* Boston: Little, Brown, 1939.

Crary, Catherine S., ed., *The Price of Loyalty, Tory Writings from the Revolutionary Era.* New York: McGraw-Hill, 1973.

Dann, John C., *The Revolution Remembered, Eyewitness Accounts of the War for Independence.* Chicago: Univ. of Chicago Press, 1980.

Dorson, Richard M., ed., *America Rebels, Personal Narratives of the American Revolution.* New York: Pantheon, 1953.

Emerson, William, *Diaries and Letters of William Emerson*

1743-1776. Edited by Amelia Forbes Emerson. Boston: Thomas Todd, 1972.

Evans, Elizabeth, ed., *Weathering the Storm, Women of the American Revolution.* New York: Scribner's Sons, 1975.

Hart, Albert Bushnell, ed., *American History Told By Contemporaries,* v. 2. New York: MacMillan, 1898.

Heath, William, *Heath's Memoirs of the American War.* New York: A. Wessels, 1904. Edited by Rufus Rockwell Wilson.

Huntington, Jedidiah, *Letters* home from Roxbury, Mass., during the blockade of Boston, 1775-1776. Connecticut Historical Society Collections, v. XX.

Mackenzie, Frederick, *Diary of Frederick Mackenzie, Giving a Daily Narrative of his Military Service as an Officer of the Regiment of Royal Welsh Fusiliers During the Years 1775-1781 in Massachusetts, Rhode Island and New York.* Two volumes. Cambridge, Mass.: Harvard University Press, 1930.

Moore, Frank, ed., *Diary of the Revolution, from Newspapers and Original Documents.* New York: Scribner, 1860.

Murray, James, *Letters from America 1773-1780, Being letters of a Scots officer, Sir James Murray, to his home during the War of American Independence.* Edited by Eric Robson. Manchester, England: Manchester University Press, 1951.

Niles, Hezekiah, *Principles and Acts of the Revolution in America.* New York: A. S. Barnes, 1876.

Padelford, Philip, ed., *Colonial Panorama 1775, Dr. Robert Honyman's Journal for March and April.* San Marino, Calif.: Huntington Library, 1939.

Peckham, Howard H., ed., *Sources of American Independence, Selected Manuscripts from the Collections of the William L. Clements Library,* v. I and II. Chicago: University of Chicago Press, 1978.

Percy, Hugh, *Letters of Hugh Earl Percy from Boston and New York, 1774-1776.* Edited by Charles Knowles Bolton. Boston: Gregg Press, 1972.

Phelps, Elihu, *Letter* from Cambridge, Mass., dated June 19, 1775, to his mother in Wethersfield, CT. Unpublished manuscript in Conn. State Library.

Pole, J. R., ed., *The Revolution in America, 1754-1788*. Stanford, Calif.: Stanford University Press, 1970.

Potter, Israel R., *Life and Remarkable Adventures of Israel R. Potter*. New York: Corinth Books, 1962.

Putnam, Daniel, *Letter* about the role of his father, Israel Putnam, at Bunker Hill. Connecticut Historical Society Collections, v. I.

Rankin, Hugh F., *The American Revolution*. New York: Putnam's Sons, 1964.

Ryan, Dennis P., ed., *A Salute To Courage, The American Revolution as seen through Wartime Writings of Officers of the Continental Army and Navy*. New York: Columbia University Press, 1979.

Scheer, George F., and Hugh F. Rankin, *Rebels and Redcoats*. Cleveland: World Publishing Co., 1957.

Scull, G. D., ed., *Memoir and Letters of Captain W. Glanville Evelyn, of the 4th Regiment ("King's Own") from North America, 1774-1776*. Oxford, England: James Parker & Co., 1879.

Thacher, James, *A Military Journal During the American Revolutionary War, from 1775-1783*. Boston: Cottons & Barnard, 1827.

Van Doren, Carl, ed., *The Patriotic Anthology*. New York: Literary Guild, 1941.

Washington, George, *The Writings of George Washington*, v. IV. Edited by Jared Sparks. Boston: Russell, Odiorne and Metcalf, 1834.

Wheeler, Richard, *Voices of 1776*. New York: Crowell, 1972.

Willard, Margaret Wheeler, *Letters On The American Revolution, 1774-1776*. Port Washington, N.Y.: Kennikat Press, 1968.

Wright, Esmond, *The Fire of Liberty*. London: The Folio Society, 1983.

Secondary Sources

Albanese, Catherine L., *Sons of the Fathers, The Civil Religion of the American Revolution*. Philadelphia: Temple University Press, 1976.

Bakeless, John, *Turncoats, Traitors and Heroes*. Philadelphia: Lippincott, 1959.

Becker, Carl, *The Spirit of '76 and Other Essays*. New York: Augustus M. Kelley Publishers, 1966.

Bowman, Allen, *The Morale of the American Revolutionary Army*. Port Washington, N.Y.: Kennikat Press, 1964.

Bradley, Francis, *The American Proposition, A New Type of Man*. New York: Moral Re-Armament, 1977.

Bridenbaugh, Carl, *Silas Downer: Forgotten Patriot, His Life and Writings*. Providence, R.I.: Bicentennial Foundation, 1974.

Burnett, Edmund Cody, *The Continental Congress*. New York: MacMillan, 1941.

Birnbaum, Louis, *Red Dawn at Lexington*. Boston: Houghton Mifflin, 1986.

Chidsey, Donald Barr, *The Great Separation, the story of the Boston Tea Party and the beginning of the American Revolution*. New York: Crown, 1965.

Christie, Ian R., and Benjamin W. Labaree, *Empire or Independence 1760-1776*. New York: Norton, 1976.

Coburn, Frank Warren, *Fiction and Truth about the Battle on Lexington Common, April 19, 1775*. Lexington, MA: F. Coburn, 1918.

Cook, Don, *The Long Fuse, How England Lost the American Colonies, 1760-1785*. New York: The Atlantic Monthly Press, 1995.

Cumming, William P., and Hugh Rankin, *The Fate of a Nation, The American Revolution through contemporary eyes*. London: Phaidon Press, 1975.

Davis, Kenneth S., "In the name of the Great Jehovah and the Continental Congress!" *American Heritage*, v. XIV, no. 6, Oct., 1963.

Fiore, Jordan D., *Days of History, 200 Years Ago, Revolutionary Era*, v. 1, 1775. Taunton, MA: Historic Reproductions, 1974.

Fischer, David Hackett, *Paul Revere's Ride*. New York: Oxford University Press, 1994.

Fisher, Sydney George, *The Struggle for American Independence*, v. 1. Philadelphia: Lippincott, 1908.

Fleming, Thomas J., *Now We Are Enemies, The Story of Bunker Hill*. New York: St. Martin's Press, 1960.

Fleming, Thomas J., "Verdicts of History I: The Boston Massacre," *American Heritage*, v. XVIII, no. 1, December, 1966.

Forbes, Esther, *Paul Revere & The World He Lived In*. Boston: Houghton Mifflin, 1942.

French, Allen, *The First Year Of The American Revolution*. Cambridge, MA: Riverside Press, 1934.

French, Allen, *Taking of Ticonderoga in 1775: the British Story*. Cambridge, MA: Harvard University Press, 1928.

Frothingham, Richard, *History of the Siege of Boston, and of the Battles of Lexington, Concord, and Bunker Hill*. New York: DaCapo Press, 1970.

Furneaux, Rupert, *The Pictorial History of the American Revolution as told by Eyewitnesses and Participants*. Chicago: J.G. Ferguson Pub. Co., 1973.

Gonbold, E. Stanly, Jr., and Robert H. Woody, *Christopher Gadsden and the American Revolution*. Knoxville: University of Tennessee Press, 1982.

Griffith, Samuel B. II, *In Defense of the Public Liberty, Britain America and the Struggle for independence from 1760 to the surrender at Yorktown in 1781*. Garden City, N.Y.: Doubleday, 1976.

Hamilton, Edward P., *Fort Ticonderoga, Key to a Continent*. Boston: Little, Brown, 1964.

Handlin, Oscar, and Lilian Handlin, *A Restless People, Americans In Rebellion 1770-1787*. Garden City, N.Y.: Anchor Press/Doubleday, 1982.

Hansen, Harry, *The Boston Massacre, An Episode of Dissent and Violence*. New York: Hastings House, 1970.

Hargreaves, Reginald, *The Bloodybacks, The British Serviceman in*

North America and the Carribbean 1655-1783.   New York: Walker and Co., 1968.

Hibbert, Christopher, *Redcoats and Rebels, The American Revolution Through British Eyes*. New York: Norton, 1990.

Higginbotham, Don, *The War of American Independence, Military Attitudes, Policies, and Practice, 1763-1789*. New York: MacMillan, 1971.

Jensen, Merrill, *The Founding of a Nation, A History of the American Revolution, 1763-1776*. New York: Oxford University Press, 1968.

Ketchum, Richard M., *Decisive Day: The Battle for Bunker Hill*. Garden City, N.Y.: Doubleday, 1974.

Labaree, Benjamin Woods, *The Boston Tea Party*. New York: Oxford University Press, 1964.

Lancaster, Bruce, *From Lexington to Liberty, The Story of the American Revolution*. Garden City, N.Y.: Doubleday, 1955.

Ludlum, David M., "The Weather of American Independence - 2: The Siege of Boston," *Weatherwise*, v. 27, no. 4, August, 1974.

Maier, Pauline, *The Old Revolutionaries, Political Lives in the Age of Samuel Adams*. New York: Knopf, 1980.

Meigs, Cornelia, *The Violent Men, A Study of Human Relations in the First American Congress*. New York: Macmillan, 1949.

Miller, John C., *Origins of the American Revolution*. Boston: Little, Brown, 1943.

Mitchell, Joseph B., *Discipline and Bayonets, The Armies and Leaders in the War of the American Revolution*. New York: Putnam's Sons, 1967.

Montross, Lynn, *The Reluctant Rebels, The Story of the Continental Congress, 1774- 1789*. New York: Harper & Brothers, 1950.

Moore, Howard Parker, *A Life of General John Stark*. New York: H. P. Moore, 1949.

Murdock, Harold, *Bunker Hill, Notes and Queries on a Famous Battle*. Boston: Houghton Mifflin, 1927.

Murdock, Harold, "The Nineteenth of April 1775," *American Heritage*, v. X, no. 5, August, 1959.

O'Toole, Dennis, and Lisa W. Strick, "In the Minds and Hearts of the People," *Five American Patriots and the Road to Revolution*. Washington: Smithsonian Institution, 1974.

Pearson, Michael, *Those Damned Rebels: The American Revolution As Seen Through British Eyes*. New York: Putnam's Sons, 1972.

Peckham, Howard H., *The War For Independence, A Military History*. Chicago: University of Chicago Press, 1958.

Perret, Geoffrey, *A Country Made By War, From the Revolution to Vietnam - the Story of America's Rise to Power*. New York: Random House, 1989.

Randall, Willard Sterne, *Benedict Arnold, Patriot and Traitor*. New York: William Morrow, 1990.

Robson Eric, *The American Revolution In Its Political and Military Aspects*. New York: Norton, 1966.

Royster, Charles, *A Revolutionary People at War, The Continental Army & American Character 1775-1783*. New York: Norton 1979.

Sabine, David B., "Ethan Allen and the Green Mountain Boys," *American History Illustrated*, v. XI, no. 9, January 1977.

Scott, John Anthony, *Trumpet of a Prophecy, Revolutionary America 1763-1783*. New York: Knopf, 1969.

Shy, John, *A People Numerous And Armed, Reflections on the Military Struggle for American Independence*. New York: Oxford University Press, 1976.

Smith, Page, *A New Age Now Begins, A People's History of the American Revolution*, v. 1. New York: McGraw-Hill, 1976.

Stout, Neil R., *The Perfect Crisis, The Beginnings of the Revolutionary War*. New York: New York University Press, 1976.

Tourtellot, Arthur Bernon, *William Diamond's Drum, The Beginning of the War of the American Revolution*. Garden City, N.Y.: Doubleday, 1959.

Troiani, Lon, "Lexington and Concord," *American Heritage*, v. XXV, no. 3, April, 1974.

Ward, Christopher L., *The War of the Revolution*. Two volumes. New York: MacMillan, 1952.

INDEX